LEADING THE PACK

Library and Archives Canada Cataloguing in Publication

Title: Leading the pack : 50 years of Sudbury Wolves history / Scott Miller ;
    foreword by Mike Commito.
Names: Miller, Scott (Writer on local history), author. | Commito, Mike,
    writer of foreword.
Identifiers: Canadiana (print) 2022023924X | Canadiana (ebook)
    20220239258 | ISBN 9781988989495 (softcover) | ISBN
    9781988989501 (EPUB)
Subjects: LCSH: Sudbury Wolves (Junior hockey team)—History.
Classification: LCC GV848.S79 M55 2022 | DDC
    796.962/6209713133—dc23

Printed and bound in Canada on 100% recycled paper.

Cover Design: Laura Boyle Design

Published by:
Latitude 46 Publishing
info@latitude46publishing.com
Latitude46publishing.com

SCOTT MILLER

LEADING THE PACK

FOREWORD BY MIKE COMMITO

50 YEARS OF SUDBURY WOLVES HISTORY

CONTENTS

FOREWORD

You never forget your first Sudbury Wolves game. Whether your initial visit was during the team's high-flying days in the 1970s or more recently during the dynamic but brief Quinton Byfield era, there's something about catching Wolves hockey in the old barn on Elgin Street that sticks with you.

Even if the Wolves didn't win that game, that experience probably made you a lifelong fan. It might have been the smell of popcorn wafting through the building (now over seven decades old) or the fact that team benches are on opposite sides of the ice, but it was probably more precisely right after the Wolves scored a goal, summoning a stuffed wolf on a wire that made its way high above the ice to taunt the opposing team's bench. It doesn't matter how old you are, seeing that wolf run its course for the first time is nothing short of magical. There are few things better than scanning the arena after that wolf rears its mangy head and seeing the expression on people's faces.

You can tell who is seeing it for the first time and it brings you back to your earliest memories of Sudbury Wolves hockey. Sure, some might refer to it as tacky, but it has become synonymous with the team and is in many ways emblematic of the community's hard-rock approach to life: we don't care if you don't like it, we don't want you anyway.

That stuffed wolf is just one of the reasons I love the Wolves and reading through Scott Miller's *Leading the Pack: 50 Years of Sudbury Wolves History* brings back so many memories—and, more importantly, all the other reasons I root for the team. While I might not have been around to experience the team's humble beginnings or its resurgence in the early 1990s (I was still living in Southern Ontario at that time), I do have vivid memories of the deep playoff run the club made in 2007. During that playoff season it was nearly impossible to get a seat in the Sudbury Arena. The only tickets you could get were for the standing-room only section along the railings on the upper concourse. Of course, even there, it was three rows deep so you had to get there early if you wanted to catch the game from a decent angle. I'll never forget how the arena felt when the music came on and the team skated through the inflatable wolf head. If you had your hands on the railings, you might as well have been holding a live wire because it truly felt like electricity was coursing through the building. It was a hair-raising experience and I have yet to attend another live sporting event at any level that rivalled the excitement on Elgin every time the Wolves took to the ice that postseason.

And I know I am not alone in that thinking. There are hundreds if not thousands of people out there who have that run etched into their memories. Even if the Wolves fell short of hoisting the J. Ross Robertson Cup that year, the community put its full weight behind the team and experienced the highs and lows of the campaign together. The Sudbury Wolves are more than a hockey team, they are a community. For me, that's the biggest take-away from Miller's book. The club's history demonstrates that they have been woven into the fabric of the city and there is nothing quite like witnessing how the club can bring people together.

While this is unquestionably Miller's book, he has made something that the Wolves community would be proud to call their own. Whether you remember Mike Foligno scoring in green and white or Jamie Rivers setting teammates up in blue and white, this is the book for you. We can all only hope that one day, perhaps in the not-too-distant future, Miller will be called upon to write an addendum that includes a Memorial Cup championship. But until then, *Leading the Pack* should tide you over and get you excited for Sudbury Wolves hockey with every turn of the page.

Mike Commito
Team Historian for the Sudbury Wolves and author of the *Hockey 365* series

INTRODUCTION:

SUDBURY AND THE WOLVES, A SYNONYMOUS HISTORY

In April 1932, the people of Sudbury, Ontario, a mining community of about 20,000 residents, listened anxiously to a radio broadcast of the final game of the Memorial Cup championship series hosted in Winnipeg, Manitoba. The Sudbury Cub Wolves were battling the Winnipeg Monarchs, and the winner of this third match between the two clubs would be crowned Canada's junior hockey champions. The Wolves ultimately emerged victorious by a one-goal margin and captured the city's first—and to date only—Memorial Cup title. When the news crossed the airwaves and reached Sudbury, fans "rushed into the streets … shouting, singing, and dancing around bonfires." For the city of Sudbury, it was, in the words of one local historian, "a scene matched only by the celebrations at the end of the Second World War."[1]

While the City of Greater Sudbury has undergone a wholesale transformation since that fateful day in 1932, the significance of the Sudbury Wolves in community life has remained unchanged. The modern franchise has existed since 1972 as a member of the Ontario Hockey League (OHL), but the club's identity dates back to the years following the First World War. In September 2022, the Sudbury Wolves organization will celebrate exactly fifty years since it dropped the puck for its first game. This book serves as a commemorative history of the Sudbury Wolves in celebration of this milestone, and in doing so it highlights the franchise's achievements and the central role it has played in the community over the last half-century.

Moreover, this book aims to demonstrate that the histories of both Sudbury and that of the Wolves are in many ways synonymous, reflecting the city's status as a first-rate hockey town. As cliché as it has become to romanticize hockey's place in Canadian culture, the development of the quintessential hockey town, inhabited by fans who love the game in general and its local teams and players in particular, is an observable historical process.[2] Take, for example, Frank S. Sarlo's book *Hound Town: One of the Greatest Hockey Towns Anywhere*, which covers the history of the Sault Ste. Marie Greyhounds, the Wolves' oldest rival. Sarlo contends that the city of Sault Ste. Marie, Ontario, located about 300 kilometres west of Sudbury and often referred to simply as "the Soo," is "a real hockey town" permeated by a "special relationship among Sault Ste. Marie, its people, and its hockey team, the Soo Greyhounds." He adds that the Greyhounds have been a rallying point for the city during turbulent times, stating that "Sometimes the community supports the hockey team and sometimes its vice versa."[3]

The Sudbury Wolves and its host city have had a similarly close-knit relationship, one underscored by Sudbury's unique position in the world. As the largest community in Northern Ontario by population, Sudbury is a regional hub of over 160,000 residents that attracts people who come from all over in search of jobs, education, leisure, medical treatment, and more. Since the late nineteenth century, nickel has been an especially important commodity for Sudbury, driving the local economy and giving rise to the nicknames "Nickel City" or "Nickel Capital." This prosperity came with a price, however. Having been devastated by decades of relentless mining pollution, Sudbury's landscape was notorious for being blackened and devoid of vegetation for much of the twentieth century. A visit in 1971 by the Apollo astronauts led to an enduring legend that Sudbury's desolate landscape was being used to simulate walking on the cratered, uninhabitable moon.[4]

Then there is the city's central but often forgotten role in the environmental movement. Beginning in the 1970s, governments, academics, companies, and volunteers from all walks of life banded together to undertake what is now known as one of the most successful land reclamation projects ever completed. In 1972, the International Nickel Company (INCO), now Vale, constructed the 1,250-foot-tall chimney known as the Superstack, which remains one of the tallest freestanding structures in the Western hemisphere, to help disperse its emissions away from the Sudbury area. Although it is set to be demolished by Vale in the near future, the Superstack has long served as a symbol of Sudbury's industrial heritage and subsequent environmental turnaround. Indeed, the city's re-greening effort has garnered international praise, and allowed Sudbury to shed its reputation as a sulphur-stricken mining town on the fringes of the Canadian Shield and became known as a modern, environmentally friendly city no longer wholly-dependent on a single industry for survival.

Throughout all this growth and change, Sudburians' love for hockey and the Sudbury Wolves has remained constant, and this has led to the Wolves to become linked with the city in the same way as nickel. "If you go from coast to coast, people will associate Sudbury with a handful of things," says Sudbury native, former Wolves captain and current head coach Craig Duncanson. "One would be the Superstack. Two would be the that the astronauts trained here … when we had no vegetation. And the other has to be, that it's the home of the Sudbury Wolves, where the wolf comes out. And people all across the country know that."[5] For the last seventy years, whenever the Wolves score a goal at the Sudbury Community Arena a stuffed grey wolf descends from the rafters along a pulley system and glares at the opposing team's bench. Furthermore, Sudbury's bluc, white and grey jerseys – which were green and white in colour until the late 1980s – emblazoned with the wily, bloody-mouthed wolf head in the centre have become one of the most recognizable logos in the Canadian Hockey League (CHL), the umbrella organization overseeing the OHL, the Western Hockey League (WHL), and the Quebec Major Junior Hockey League (QMJHL).

For fifty years the Sudbury Wolves have produced players known to hockey fans around the world. Quinton Byfield, Randy Carlyle, Pat Verbeek, Mike Foligno and his sons Nick and Marcus, Marc Staal, Mike Fisher—these and many other players all forged their paths to the National Hockey League (NHL) with the Sudbury Wolves. In fact, the franchise is among the world's leading producers of professional hockey players. A study released by *The Hockey News* in 2015 combed through every NHL draft from 1990 to 2014 in an effort to determine which National Collegiate Athletic Association (NCAA) programs and CHL teams developed the most NHL players. The magazine concluded that the Sudbury Wolves were "the top development franchise in major junior over the past 25 years" and were "a model of consistency when it comes to producing NHL talent" among players with at least 200 NHL games to their name. Since 1973, over 120 Wolves players have been drafted to the NHL.[6]

Members of the Sudbury Wolves, past and present, have regularly commented on the superb quality of the team's fanbase, and have often taken an active role in giving back to the city in which they played. "I had a great opportunity to play junior and minor hockey here in Sudbury, and it prepared me for the pro game," once explained local product Zack Stortini, the longest-serving captain in Wolves history and retired NHL forward who now works as an assistant coach for the team. "It's such a great hockey town that loves and supports the team," he told *The Sudbury Star*.[7] Whether it be through public appearances for autographs and pictures with fans or fundraisers for charitable causes, for years the Wolves organization and its members have embraced its role as a pillar of the Sudbury community. "I'm very proud of them," says legendary Toronto Maple Leafs broadcaster Joe Bowen, a Sudbury native who began his career covering the Sudbury Wolves on local radio in the 1970s and whose son, David, was drafted by the club in 2016. "The guys are out in the community. They're going to schools. They have special events in the arena … These guys become pretty famous people in the community, and they have to understand that's part of the job."[8]

The Sudbury Wolves serve as a lightning rod for the city's passion for the game. With more than a dozen public arenas and over 50 outdoor rinks in the Greater Sudbury area, the local residents have ample opportunity to indulge in the sport themselves, either as participants or as spectators. Since 1951, fans have gathered at the downtown barn on Elgin Street to watch the Wolves take on their opponents, and these games have inspired countless Sudburians to fall in love with hockey. "I have been a fan of the Wolves for as long as I can remember and some of my fondest memories deal with our local OHL club," one fan wrote to *The Sudbury Star* in 2006. "I feel at home whenever I walk into the Sudbury Community Arena, hearing the roar of the crowd and the sounds of skates and hockey sticks on the ice … My Sudburian pride will never leave me."[9]

Current and former owners of the franchise have always understood the importance of the Sudbury Wolves in the community. "Hockey in Sudbury is like a religion," says Joe Drago, who served as an executive, coach, and part-owner of the club from the early 1970s until the mid-1980s. "Sudbury fans are difficult fans because they want a winner and they don't accept losing."[10] Mark Burgess, whose family previously owned the team for 31 years, once remarked that "The team is a calling card for this city. Being an OHL city gives a stamp of identity to any community, and gives us national and international exposure."[11] The current owner of the franchise, Dario Zulich, who purchased the team in 2016, echoes these sentiments: "I think the Sudbury Wolves is a reflection of the spirit of the community … We are a hard-working city, and we have a hard-working team, and I believe we reflect the spirit of our city."[12]

At the same time, supporters of the Wolves have been wringing their hands and shaking their fists over the club's failure to win an OHL championship or the coveted Memorial Cup over the last number of decades. Since 1919, the Memorial Cup has been awarded to the best junior hockey team in Canada, and today it serves as one of the most coveted trophies in North American sport as teams from the United States have also been brought into the fold. Each spring since 1972, the champions of the OHL, the WHL and the QMJHL compete in a round-robin series overseen by the CHL to determine who gets to take home the Memorial Cup.[13] Junior hockey players themselves are quite young, ranging from 15 to 21-years-old, and they must endure a tremendous amount of pressure each season to capture this championship for their respective teams; realizing this goal requires a huge amount of determination and maturity. Since 1932 the Sudbury Wolves have not won the Memorial Cup, nor have they captured the J. Ross Robertson Cup—emblematic of the OHL championship and named after former Ontario Hockey Association (OHA) president John Ross Robertson—since joining the league.

In an almost perverse way this has fuelled the passion of the Wolves fan-base, comparable to those who supported Major League Baseball's Chicago Cubs during their 108-year World Series drought, or those who currently back the Toronto Maple Leafs in their annual quest for their first Stanley Cup since 1967. "Although Sudburians are very proud anyway, Sudbury deserves a championship team," says Dario Zulich. "And so, I take a lot of responsibility."[14] Joe Bowen has made a few trips back to the Sudbury Arena in recent years to watch his son, a goaltender, play for the Wolves, giving him renewed exposure to the devotion of the fans in spite of the team's long-standing championship shortfall. "When it does happen, and I really hope it does for the Wolves," Bowen states, "I mean, it's going to be … literally, people going to graveyards and gravesites to tell great-grandpa, or dad, or whoever, that 'You'll never guess what finally happened.' And it will, it will."[15]

The Sudbury Wolves did come remarkably close to making an appearance in the Memorial Cup tournament as recently as the 2006-07 OHL season, and despite missing the mark that year the experience demonstrated the magnitude of the team's place in the lives of Sudburians. After a mediocre regular season, the Wolves went on a Cinderella run to the 2007 OHL Finals, narrowly losing in Game 6 to the now-defunct Plymouth Whalers. Coached by Sudbury native Mike Foligno, who played for the team in the 1970s and became known as one of greatest players in franchise history, the Wolves gave hope to fanatical local hockey fans that the club could be champions once again. "This whole community is electrified," Foligno said in May 2007 as his team prepared for Game 3 of the finals. "This run has been really special for the North. It's special for the ownership and the community."[16]

Foligno's choice of words was noteworthy. Why was the Wolves performance special for "the North" and not just Sudbury itself? When the Windsor Spitfires won back-to-back Memorial Cup titles in 2009 and 2010, for instance, did locals celebrate it as an accomplishment for "the South"? Certainly not, and there is a specific set of reasons behind this distinction, embedded in a regional identity that has shaped the Sudbury Wolves from their earliest beginnings. In 1932, the "Cub Wolves of the North" were portrayed not only as the champions from Sudbury, but from the wider region of Northern Ontario. During the Wolves' championship series against Plymouth in 2007, a fan of the Soo Greyhounds wrote to *The Sudbury Star* to wish the Wolves luck, proclaiming that "The support by Northern Ontario fans is legendary, so let's get the [Memorial Cup] back up here where it belongs—in front of true hockey fans."[17]

The region of Northern Ontario— traditionally defined as the area of the province lying north and west of a line running roughly from Lake Huron, the Mattawa River, Lake Nipissing, and the French River—has historically differentiated itself from the rest of the province in a way that stretches beyond mere geography, and this phenomenon has naturally spilled over into the realm of sporting. "I think the game of hockey is part of the fabric of the North," says Sudbury native and Wolves legend Randy Carlyle, who went on to have a decorated playing and coaching career in the NHL. "It's part of the community, it's part of the fabric. It's part of what we do when we live in Northern Ontario and you attend the games. And attendance is one thing, but everyone's got an opinion," he explains further. "They might not have watched the game, but they watched the highlights, or they read the newspaper, or they read the Internet—they are involved, they are committed to following the team, good or bad."[18] Without getting too sidetracked about the implications of Canadian regionalism—Prime Minister William Lyon Mackenzie King once said that "If some countries have too much history, we have too much geography"—we will see throughout this book that the language of "the North" has been evoked by fans and observers of the Sudbury Wolves for decades, giving the team an added layer of meaning to the community to which it belongs.

This book weaves all these ideas into the big wins, heartbreaking losses, legendary players, lively coaches, and rabid fans who have played their part in creating the history of the Sudbury Wolves. It is hoped that it will be a source of reminiscing for long-time fans and one of inspiration for the next generation of supporters. Rick Bartolucci, Member of Provincial Parliament for Sudbury from 1995 to 2014, perhaps best captured the synonymous relationship between Sudbury and the Wolves when he wrote, "The resiliency, perseverance and dedication of the Sudbury Wolves represent characteristics of the community at-large … It is this strong connection that will surely help the Sudbury Wolves achieve even greater success in the future."[19]

CHAPTER 1:

WOLVES OF THE NORTH, 1892-1972

In March 1920, the Collingwood Hockey Club, the five-time OHA intermediate champions, prepared to face off against an unfamiliar opponent. Collingwood had earned the chance to play for the Allan Cup, the coveted Canadian senior national ice hockey championship, and the team's next opponent was the top club from the Northern Ontario Hockey Association (NOHA), a league affiliated with the OHA. A Toronto-based journalist remarked that "southern fans are 'shaking in their shoes'" at the prospect of Collingwood facing a team which was "reputed as the best that ever came out of the North."[1] These concerns proved valid when the two teams clashed just a few days later at the Toronto Arena Gardens. The northerners completely overpowered Collingwood both physically and on the scoresheet, racking up a lopsided 11-2 victory before a disgruntled crowd. *The Globe* explained in its postgame analysis that "Collingwood may be invincible in the Ontario Hockey Association intermediate series, but they certainly went out of their class when they met … the N.O.H.A titleholders, here last night." The newspaper added that the rough, highly-skilled NOHA champions had certainly lived up to their increasingly popular nickname: "Wolves of the North."[20] These so-called "Wolves of the North" actually hailed from Sudbury, and it was on that evening in 1920 that the spirit of the Sudbury Wolves became entrenched in the minds of hockey fans across Ontario.[21]

The early history of the Sudbury Wolves can be somewhat convoluted. The city of Sudbury has had a hockey team named the Wolves or Cub Wolves nearly every season since the end of the First World War, but these clubs existed in various forms and competed at different levels of the game over the course of the twentieth century. In 1932, for example, the junior Cub Wolves won the Memorial Cup, and then stormed all the way back to the finals again in 1935. In the late 1930s, a senior version of the Wolves won the Ice Hockey World Championships in Europe. In 1959, a professional Wolves team played the Eastern Professional Hockey League (EPHL), a minor league run by the NHL. Although the EPHL folded in 1963, by that time the Cub Wolves had re-emerged as members of the NOHA Junior 'A' league. Finally, in 1972, businessman Mervin "Bud" Burke purchased the Niagara Falls Flyers of the OHA Junior 'A' league (predecessor to the OHL) and relocated the team to Sudbury, ushering in the modern Wolves organization. With all this in mind, this era in Wolves' history can at times be challenging to follow. Nonetheless, the many successes of these early Wolves teams played an essential part in transforming Sudbury into a true hockey town and continue to provide fans with a sense of collective memory that has transcended generations.

EARLY HISTORY OF THE PACK

Since the late nineteenth century, at least two things have remained constant in Sudbury: mining and hockey. Originally established in 1883 as a temporary campsite for workers building the Canadian Pacific Railway (CPR), the trajectory of the Sudbury area was forever altered by the discovery of rich copper ore bodies that contained significant amounts of nickel, also known as "devil copper." By the early 1890s, nearly 2,500 people resided in the blossoming mining community, and in 1892 a local hockey club was founded.[22] In 1899 it began competing against teams from North Bay, Mattawa, Warren, and Sturgeon Falls for a district championship.[23]

Hockey in Sudbury began charting a new course in the early twentieth century. In 1903, Sudbury joined the OHA, the governing body overseeing amateur ice hockey play in Ontario since 1890.[24] The OHA oversaw three separate levels of play—junior, intermediate, and senior—which were distinguished by age and skill-level. Sudbury was slotted into an intermediate division and competed at that level with moderate success for the next four years. Local leagues flourished in Sudbury during the 1910s, most notably in 1915 when a squad of Sudbury's all-stars won the Gordon Cup as the champions of the District of Nipissing.[25] It was during this time that hometown superstars Alex McKinnon and Wilfred "Shorty" Green burst onto the scene. Sudbury's team also launched its long tradition of donning green and white jerseys. The colour choice allegedly stemmed from the fact that most players from that 1915 championship team happened to play for a team in a local league that wore green and white sweaters.[26]

There was a slight lull in Sudbury hockey during the First World War (1914-18), but in the aftermath of the conflict the town solidified its position as both a strong mining and hockey hub. By 1913 Sudbury had emerged as the world's leading supplier of nickel, and this was further enhanced by the skyrocketing demand for this wartime metal in the production of weaponry, armour, and other military equipment; it was not long before the town was known as the "Nickel City" or "Nickel Capital." At the same time, the pollution emitted from the operations of mining giants such as INCO had a devastating impact on the natural surroundings, giving Sudbury the image of a blackened landscape that endured for much of the twentieth century.[27] In terms of hockey, in 1919 Sudbury entered the OHA junior loop, which was reserved for players under twenty years of age, and shortly thereafter the NOHA was formed as a sister organization of the OHA. Sudbury promptly entered teams in both the NOHA junior and senior series alongside teams from Sault Ste. Marie, North Bay, New Liskeard, and elsewhere across the north. Sudbury sported superb players at both levels, including McKinnon, Shorty Green, his younger brother Christopher Redvers "Red" Green, and Sam Rothschild, who went on to become the first Jewish player in the NHL.[28]

Sudbury earned the "Wolves" moniker for its hockey teams around 1920.[29] The Sudbury juniors and seniors each won their respective NOHA titles that year to gain a spot in the OHA playdowns against teams from southern Ontario. Although the juniors, which featured Rothschild on its roster, were eliminated by Toronto, the Sudbury seniors easily defeated Collingwood in the aforementioned "Wolves of the North" match. After trouncing Collingwood, Sudbury, which included players like McKinnon and both the Green brothers, advanced to face the Toronto Granites. The winners would represent eastern Canada in the Allan Cup finals, making it the most important match in Sudbury hockey history up to that point. About five hundred Sudburians travelled southward to watch the first of two Sudbury-Toronto games, while those in town received updates from the CPR telegraph office. In the first game, Sudbury soundly beat the Granites by a score of 6-2.[30] According to sportswriter Frank Pagnucco, during the third period of this game an unidentified CPR telegraph operator coined the phrase "Wolves of the North" while providing updates to eager fans in Sudbury, likely as a reference to the "voracity and tenacity that typified the play of these men from Sudbury."[31]

It is not entirely clear if this mysterious CPR employee deserves full credit for conceiving the "Wolves of the North" nickname, however. In 1974, an elderly Sam Rothschild stated in an interview with *The Northern Life* that the "first Sudbury Wolves hockey team was formed back in 1913" and competed "in a small league with only Sudbury, North Bay and the Soo." Yet Rothschild also claimed that Sudbury won the Gordon Cup in 1913, when in reality North Bay captured the title that year. It is possible that in his old age Rothschild's memory was a tad foggy. He may have been merely trying to explain that players such as McKinnon and the Green brothers had begun playing together around 1913 before becoming team-mates on the 1920 "Wolves of the North" squad. It is therefore uncertain if the "Sudbury Wolves" name itself was formally used prior to the First World War, as other sources confirming this remain uncovered.[32]

Regardless, the "Wolves of the North" label did appear in Toronto newspapers during the lead-up to Sudbury's match against Collingwood in 1920, before it was apparently transmitted during coverage of the game versus the Granites. Moreover, it has been documented that Sault Ste. Marie began using its own historic hockey team name—the Greyhounds—in 1919 in direct reference to the Wolves. Shortly after the First World War, an unnamed hockey club based in the Soo had been set to join the now-defunct Upper Peninsula Hockey League. The head coach allegedly requested "that the team be called the Greyhounds because 'a Greyhound is much faster than a wolf,' a reference made to the already established rival club, the Sudbury Wolves."[33] It seems more likely, then, that the CPR employee may have merely popularized "Wolves of the North," which in later years was simply shortened to the Wolves. Indeed, in the words of sports historian Joe Greaves, the year 1920 marked the beginning of "the illustrious history of the Sudbury Wolves."[34]

The Sudbury Wolves fanbase experienced its first big heartbreak during the OHA playdowns in 1920. On March 20, Sudbury again made short work of the Granites, toppling the home team and making a lasting impression on the Ontario hockey community. "Wolves of the North they were named and Wolves of the North they turned out to be," wrote *The Globe* in its postgame coverage. "For years the Northerners have awaited the time when they could demonstrate their strength. Their hour came Saturday night, and over six hundred Sudbury fans, who had made the trip especially for the occasion, were on hand to see their favorites crush Granites' hope."[35] The Wolves had earned the opportunity to represent eastern Canada in the Allan Cup finals—or so they thought. The University of Toronto, the reigning intercollegiate champions, suddenly insisted that they be allowed to challenge Sudbury for the opportunity to play in the national amateur championship. Despite lingering doubts about the legitimacy of its request, Toronto was granted the chance to play a tired and unprepared Sudbury team. The first game ended in a 2-2 draw.[36] In the final sudden-death match that followed, Sudbury rallied back from a three-goal deficit to send the game into overtime, but it was the University of Toronto that scored in the extra frame to send themselves to the Allan Cup against Winnipeg.

For Sudbury fans the whole scheme had been a grave betrayal, robbing their team of what was believed to be its rightful place in the national title game. The Wolves of the North were still warmly received by the people of Sudbury and were presented with medals, individual diamond rings, and the NOHA trophy at a banquet upon their return.[37]

In 1921, the Wolves of the North acquired its first mascot, albeit an unusual and potentially dangerous one. In October, a local fan named Bob Stevens purchased a live wolf from a farmer near Espanola who had accidentally captured the canine when it wandered into a bear trap he had set. Stevens then decided to give it to the team to serve as the "mascot of the 'Wolves of the North.'" The wolf was expected to be muzzled and kept on a chain while in public, although the farmer who captured him allegedly was able to pick it up in his arms and pat it. "There is no doubt but that the mascot will be a unique addition to the team," wrote *The Sudbury Star*. "When the Wolves of the North go after the hockey honors this winter it will likely be the proudest wolf in the entire North Country."[38] The newspaper later held a contest inviting readers to suggest a name for the wolf, with the name "Ki-I" emerging as the name of choice. The origin of this name was not provided, but the Sudbury resident who proposed it included a brief poem which concluded "And when we play the final game, Let it be said that people came, To see young Ki-I, mascot pup, Annex with ease, the Allan Cup."[39] Whatever became of the Wolves' first mascot remains unknown.[40]

The rest of the Roaring Twenties were less eventful for the Wolves of the North. Starting in 1923, a number of Sudbury's best players were lured out of town by professional contract offers. Alex McKinnon and the Green brothers, for example, went on to play for the Hamilton Tigers of the NHL. These moves decimated the Wolves lineup and led the team to withdraw from NOHA senior competition for that year.[41] During the 1924-25 NHL season, meanwhile, the Tigers, led by captain Shorty Green, initiated the first strike in league history over playoff compensation. The NHL fined the players for their defiance, though the landmark labour dispute did see many Tigers players receive raises following the team's subsequent relocation to New York.[42] In 1924, Sam Rothschild also departed for the NHL when the Montreal Maroons offered him a two-year contract worth $3,500 per season; he became the first Sudburian to win a Stanley Cup in 1926.[43]

Back in Sudbury, the Nickel Belt Hockey League (NBHL) was formed in the mid-1920s to help develop local hockey players, provide fans with a league to follow and feed regional clubs (namely the Sudbury Wolves) with talent. W.E. Mason, owner of *The Sudbury Star*, served as president of the NBHL. There were up to eight teams in the league, with companies such as INCO, the CPR, and Falconbridge Nickel Mines Limited, founded in 1928, sponsoring the league and recruiting men from wide and far to come to the area as employee-athletes. In the spring, the best players from the NBHL were selected to form an all-star team to compete nationally under the name of the Sudbury Wolves, whether at the senior or junior level. It was through the NBHL that some of the greatest moments in Wolves history occurred.[44]

NORTHERN CHAMPIONS

Sudbury was to some degree sheltered from the economic downturn of the Great Depression that sent shockwaves across the rest of Canada in the 1930s. While roughly one-third of Canadian workers lost their jobs, people actually moved *to* Sudbury—which officially became a city in August 1930—in search of employment opportunities.[45] Worldwide demand for nickel remained strong for much of the decade; the city's population grew from about 18,000 to over 30,000. One of the most enduring memories of this era for Sudbury's history, however, is the on-ice success of multiple Wolves teams. These victories during the 1930s helped form the basis of Sudbury's reputation as a hockey-mad city that persists to this day.[46]

The highlight of the decade was undoubtedly the Cub Wolves run to the Memorial Cup in 1932. The team was run by Max Silverman, a local businessman who began his tenure with the Sudbury hockey club in 1919 as a water-boy and rose to the role of manager and coach by 1930.[47] Small in stature but with a big personality, Silverman was active in the Sudbury hockey community his entire adult life. "In hockey Maxie became a living legend of the North," once read *The Globe and Mail*.[48] He was elected mayor of Sudbury in 1965 but succumbed to cancer the next year while still in office.[49] In 1932, Silverman decided to put together a star-studded junior

Wolves team to vie for the Memorial Cup. He delegated the coaching job to Sam Rothschild, who had returned to his hometown years earlier to work as a liquor salesman after his NHL career was cut short by a knee injury. Rothschild had also been coaching Falconbridge in the NBHL for the last few seasons.[50] "They had good hockey players," Rothschild told *The Northern Life* in 1974. "Max Silverman came to me and said 'how'd you like to coach the team. I'll be the manager and you can coach.' It sounded okay to me."[51]

Together Silverman and Rothschild built a crew of dynamic junior players to form the nucleus of a Memorial Cup contender. The squad was led by top forwards Dalton "Nakina" Smith, Adelard Lafrance, and Jack McInnes. The equally impressive second line was anchored by Coniston native Joseph Hector "Toe" Blake, the future Montreal Canadiens legend and ten-time Stanley Cup champion, alongside Max Bennett and Larry Lafrance. The backend was held down by the likes of team captain Red Porter and his bruising defence partner Bob McInnes, with Anthony "Ant" Healy standing between the pipes. Others included Borden Caswell, Gordon Grant, Ivan Fraser, Don Price, Maurice Dabous, A.J. Powell, and Peter Fenton. Most of these young men had played for Silverman during the NBHL season, while Smith, Blake and Bennett were add-ons recruited by Rothschild from his Falconbridge team.[52]

The 1932 Cub Wolves began their journey to the Memorial Cup in January against their NOHA rival Soo Greyhounds. Sudbury won the first game by default after the Soo forfeited the match because they claimed they had been unable to practice due to a lack of a suitable ice surface. When the two teams finally met in late January, the Wolves annihilated the Greyhounds by a score of 11-2. Sudbury then won the following meeting by a narrower margin to advance to the NOHA semi-finals. *The Sudbury Star* basked in the glory of the Soo's demise, declaring that the "Sudbury Kids Score Revenge for Anything Soo's Ever Done."[53]

Sudbury rolled through the rest of the NOHA without much difficulty. On February 22, the Cub Wolves crushed the Chapleau Huskies 14-0, with Smith posting eight points on the night.[54] The Wolves then travelled to Monteith, near Iroquois Falls, for the opening game of the

NOHA championship. The series would be decided by the aggregate score, meaning the team with the most goals over the two games played would win the title. On the road Sudbury rolled over its opponent by a score of 5-0. Five days later, Monteith arrived in the Nickel Capital and eked out a 3-2 win at Sudbury's Palace Rink, but it was not enough to outscore the Wolves in the round. *The Star* proudly announced that "the Woofers are the junior champions of the Northern Ontario Hockey Association and the regions lying beyond Moosonee."[55]

The Cub Wolves were slotted to face the OHA-champion Toronto Marlboros to decide who would qualify for the Eastern Canada semifinals. The city of Sudbury rallied around the underdog Wolves as they prepared to "invade the sub-Arctic regions of Toronto in quest of the Memorial Cup."[56] Both games were played in mid-March at Maple Leaf Gardens, a now iconic building that had just opened in November 1931 as the home of the Toronto Maple Leafs.[57] The Cub Wolves stunned the Marlboros in the opener with a decisive 3-0 victory in front of 6,000 fans. Ant Healy was unbeatable in net while Nakina Smith registered a goal and an assist. The win was of major significance to the people of Sudbury. "Sudbury's Cub Wolves of the North … hold a record that no other junior aggregation from the north has ever attained," wrote *The Sudbury Star*. While other Northern Ontario clubs had defeated southern contenders in the past, "they were never able to whip them to a frazzle and then rub their noses with whitewash like the Cub Wolves did."[58]

The second game was more nerve-wracking for Wolves' fans as 13,000 people packed the Gardens for another gripping match. Toronto's Jack Shill sniped four goals on the night—three of them coming in a span of 26 seconds—to give the Marlboros a 4-1 lead at the end of the game. With the aggregate score tied 4-4, overtime was necessary. Seven minutes into the extra frame, Bennett snapped the series-winning goal behind the Toronto goaltender.[59] The Wolves had defied the odds and conquered the OHA champions; the best was yet to come, however.

Clubs from Ottawa and Montreal were the last obstacles in Sudbury's march toward the Memorial Cup finals. The Cub Wolves opened the next round by beating the Ottawa Shamrocks 2-0 before stumbling out the gate in the second game. Although Ottawa took an early two-goal lead, *The*

Star maintained that "the Cub Wolves of the North never lost control of the situation, and their comeback was just another thrilling page in their thrilling history." In the second period, Nakina Smith tucked the Wolves' first goal of the game to put his team up 3-2 on the round. After Bennett had already set-up Adelard Lafrance for another one, Smith sealed the deal by scoring "the prettiest goal of the evening" to end the round at 5-2 in Sudbury's favour.[60]

The Wolves then advanced to the Eastern Canada finals versus Montreal A.A.A., with the winner clashing against the Western titleholders for the coveted Memorial Cup. The first match in Montreal ended in a tie, leading to a winner-take-all scenario at Maple Leaf Gardens in late March. Early in the second period, the unstoppable Smith dangled his way around the Montreal defence and scored the go-ahead marker. Only minutes later, Larry Lafrance rifled a shot at Montreal's goaltender, striking him in the face and causing the netminder to stare "straight ahead in bewilderment." Lafrance then pounced on the loose puck and put the Cub Wolves up 2-0. Sudbury closed out the game with a third goal to capture the George Richardson Memorial Trophy and earn a berth in the Memorial Cup finals as the champions of Eastern Canada.[61]

By this time the people of Sudbury were engulfed by a sense of "Woofer-Mania," the likes of which the city had never seen before. Fans had been closely following the Cub Wolves along their journey, receiving reports via telegraph or by calling *The Sudbury Star* on game-nights for updates. A few hundred fans even followed the team throughout eastern Canada to offer support on the road. Given that Sudbury lacked a permanent radio station at the time, *The Star* secured a special licence to set-up a temporary station to broadcast the games. Virtually the whole city came together in support of the local junior phenoms, providing a temporary escape from the economic hardships of the Depression. When the Cub Wolves stopped briefly in Sudbury on their way westward by train to face the Winnipeg Monarchs, they were met with the cheers of some five hundred ecstatic supporters. The Cub Wolves had cemented themselves as "the best junior team the north has ever produced," wrote *The Star* on March 30, "and they're as good right now as any Memorial Cup team ever was."[62]

The Cub Wolves and the Monarchs played the whole best-of-three Memorial Cup final series at Shea's Amphitheatre in Winnipeg. The Monarchs drew first blood on March 31 with a 4-3 win before the home crowd. Sam Rothschild remained calm entering the second game as Sudbury faced elimination, telling a reporter that he expected his club to tie the series. The fiery Max Silverman, on the other hand, was less composed once the match got underway. It was a wild outing that saw Smith leave the game in the first period after suffering a broken cheekbone. Blake was charged with filling the void at centre and did so admirably, feeding a pass to Grant who deposited the puck behind Monarchs' goalie Art Rice-Jones to give Sudbury a 1-0 lead. In the second period, Silverman jumped out of the stands onto the ice and punched Winnipeg's George Brown on the chin after it appeared Brown was about to attack a Wolves player for accidentally clipping him with his stick. A fight subsequently broke out on the ice that required police intervention to restore order. Overtime was called after Winnipeg tied things up 1-1 late in the third period. In the extra frame, Cub Wolves' captain Red Porter carried the puck end-to-end before dishing a pass to Adelard Lafrance, who tucked the game-winning goal into Winnipeg's net and sent the series to a third and deciding match.[63]

The outcome in early April provided Sudbury with one of the most celebrated moments in the city's history. Tickets were difficult to get for those in Winnipeg, with some people willing to dish out as much as ten dollars to scalpers for a seat. The Memorial Cup championship final was radio broadcast all the way from Manitoba to Sudbury, and fans listened nervously and hoped for a big victory. The Cub Wolves did not disappoint. Smith returned from injury and came up clutch early in the first period, skating around Winnipeg's defence and picking "the corner on the twine before the goalie had a chance to spot it." The 5,500 fans at the Shea's Amphitheatre did not see another goal for the remainder of the game. Sudbury's Healy was "invincible" in net and stopped every puck he faced, even after the Monarchs unsuccessfully attempted to get him disqualified by accusing him of using illegal equipment. The Cub Wolves won 1-0 and were the Memorial Cup champions.

People poured into the streets of Sudbury in jubilation. "Sudbury's Cub Wolves of the North are the best junior hockey players in Canada," boasted

The Sudbury Star. "For the first time in history the cherished silverware comes to rest in Northern Ontario."[64] The Cub Wolves were greeted with applause and admiration that extended across Northern Ontario as the team travelled from Winnipeg to Sudbury along the CPR. At home thousands of people congregated in the streets to welcome their hockey heroes as the players were paraded through Sudbury on a firetruck. A civic banquet was held in April to commemorate the Cub Wolves, and mayor Peter Fenton even presented the team's players with keys to the city.[65]

Ninety years later, the pennant memorializing the triumphant 1932 Cub Wolves still hangs in the rafters of the Sudbury Arena as a reminder of the team's impact on the history of the community. The Memorial Cup title brought attention and prestige to the city of Sudbury, as well as the reputation of being a producer of top-notch hockey talent. Along with Blake, teammates Bennett, Smith, and Adelard LaFrance all went on to play in the NHL. While winning the Memorial Cup remains unmatched by any Wolves team since, the legendary rise of the Cub Wolves of the North roughly nine decades ago has kept fans hopeful of enjoying another grand Memorial Cup party in the Nickel City.

THE PACK & THE SILVER FOX

The Cub Wolves nearly replicated their success just three years after the glorious 1932 campaign. A rift between Silverman and Rothschild led the two men to sever their working relationship not long after winning the national title, with Silverman taking control of the Cub Wolves while Rothschild assumed the coaching duties of Sudbury's senior hockey crew. In 1935 both the junior and senior clubs captured their respective NOHA titles. The junior Cub Wolves wrecked South Porcupine in the NOHA finals, leading *The Star* to comment that the "green-shirted Sudbury Juniors had too much power, too much speed for … the Porkies." Though the senior Wolves were eliminated from Allan Cup contention relatively early on, the Cub Wolves began another drive toward the Memorial Cup. Silverman, dubbed "the nickel city hockey wizard," was coaching a junior Wolves team that included goaltender Dave Kemp and future NHL players Chuck Shannon, Wilbert Carl Hiller, and Don Grosso.[66]

The Cub Wolves travelled to Toronto to play the Oshawa Majors in the Ontario championship finals. After falling behind 3-0 in the game, Sudbury charged back on a hat trick by Grosso to tie it up. Late in the third period, defenceman and team captain Shannon scored the game-winning goal for the Wolves. Following the match, however, the OHA executive ordered that the game be replayed because it claimed that Silverman had violated league rules regarding player transfers. In the ensuing kerfuffle, the Cub Wolves were forced to drop one of their players and a rematch against Oshawa was mandated. With only eight regulars in the lineup, the Wolves defeated the Majors 5-3, and would thus represent the province in the Memorial Cup tournament. "The handling of the Cub Wolves in the sudden-death game with Oshawa Majors was the hardest coaching job I ever had," Silverman later said.[67]

The Wolves had to prove that they were the best club in eastern Canada before earning a berth in the Memorial Cup finals. The team first faced the Verdun Maple Leafs, the junior champions of the Quebec Amateur Hockey Association, in a two-game aggregate series. Sudbury beat Verdun at Maple Leaf Gardens by a score of 9-4, and in the next game sealed the deal with an 11-7 victory at the Montreal Forum to advance.[68] Next in line were the powerhouse Ottawa Ottawas. In late March, again at Maple Leaf Gardens, which had essentially served as the Cub Wolves' home arena due to a lack of artificial ice in Sudbury, the Greenshirts upset the Rideaus by a score of 3-0 on a shutout by Kemp and two goals by forward Art Stuart. In early April in Ottawa in front of 5,500 fans, the Wolves again defeated Rideau 7-4, with Hiller scoring three goals. The Wolves had again won the George Richardson Memorial Trophy as the champions of Eastern Canada. Max Silverman received praise for his coaching and management of the team, having "accomplished what few other sport mentors would have even dared to pursue in bringing the player-shorn Greenshirts to the very top rung of junior hockey in Canada."[69]

The 1935 Memorial Cup title series was a rematch between the Sudbury Cub Wolves and the Winnipeg Monarchs. Unlike 1932, the Wolves were seen as the favourites this time around, having gone undefeated in the postseason. In the first game at Winnipeg's Amphitheatre, the Monarchs skated to a 7-6 win over the visiting Greenshirts. After the loss, a frustrated Silverman got into a physical confrontation with at least one taunting Winnipeg fan. Sudbury won the second meeting with Winnipeg by a score of 7-2, but it was the conduct of the Monarchs that stole the show. Sensing imminent defeat, Winnipeg resorted to dirty tactics in the third period, ruthlessly slashing and pushing around the Wolves. By the final fifteen seconds of the game, the Monarchs had four men in the penalty box and only their goalie and a defenceman left on the ice. Winnipeg's own fans turned against them for their unsportsmanlike behaviour, so much so that the police had to escort the Monarchs to safety after the game. "It was one of the most unusual happenings ever witnessed by the small contingent of Sudbury supporters," wrote *The Sudbury Star*.[70]

With the series tied one game apiece, the Cub Wolves and the Monarchs had a final showdown on a dreary night in mid-April. As rain poured through the gaps of the Amphitheatre's roof onto the players and the ice, the city of Sudbury's hopes for a second Memorial Cup were drowned. The Monarchs defeated the Cub Wolves by a score of 4-1 in the decisive match-up, handing Winnipeg its first Memorial Cup championship. When the dejected Greenshirts arrived back in the Nickel City, the sound of "2,000 throats roared a welcome that was reminiscent of the wild scenes which attended the arrival of the victorious Woofers of 1932." Notwithstanding their defeat, the people of Sudbury greeted their junior hockey warriors with a live band, parade, and celebratory feast.[71]

The Sudbury Wolves gained international recognition in 1938, and again in 1949, when Max Silverman led Canadian teams overseas to play in the Ice Hockey World Championships. In 1937, Silverman received permission from Canada's amateur hockey governing bodies to organize a squad of players from across Canada to travel to Czechoslovakia to represent the country in the international tournament. Stylized as the Sudbury Wolves, the team played over thirty exhibition games throughout Europe (winning all but two of them) before heading to Prague in February 1938. The Wolves dumped Germany and the host Czechs to earn the right to play Great Britain in the final, winning that game 3-1 on goals by Reg Chipman, Pat McReavy, and Johnny Godfrey. The Wolves returned to

Canada in March with a statue to signify their status as the world's best amateur ice hockey team.[72]

The Wolves' World Championship appearance more than ten years later was less magical. In 1949 Silverman once more pieced together a roster of players from throughout Canada to enter the international tournament, this time held in Stockholm, Sweden. The Wolves kicked off with an unfathomable 47-0 victory over Denmark. The Canadians drew the ire of European observers for their aggressive play all tournament long, with the Swedish press dubbing them "dangerous men." Before the Wolves' game against Sweden on February 16, a rambunctious crowd outside Stockholm's Olympic Stadium got out of hand, creating a scuffle that sent fourteen people to the hospital. The game ended in a 2-2 tie. The Wolves finished the World Championships with a record of 2-1-2, placing second behind Czechoslovakia. Silverman publicly denounced the tournament before it was even over, opining that "it will be very foolish to send another Canadian team over here under the present conditions. There's too much politics. They don't want Canada to win."[73]

The years immediately following the Second World War (1939-45) witnessed major changes in Sudbury, and this naturally affected the development of the Wolves. Booming industrial and commercial activity during and after the war brought enormous economic benefits to the city as the demand for nickel grew exponentially.[74] The population exceeded 42,000 by 1951, the same year that the roughly 5,000-person capacity Sudbury Community Arena was opened. Located on Elgin Street in the downtown core, the Sudbury Arena was built on the site of the former Central Public School. It replaced the old Palace Rink, which had been demolished in the late 1930s. In the interim, the Stanley Stadium in Copper Cliff had hosted much of Sudbury's hockey activity. The senior Wolves had disbanded by the early 1950s due to the exodus of prime talent from the Sudbury area, though Silverman had continued to oversee a junior incarnation of the team. The senior Wolves were granted the right to call the Sudbury Arena their new home, and soon Silverman had resurrected the team within the NOHA. The Wolves and other NOHA teams were affiliated with NHL organizations, such as the New York Rangers, throughout the 1950s.[75]

By 1953 the Wolves had been reborn as a formidable force that received widespread support from Sudbury's hockey fans. The players—including the high-scoring Gordon Heale, goaltender Allan Millar, and forward John "Yacker" Flynn—often worked jobs at INCO or elsewhere while playing for the Wolves, but the club also paid them on a weekly basis. During the 1953-54 season, the Wolves broke several NOHA attendance records, averaging over 5,000 fans per game.[76] Silverman alone was a draw for many spectators, sometimes leading the "Silver Fox" to get booed by contemptuous onlookers; his appetite for fighting crowd members became almost mythical and gave the coach a mark of notoriety.[77]

A couple of long-standing traditions in Wolves' history simultaneously began that year as well. In November 1953, the late Berk Keaney started his nearly sixty-year career as the Wolves' public address announcer and well-regarded voice of the team. Likewise, the familiar sight of a stuffed wolf descending from the rafters of the Sudbury Arena after each Wolves goal—first through a trap door and later along a pulley system—began around this time after *The Sudbury Star* donated a stuffed wolf to the team as a token of appreciation.[78] Sudbury capped a strong NOHA season by defeating archrival Soo Greyhounds to win the league championship. The next game took place against the Owen Sound Mercurys in the Ontario finals. Hockey fans rushed to the Sudbury Arena to get tickets for the seven-game series. The Wolves won it in Game 7 at the Sudbury Arena to become the inaugural winners of the W.A. Hewitt Trophy as the province's best senior amateur hockey team.[79]

Silverman and the Wolves turned their sights toward the Allan Cup after slaying Owen Sound. The team travelled to the Gaspé Peninsula in Quebec to take on the Matane Red Rocks in another gruelling best-of-seven contest to decide who would be champion of Eastern Canada. The Wolves beat the Red Rocks in a back-and-forth series, propelling Sudbury to the Allan Cup finals in British Columbia versus the pesky Penticton Vees. The Wolves seemed poised to win it all after taking a 3-1 series lead. In Game 5, Sudbury went ahead by a score of 5-2. After the second period, Silverman, boldly assuming his team had the Allan Cup in the bag, infamously cancelled their hotel rooms and had the team plane refuelled and stocked with sandwiches and champagne in preparation for a joyous flight home. The Vees had other plans, however, storming back and winning the game in overtime by a score of 6-5.[80]

The Vees won the next match as well and pushed the 1954 Allan Cup to a seventh game. "Looking out at Sudbury that night in the final game … the whole city of Sudbury was lit up at midnight," reminisced Berk Keaney upon his retirement in 2011.[81] The Wolves gave up three goals in the early going of the game before scoring two to put themselves back in it. The final period has been described as "the most scintillating 20 minutes in Allan Cup history," as the Wolves tried desperately to even the score. Sudburians tuned to the radio broadcast at home listened attentively in hopes of a miracle comeback. In the end, Penticton held on to its 3-2 lead and hoisted the Allan Cup in front of their own adoring fans in the Okanagan Valley.[82] The city of Sudbury commended what was nonetheless a fantastic season for the Wolves, recognizing the team with a host of festivities.[83]

HOWLS OF VICTORY

Although senior hockey fizzled out in Sudbury not long after the Allan Cup run, minor professional hockey came to town in 1959 under the auspices of the EPHL. The six-team league was a farm system for the NHL and included clubs from Ontario and Quebec until its collapse in 1963 owing to financial problems.[84] The Wolves enjoyed considerable success in the EPHL, finishing first in the 1959-60 regular season before losing the championship title in seven games to the Montreal Royals. Sudbury returned to the finals in 1963, this time falling short to the Kingston Frontenacs.[85] Notable figures to suit up for the Wolves over those four EPHL seasons included Leafs legend Dave Keon, Hockey Hall of Fame goaltender Gerry Cheevers, and former *Coach's Corner* host Don Cherry.[86]

Fortunately for Sudbury's hockey fans, the decline of the EPHL coincided with a return of junior competition to the city. In the early 1960s the Wolves joined the newly formed NOHA Junior 'A' league, predecessor to the modern Northern Ontario Junior Hockey League (NOJHL), through the efforts of a group of local sportsmen that included the late Leo Gasparini.[87] This northern loop was a step below the OHA Junior 'A' league, which itself served as a breeding ground for world class players such as Bobby Orr of the Oshawa Generals. These young Sudbury Wolves teams were a popular source of entertainment for hockey fans during the 1960s and early 1970s. The Sudbury Arena was often packed to the brim with spectators seeking to indulge in fierce, old-school hockey between the Wolves and the Sault Ste. Marie Greyhounds, North Bay Trappers, and a handful of other northern clubs. It was not uncommon for NOHA Junior 'A' games to get rowdy and even completely out of hand. In November 1971, for instance, referees dished out ten major penalties and nine game misconducts as the Wolves thumped the Trappers by a score of 14-1.[88]

Bad blood between Sudbury and the Soo in particular reached new heights in the late 1960s to early 1970s. The Wolves, led by coach Marcel Clements and later Barry Mackenzie, a former NHL player who represented Canada at the Winter Olympics in 1964 and 1968, met the despised Greyhounds in the NOHA Junior 'A' finals every year from 1969 to 1972. Sudbury bested the Soo in 1969 and 1971 to win the McNamara Trophy as league champions.[89] During this period players like Sudbury native Al Blanchard, who tied an NOHA Junior 'A' record with 65 goals in the 1970-71 regular season, certainly provided Wolves fans with the chance to watch some of Ontario's top talent, but many believed there was still a market for an even higher level of junior hockey in Sudbury.[90]

Local entrepreneur Mervin "Bud" Burke—a nickname which he says he carried from childhood due to his older sister calling him her "buddy"—led the charge to bring an OHA Junior 'A' club to Sudbury. A native of Quebec, Burke moved to Sudbury in the early 1950s where he built a successful plumbing and heating business. He later expanded into a wide range of ventures, including real estate, a roller-skating rink, and horseracing.[91] Burke was also involved in hockey team operations as a shareholder in the NOHA Wolves, and then became well-known in the community as the outspoken public figurehead of the Sudbury Wolves organization during its first seasons in the OHA. Now in his early-nineties and residing in Ottawa, Burke affirms that "I've never had a lack of being straight up about things."[92] All these years later he has left a lasting impression on many of those who knew him during his time as the Wolves' majority owner. "Bud was a character," says Randy Carlyle, who began his journey to the NHL with the Wolves in the 1970s. "He was very visible. He was in the office all the time. He was around the rink. He was not absentee ownership. He had a huge presence."[93]

Sudbury's path toward gaining an OHA Junior 'A' franchise of its own was by no means straightforward. Burke and his associates attempted to gain entry into the upper tier of Ontario junior hockey as early as 1969. That year, Burke and his associates provided the OHA with a $30,000 down payment to begin the process, but under Canadian Amateur Hockey Association rules the NOHA was able to block the deal, fearing the move would force the league to fold because it would lose one of its most important teams. At the same time, a separate faction, led by Sudbury native and former Boston Bruins forward Jerry Toppazzini, also began lobbying the OHA to consider expanding into Sudbury.[94] Rumours flew over the next few years, and by the early 1970s *The Sudbury Star* remarked that there was "a lot of talk around Northern Ontario about teams getting into the Ontario Hockey Association Junior 'A' and thereby keep the northern players at home."[95]

The movement reached a boiling point in 1971. In March of that year, Burke's group presented a letter to the NOHA to seek permission to submit a formal application for the purchase of an OHA franchise. The matter proved to be a contentious issue at the NOHA's annual meeting in North Bay that April. Lou Farelli and Angelo Bumbacco, owners of the North Bay Trappers and Soo Greyhounds respectively, were vocal opponents of Sudbury's prospective jump to the OHA. Bumbacco allegedly stormed out of one of the meetings in anger, and Farelli publicly stated he would file a lawsuit if the Wolves were awarded a franchise. Their concerns were not without merit. It was generally believed that Sudbury's departure from the NOHA would spell the end of the league itself because the Wolves generated more revenue than any other team, providing funds which were essential to supporting the smaller clubs. Although the league's executive initially voted 5-4 in favour of permitting Sudbury to apply for an OHA franchise, the decision was overruled by NOHA president Terry Talentino, who claimed that his decision to abstain invalidated the entire vote. Talentino later came out against the motion, leaving the issue evenly split among members of the NOHA executive.[96]

Things were far from settled, however, and only became more convoluted over time. When OHA president Clarence "Tubby" Schmalz caught wind of the stalemate, he explained that "to his knowledge no president of the NOHA has ever cast a vote" on a league issue. *Sudbury Star* writer Ted Saunders expressed similar doubts, stating that in his seven years of covering NOHA executive meetings he could not recall the league president ever voting on any important business that arose. A few days later it was reported that the members of the NOHA executive had once again met in North Bay and voted in favour of allowing both the Burke and Toppazzini groups to seek approval to enter the OHA, apparently contingent on the condition that any such franchise be wholly owned by residents of Sudbury for the first five years of operation. Oddly, NOHA president Talentino later denied that the topic had even been discussed at all. "As far as we are concerned, it's none of our business who owns a Sudbury franchise in the OHA league … At no time did we discuss it Saturday because we didn't want to tie anyone down," he told *The Star*. In the end the decision was left to the OHA, which reached a final verdict on April 20; it would not grant Sudbury an expansion team for the upcoming season.[97]

Sudbury's dream of an OHA franchise had not yet been squashed, however. Although the OHA executive had ruled against granting the city an expansion team, it had left the door open for an existing franchise to be relocated. Over the previous two months there had been speculation that the owner of the Niagara Falls Flyers, retired NHL player and southern Ontario resident Leighton Alfred "Hap" Emms, was considering moving his franchise northward. It was believed that Emms might want to form a partnership with Burke, something that would have violated the NOHA's stance on Sudbury-based ownership.[98]

Burke's struggle to bring an OHA Junior 'A' team to Sudbury at last came to fruition in May 1972. Emms eventually decided to sell the Flyers outright to a group consisting of Burke, Bill Plaunt, who operated the local television and radio station CKSO, and Barry Mackenzie, who was also named head coach, for approximately $225,000. Unsurprisingly, the team was rebranded as the Sudbury Wolves, and the newly minted organization swiftly signed a three-year rental deal with the Sudbury Arena. The

Wolves were set to inherit eleven players from the old Flyers squad. Burke arranged the option for fans to buy season tickets through the local Toronto Dominion Bank branch, with the cost of two seats going for around $189; Gord Ewin, a local teacher who would later become part-owner of the club, was the Wolves' first-ever season ticket holder.[99] Shortly thereafter, Sault Ste. Marie was also awarded an OHA Junior 'A' franchise of its own after the Montreal Junior Canadiens were relocated to Northern Ontario, thereby opening a new chapter in the historic Wolves-Greyhounds saga.[100]

Hockey teams competing under the Sudbury Wolves banner were central components of community life in the Nickel City for decades prior to the arrival of the OHA Junior 'A' organization in 1972. The years after the First World War marked the rise of the "Wolves of the North" as the defining cornerstone of Sudbury's hockey culture, and this identity was only strengthened as the Cub Wolves rose to the upper echelons of junior hockey in the 1930s. Senior and professional hockey in Sudbury provided yet another platform for the Wolves' brand to connect with fans in the postwar era, especially with the opening of the Sudbury Arena and the charge toward the Allan Cup in the early 1950s. The NOHA Junior 'A' league brought junior hockey back to prominence in Sudbury starting in the 1960s, revitalizing an already passionate Wolves fanbase. By the time the OHA Junior 'A' circuit had come to town, the Wolves were so intertwined with Sudbury that the transition felt seamless. The stage had been set for another exciting half-century of Wolves hockey.

CHAPTER 2:

TRIAL BY ICE, 1972-1976

The owners, management, players and fans of the brand-new Sudbury Wolves franchise soon realized that the OHA Junior 'A' league was a beast of a different nature. The ten-team association was arguably the most important stepping-stone to the ever-expanding NHL, and it thus brought a level of junior hockey to the Nickel City that it had never seen before. For reasons that will become clear, the Wolves' first OHA season was not exactly a smashing success. Moreover, Sudbury's mining industry endured layoffs, strikes, and cutbacks that hurt the local economy during the 1970s. As a result, local hockey enthusiasts did not always flock to the Sudbury Community Arena in massive numbers in the Wolves' early years.[1] The team and its fans managed to overcome these hurdles, however, and in the process took the budding Wolves organization to new heights by the midway point of the decade. In dealing with navigating these unchartered waters, those closely involved with the Sudbury Wolves during this period underwent a trial by fire, or perhaps more fittingly, a trial by ice.

RUDE AWAKENING

In May 1972, the Wolves were sitting in the enviable position of owning two first round picks back-to-back in the OHA Junior 'A' draft. With the third and fourth overall selections, Sudbury chose defenceman Greg Neeld of the Markham Waxers and left winger Mike Marson of the Chatham Maroons as the first two draft choices in modern Wolves history.[2] Neeld proved to be a controversial choice from the get-go. In 1971, the teenage blueliner had been signed by the Toronto Marlboros of the OHA after his family had relocated to Ontario from British Columbia. Toronto assigned Neeld to its minor affiliate in Markham, hoping it could protect him from the upcoming 1972 draft. When the OHA executive ruled that Neeld was actually still eligible to be drafted, the Wolves picked him and initiated a "rights war" with the Marlboros that extended into the 1972-73 season.[3] In Marson, the Wolves had gained a skilled, physical forward and one of the few black players in Canadian junior hockey at the time. "I was just a kid. When you're sixteen, you're really only like, eight, as far as sports go," laughed Mike Marson forty years later when reflecting on his time in Sudbury in an interview with the Canadian Broadcasting Corporation (CBC). "The first year, it was so cold … and many, many times when it was minus a hundred, I wondered what I was doing."[4]

The Wolves were projected by many to have a solid inaugural season in the OHA Junior 'A' league. Over 100 players showed up to training camp in September in hopes of earning a roster spot, including veterans from the former Niagara Falls Flyers, fresh-faced rookies, and various local products.[5] "It was kind of a pressure situation for everybody," remembered Marson. "It was pretty intense. Bud Burke … coach Barry Mackenzie … these guys were serious guys, you know. It's different to go from being coached as a player in the amateur ranks, to dealing with the very tough and the very systematic teaching that the old pros in those days had."[6] Bud Burke himself remembers it as an exciting time, "but it was tough, too."[7] Mackenzie whittled the opening night roster down to fifteen players, including former Flyers Tom Colley, Eric Vail, Morris Titanic, and Wayne Chrysler. Rookies included Marson, Geoff Green, Norm Martel, Dan Johnson and Mark Sullivan. Neeld, on other hand, was unable to play any regular season games until the Wolves' dispute with the Marlboros had been settled. In net were the tandem of Bob Volpe and Mike Ryckman.[8] Management kept with tradition and dressed the team in green and white uniforms with gold trim and the famous wolf logo front and centre.

Since 1972, dozens of young men have had the honour of serving as captain of the Sudbury Wolves, but it should be noted that exactly who can lay claim to being the first in franchise history is not crystal clear. Official team history indicates Colley was team captain during that inaugural season, yet the historical record provides some conflicting evidence. It appears that the first mention in *The Sudbury Star* of anyone wearing the 'C' was Eric Vail in November 1972.[9] The local newspaper would later report at least two changes to the captaincy throughout the season, with no apparent mention of Colley ever serving in that role. Regardless, Colley is presently credited as the first captain in the history of the Sudbury Wolves.

The first game in the history of the modern Sudbury Wolves was played at the Sudbury Community Arena on September 29, 1972 versus the Ottawa 67's. That year coincidentally marked the fortieth anniversary of Sudbury's last Memorial Cup championship. Some members of that famed 1932 Wolves team were present for the festivities, including Sam Rothschild, who dropped the puck for the ceremonial opening faceoff.[10] Unfortunately for the Wolves and their fans, the home team lost the game by a score of 6-3. Rookie Mark Brazeau scored the first goal in Wolves' franchise history in the first period, but it was not enough to uplift a team that looked out of its element for much of the game. As *The Sudbury Star* described it, the 67's had given the Wolves a "rude lesson in the difference between Ontario Hockey Association major Junior 'A' hockey and the old Northern Ontario Junior Association Tier Two Junior 'A' of the past 10 seasons."[11]

The rest of the 1972-73 season did not get much easier, though there were some milestones worth celebrating. On October 3, Sudbury, backstopped by Bob Volpe, recorded its first win in the OHA with a 5-2 road victory over the Hamilton Red Wings.[12] Two weeks later the team won its first game at home as Titanic scored a hat-trick and the Wolves overcame the Kitchener Rangers by a score of 9-6. Overall, the team struggled defensively, allowing fifty-five goals in its first 11 games. Some help came in mid-October when Sudbury finally wrestled Neeld away from the stubborn Marlboros, but only after Burke reluctantly surrendered two draft picks as compensation. Although Neeld scored in his Wolves debut versus the St. Catharines Black Hawks on October 20, his team lost 6-4 and was met with a chorus of boos from an upset home crowd. This loss proved that the "the honeymoon between fan and warrior is over"; Wolves' supporters expected results.[13]

It was not long before the finger-pointing began. The highly anticipated first OHA Junior 'A' game between the Wolves and the Soo Greyhounds took place at the Sault Memorial Gardens on November 14. The Soo, a team that ultimately finished in last place that season, completely controlled the play from the opening faceoff, crushing Sudbury 9-2 in what coach Mackenzie called "the worst game I've ever been involved in."[14] In early December, *Sudbury Star* reporter Chuck Kruse wrote a piece suggesting that Burke "turn over the reins to those more qualified hockey-wise." Burke responded by temporarily suspending Kruse from any further contact with the club. It was the beginning of Burke's often contentious relationship with *The Star* and its sportswriters, leading the Wolves' owner to periodically re-strict the local newspaper's access to the team over the years.[15] "There w[ere] media problems, for sure," says Bud Burke nearly fifty years later. "I guess in the newspaper business, you have to sort of stretch this, and stretch that. Well, I'm not rubber, and I don't stretch."[16]

The Wolves eventually made changes on and off the ice. By January 1973 the team had an entirely new goaltending tandem after Ryckman was waived and Volpe sat awaiting a trade. The Wolves turned to netminders Dennis Higgins, acquired in a trade with Hamilton, and Detroit native Doug Nowels.[17] The Wolves also moved Mackenzie into the role of general manager and hired Sudbury local Larry Rubic as the new head coach. Not long after apparently being voted as the new captain by his teammates, Chrysler was dealt to St. Catharines for winger Max Hansen and two other players; veteran defenceman Randy Holt was reportedly then hand-ed the 'C.' Sudbury then called up 15-year-old forward Dale McCourt from the Coniston Cubs NOHA Junior 'B,' the Wolves' minor affiliate, making him the first local player to earn a full-time spot with the Wolves franchise.[18] "That was a good team," remembers Tim Stortini, a Sudbury native who played alongside McCourt on the Cubs before making the jump to the Wolves' roster for the 1973-74 season, "we ended up beating the Wolves."[19] Indeed, in January the Junior 'B' Cubs defeated the Wolves by a score of 6-4 in an exhibition match, casting doubt on the Wolves' readiness for the OHA Junior 'A.'[20]

The turnover continued as the team struggled to hang on to a play-off spot. In early February, after exactly five weeks behind the bench, Rubic was fired. He was replaced as coach by Wolves director of player personnel and Falconbridge Nickel Mines electrician Trevor Boyce, who oversaw a 6-4 win against the Rangers in his coaching debut. Difficulties aside, Sudbury ultimately finished seventh (21-32-10) in the standings and earned a postseason berth.[21] Titanic led the Wolves with 121 points and also finished with 61 goals, the second-most in the league that season, a stellar campaign he attributed to Barry Mackenzie. "He was very instrumental in me developing into the kind of player he thought I could be. He gave me lots of confidence and opportunities," Titanic recollected in an interview with historian Mike Commito in 2020.[22]

The Wolves ended their inaugural season the same way they had started it by falling to the Ottawa 67's. The franchise's first OHA playoff series was not even close. Led by future NHL legend Denis Potvin, the 67's overwhelmed the Wolves from start to finish. In Game 1 on March 28 in Ottawa, the 67's beat Sudbury by a score of 9-2. The second meeting was not much better for the Wolves as Nowels was chased from the net in a 7-2 loss at the Sudbury Arena. After dropping Game 3 at home by an identical score, Barry Mackenzie called out the team's veteran players for their lack of leadership, though he did give credit to Holt, Hansen, and forward Tom Colley. The team's offence had disappeared, and Ottawa was not responding to the Wolves' repeated attempts at intimidation and the instigation of fights. The 67's finished things off on April 3 in the nation's capital, rolling over the Wolves by a score of 14-2 to sweep the series in four straight games. "It was our first year and we have to work to make the second one much better. There's a lot of work to do between now and the fall," Bud Burke said after his team's postseason elimination.[23]

The Wolves' maiden voyage had not been a total failure, however, at least for some individual players. In the 1973 NHL Draft, which saw the New York Islanders take Denis Potvin first overall, a total of five Wolves were chosen by professional clubs: Morris Titanic (Buffalo Sabres, 12th overall), Eric Vail (Atlanta Flames, 21st overall), Randy Holt (Chicago Black Hawks, 45th overall), Tom Colley (Minnesota North Stars, 57th overall), Tom Young (Philadelphia Flyers, 106th overall), and Max Hansen (Minnesota North Stars, 163rd overall). In the same year's draft for the World Hockey Association (WHA)—a professional league that operated in North America during the 1970s until it merged with the NHL in 1979—Titanic and Vail were selected by the Quebec Nordiques, while Colley and Holt were nabbed by the New England Whalers. Four decades later, Titanic remembered finding out he had been drafted by Buffalo while working his summer job as a gas station attendant: "One of the grease monkeys had the radio on in the shop and he yelled out to me, 'hey, you got drafted by the Sabres.' And that was kind of the whole deal. That was as exciting as it got back then."[24]

TAKE TWO

The Sudbury Wolves organization had a lot on the line entering its second season. The team's subpar showing in its first year in the OHA Junior 'A' league had had a noticeable impact on the attitude of its fans. "You see, the hockey fans around the Sudbury area are real critics, and they won't support a club that doesn't give out and produce," wrote *Northern Life* reporter and former NHL forward Cummy Burton in September 1973. "In the years of the old fox, Max Silverman, people would sleep on the sidewalk to get tickets to see the Wolves perform, and Bud Burke … is hoping they'll be lining up to see his Wolves perform in the same fashion as the old clubs."[25] The franchise had invested in its future at the 1973 OHA draft in June, selecting left winger Rod Schutt from the Pembroke Lumber Kings fourth overall and then Sudbury native Ron Duguay with its next pick. The Wolves had hoped to get star local forward Dale McCourt, who was required to enter the OHA draft due to his age, but he was chosen second overall by the Hamilton Red

Wings. The team had hired a new bench boss, Mac MacLean, who had been coaching in the Central Ontario Junior Hockey League for the previous two years.[26] In September, it was reported that the Wolves had traded Greg Neeld to the Oshawa Generals, but he never suited up with the club and ended up playing with the Toronto Marlboros that year. Neeld lost his eye in an on-ice accident that season that helped bring attention to the need for facial protections for hockey players.[27]

It was also around this time that a young Joe Bowen began his legendary broadcasting career. After graduating from the University of Windsor, Bowen returned to his hometown of Sudbury in the early 1970s to work at CKSO radio and television station, which was owned by his late father's friend and Wolves' part-owner Bill Plaunt. Bowen worked in the promotions department for about one year before an opening came up for a sports broadcaster. "I walked down the hall and said, 'Mr. Plaunt, I would like an opportunity to apply for this.' And he says, 'No, I think you can do it.'" Bowen explains. "I'm of the opinion, and living proof, that it's not what you know, it's who you know," he adds. Bowen's job entailed travelling on the Wolves' team bus for their weekend road trips and then heading back to Sudbury to deliver morning radio sports broadcasts. He generally did not cover home games because the ownership group wanted to encourage fans to buy tickets and attend the Sudbury Community Arena in person.[28]

The 1973-74 season was a marked improvement for the Wolves from the previous year. The team opened its season on September 27 in Sault Ste. Marie, beating the Greyhounds by a score of 6-4. Bob Volpe, having returned to the fold as the Wolves' starting goaltender, stopped 41 shots while Mike Marson, the Wolves' new captain, and forward Gord McTavish each registered four points.[29] The boys in green and white kept on clicking and won six of their first ten games. Marson was the face of the team, combining "lots of hustle and plenty of hard knocks to go along with scoring ability." Head coach MacLean was particularly impressed with the 16-year-old rookie Duguay, calling him a "future superstar." Along with Duguay, who came from the Valley East area, players of local origin on the roster included Bob Blanchard, Mike Gazdic and Tim Stortini.[30] "It was a rougher, tougher game," recalls Stortini. "And Sudbury being that kind of blue-collar town, really, really embraced that style of hockey … there was a lot of excitement in the rink."[31] In spite of the team's success, Barry Mackenzie expressed concern over what he thought were disappointing turnouts at the Wolves' home games in the first half of the season.[32] A cooling nickel market may have contributed to the declining number of fans willing to shell out money for tickets; by 1974 INCO had laid off 1,500 workers and shut down its smelter for a whole month.[33]

The city of Sudbury was treated to a special match on December 26, 1973 when the Moscow Wings, a junior team from the Soviet Union, travelled to the Nickel City to play the Wolves.[34] Taking place in the midst of the Cold War, and with Canada's victory over the Soviets in the 1972 Summit Series still fresh in the minds of Canadians across the country, the outcome of this game against these foes from behind the Iron Curtain carried considerable weight for Sudburians. "We packed the place and it was a good seasonal atmosphere," says Tim Stortini of the 5,200 fans that filled the Sudbury Community arena and watched as Moscow dazzled the Wolves with their finesse and skill.[35] "They were amazing and they could really skate and they moved all over the ice," remembers Ken Campbell, Senior Writer at *The Hockey News* and Sudbury native who attended the game as a young Wolves fan.[36] The Russians potted two quick goals in the first half of the third period to go up by a two-goal margin.[37]

Down by a score of 4-2 with ten minutes left in the game, the Wolves mounted a Christmas season miracle comeback. According to Campbell, the Wolves "kind of started to lean on [the Russians] a little bit, and started to get a little physical with them—not dirty—but just sort of started to make them pay the price, and that was when they got back into the game."[38] Forwards Paul Crowley and Alex McKendry scored for the Wolves to tie it up before Duguay netted the eventual game-winner on a partial breakaway against Russian goaltender Andrei Chirkov. Additional goals by Bobby "Hustle" Russell and McTavish sealed the deal for Sudbury as the club walked away with a 7-4 victory over their Soviet guests.[39] Long after his retirement from professional hockey, Mike Marson, who recorded two assists in that game against Moscow, cited the event as the highlight of his junior career: "I remember the excitement of the fans in Sudbury. I remember the tic-tac-toe of the puck. Everything we did seemed to be magical, and it was just a tremendous outcome, and certainly one of the highest points in my life."[40]

Although the Wolves finished the year with a winning record (31-26-13) and built a reputation as a tough group, the team did not fare well in its second postseason appearance. Marson had led the team with 94 points while registering 146 penalty minutes. Wolves' defenceman Don McLean recorded more penalty minutes (305) than any other player in the OHA that season, while fellow blueliner Dave Farrish tied for fifth in the league in that same category. Sudbury met the first place Kitchener Rangers in the opening round of the playoffs. The Wolves went out swinging in Game 4 on March 31, 1974 at the Sudbury Arena, with both Russell and Wolves' defenceman Bill Best dropping the gloves in the third period in an effort to spark their team. It was not enough, however, as the Wolves lost by a score of 2-0 and were again swept in four straight games. The franchise's first ever playoff series win—let alone playoff game win—remained elusive.[41]

Multiple Wolves were drafted into the NHL and WHA in 1974, most notably Mike Marson by the NHL expansion franchise Washington Capitals. The former Wolves captain signed a five-year, $500,000 contract with the team after being chosen with the first pick in the second round of the draft (19th overall). Marson recalled watching hockey on television as a youth with his family and idolizing forward Willie O'Ree, who became the first black player in the NHL when he suited up for the Boston Bruins in 1958. "I remember the first time we all watched Willie O'Ree and I said … I want to do that. I want to be a hockey player. So, it meant whatever I had to sacrifice, that's what I had to do in order to get there."[42] Marson's dream came true on October 9, 1974 when he skated with the Capitals in the club's first ever regular season game and became the second black player in NHL history.[43]

THIRD TIME'S THE CHARM

The year 1974 brought changes to Ontario's junior hockey scene in general and the Sudbury Wolves organization in particular. Shortly after the team was eliminated from the playoffs by Kitchener, Mac MacLean resigned as head coach.[44] He was replaced by Sudbury local Stu Duncan, who had coached at the high school and Junior 'B' levels. Duncan had previously worked as a high school vice-principal and operated a sporting-goods store in town in partnership with New York Islanders coach and Sudbury native Al Arbour.[45] He was also responsible for managerial duties with the Wolves, while Barry Mackenzie served as director of player personnel and Joe Drago, another local high school principal and coach who had been involved with the team since 1972, was appointed director of operations.[46]

Meanwhile, the OHA Junior 'A' league reorganized itself into the Ontario Major Junior Hockey League (OMJHL) and began operating independently from the OHA, laying the foundation for the modern OHL. Joe Drago credits Bud Burke as the main driver behind the move. Dissatisfied with the OHA's oversight of league business, Drago states that Burke thought Ontario's major junior franchises should band together and take more direct control of their operations. "Bud didn't know much about hockey, but he was a very astute businessman," Drago asserts. "Bud thought … we're all independent owners, and we shouldn't be taking orders from a provincial organization. So, he pushed like heck to get a league office, to get a commissioner, and to run our own business as a league. In my mind, he was the catalyst to get the OHL started."[47] Tubby Schmalz served as the OMJHL's first commissioner.[48]

The Wolves entered the new season with loads of talent. Players such as Bobby Russell, Rod Schutt, Geoff Green and Ron Duguay returned to Sudbury for another year. Sophomore goalie Jim Bedard replaced Bob Volpe as the Wolves' first choice in the crease after Volpe moved on to the professional ranks.[49] Defenceman Randy Carlyle, an Azilda native who had played a handful of games with the Wolves the previous season after joining the team through a trade with Kitchener, earned an elevated role on the blue-line.[50] Coach Duncan hoped to turn the Wolves into an intimidating group comparable to the Stanley Cup champion Philadelphia Flyers—the Broad Street Bullies—but without having to resort to too much violence. "Each coach has his own philosophy … some coaches go by the myth that if you don't have the talent you got to fight your way in," he explained.[51] With the season opener weeks away, *The Northern Life* confidently predicted that "the Wolves have the stuff Memorial Cup contenders are made of."[52]

The franchise and its players really came into their own during the 1974-75 OMJHL season. The Wolves finished with exactly as many wins as the previous year, but the team took a clear step forward in its play. Around the halfway point of the season, Berk Keaney, in his seventeenth year as the Wolves' announcer while balancing his full-time job at INCO, shared his view that "This Sudbury Wolves team is the best team of juniors since the Memorial Cup winners some 40 years ago."[53] The Pack performed well at home and began drawing consistent crowds to the Sudbury Community Arena. Captain Bobby Russell rebounded from a case of tonsillitis at the start of the season to score a team-leading 51 goals.[54] Schutt broke out with 43 goals and 61 assists and was named to the league's first all-star team in April.[55] Bedard established himself as a *bona fide* starting goaltender, winning 22 games behind a sturdy back-end led by two-way defencemen Carlyle and Dave Farrish. It was a bit of a rocky year, though, leading to some mixed reviews for rookie coach Stu Duncan. "You can bet I feel it," he told a local sportswriter when asked about the pressure he faced as the Wolves prepared for the playoffs.[56]

The Wolves took on the Ottawa 67's in the first round of the postseason, a team coached by the legendary Brian Kilrea. The two clubs had met eight times during the regular season, with Sudbury winning five of those games.[57] On March 25, 1975, the Wolves franchise earned its first ever playoff game win, defeating the 67's by a score of 6-1 at the Sudbury Arena. Bedard stopped 42 shots in the victory, including a penalty shot by Ottawa superstar Tim Young.[58] The Wolves won the next two games to take a 3-0 series lead, but the 67's responded with two straight victories of their own to stay afloat. As the Wolves prepared for Game 6 in the Nickel City, coach Duncan stated that there was "no reason for us to lose tonight and the players realize this fact. It should be a whale of a game."[59] Sudbury didn't lose, but they didn't win either; the game ended in a 4-4 draw.[60]

This tie had implications that might seem unusual for modern day hockey fans. At the time the OMJHL playoffs were conducted under a points-based, seven-game series system. A win earned a team two points and a tie counted for one point, with the first club to reach eight total points winning the series. The Wolves therefore entered Game 7 in Ottawa with a 7-5 lead in points. The Wolves rallied back from a 2-0 deficit to even the score in the third period on a goal by Geoff Green. The second consecutive draw gave Sudbury the single point needed to win the series by a round total of 8-6. The Wolves organization had won its first ever playoff series since joining the league three seasons earlier.[61] Following the big victory, Duncan pronounced that "morale on the team is high, possibly the highest it's been all season. The boys want to win, they feel they can win."[62]

According to Joe Bowen, one of the more humorous moments during his time covering the Wolves came after the team's win over Ottawa. "I'll never forget this … When we won … [Bud Burke] was ecstatic, and he said to the coach, 'Take the boys out and buy them anything they want for dinner,'" he recalls. Stu Duncan told his players of Burke's offer to treat them to dinner, and made sure to emphasize that they could order anything that they wanted. "Well, in they went. And Randy Carlyle and Dave Farrish, I think, had two T-bone steaks each, a couple of pizza pies. One of the waiters came over and said 'Would you like a slice of lemon meringue?'—'No, just bring the whole pie!' I mean, I don't know what the bill was!" laughs Bowen.[63] Randy Carlyle remembers the story a bit differently, however. "Joe Bowen tells it all the time. He exaggerates," chuckles Carlyle. "He's good on the banquet circuit with it, especially when I'm in the building … But yes, we did have the ability to order what we want, and we did go over the top."[64]

The Wolves next played the Toronto Marlboros (the "Marlies"), the team that had finished in first place during the regular season. The Marlies were coached by former Toronto Maple Leafs captain and Skead product George "Chief" Armstrong, who also happened to be Dale McCourt's uncle, and were spearheaded by OMJHL leading-scorer and future NHL player and bench boss Bruce Boudreau. The winner of the series would advance to the league finals to compete for the J. Ross Robertson Cup. The Marlies won Game 1 in Toronto easily by a score of 8-1. "There's no way [the] Wolves will play that badly again, they're too fine to play two games like that in succession," predicted Armstrong after the first match. The Wolves proved him right and won Game 2 in Sudbury 6-4. The team was buoyed by Russell and the "Stud Line" centred by Ron Duguay with wingers Alex McKendry and Hector Marini.[65]

The Wolves and Marlies battled it out in a gritty, hotly contested series. After the third game ended in a tie, the Wolves took their first lead of the series on April 14 with a 5-3 win in Game 4 on a hat trick by Schutt.[66] The series resumed at Maple Leaf Gardens and ended in controversy. With the Wolves up by a score of 6-4 with three seconds left in the second period, Russell fired a long shot past Marlies' netminder Gary Carr. The red light did not flash, however, because the goal judge at the north end of the Gardens had apparently left his seat early. The clock ran out and referee Blair Graham did not award the Wolves a goal, prompting Sudbury players to engage "Graham in the biggest exchange of conversation ever heard since Muhammad Ali arrived on the sports scene a few years back." The Marlies took advantage of their good fortune and scored four unanswered goals in the third period to win the game 8-6 and tie the series at five points apiece.[67]

The Wolves were incredulous. "Absolutely bush ... just bush," said an infuriated Duncan after the loss. "This isn't sour grapes, it's fact, we got the short end of the stick tonight because a minor official blew his assignment. It cost us the game, there's no doubt about it." Bud Burke responded with fury, stating the Wolves would be seeking an injunction from the league demanding that their next road game not be played at Maple Leaf Gardens. He also insisted that either commissioner Tubby Schmalz handle the assigning of officials moving forward or that administrator David Branch, who currently carried that responsibility, resign from his position. Burke rounded out his list of accusations by claiming that Graham was biased toward Sudbury players and that Toronto's winning goal "'was at least four feet offside.'"[68]

The Wolves refused to let this injustice take the wind out of their sails, however, and fought right to the end. The Pack captured Game 6 by a score of 5-1 at home and put themselves within one point of winning the series. The Marlies replied with a 3-2 win in Game 7 at Maple Leaf Gardens with about 400 Wolves fans in attendance. "This has to be the best fan support I've ever seen ... Finer hockey fans you won't find anywhere," stated Duncan after his team fell short of closing out the semi-finals.[69] With the eight-point series deadlocked at 7-7, the Marlies had forced an eighth and final game in the Nickel City. The victor was set to play the Hamilton Fincups (formerly the Red Wings) in the OMJHL finals. The deciding game took place on the Saturday evening of April 19 at the packed Sudbury Community Arena. "People were hanging from the rafters," remembers Joe Bowen. Goaltenders Bedard and Carr duelled it out all night as the Wolves and Marlies traded goals through the first 60 minutes of play. At 13:52 in overtime with the game tied by a score of 4-4, Marlies forward John Anderson snuck past the Wolves defence and fired a shot behind Bedard to end the series.[70] "It was like someone had shot your dog right in front of you," says Bowen of the atmosphere in the Sudbury Arena after Anderson's goal. "It's something I will never, ever forget."[71]

The sting of this narrow loss for the Wolves was partially mitigated by the praise they received from supporters and opponents alike. Dozens of fans applauded the team as they left the dressing room, though one person admitted to local media that the defeat had put them on the brink of tears. Stu Duncan applauded his team's effort and stated they had made him "the happiest guy in the world." Bud Burke assured everyone that "I'm more than proud of the boys. Everybody gave everything they had and went out like champions." Even the Marlboros' head coach had nothing but good things to say about the Wolves. "I hope the Sudbury community continues to support the Sudbury club," said Hockey Hall of Fame inductee George Armstrong. "In my mind Junior 'A' hockey is in some ways better than pro."[72] Armstrong and the Marlies went on to win the 1975 Memorial Cup.

THE MAKING OF LEGENDS

For the fourth consecutive year in its four-year history, the Sudbury Wolves started the season with a new coach. Stu Duncan was let go by the club not long after the team's playoff exit and was replaced by Jerry Toppazzini. Born in the Sudbury neighbourhood of Copper Cliff, Toppazzini, who passed away in 2012, had played nearly 800 NHL games with Boston, Chicago, and Detroit before retiring from professional hockey in the late 1960s. He had spent four years working as a minor league coach and scout for the Los Angeles Kings when he returned to his hometown to coach the Wolves.[73] "Topper … was the right guy for our team. He brought a lot of character," says Randy Carlyle. "He was a guy that … you looked up to. He was firm, but fair."[74] Bowen describes the late Toppazzini as having "perpetual energy," and indicates that his team "looked a lot like its coach. They played very strong and tough."[75]

The 1975-76 Sudbury Wolves team was undoubtedly the best group ever assembled in the organization's history, setting multiple club records that remain unbeaten to this day. Rod Schutt scored a franchise record 72 goals that season, including a club record five-goal game against the Soo in February, while captain Ron Duguay registered a team record 92 assists. The Wolves went 47-11-8-0 and won the Hamilton Spectator Trophy for the best regular season record in the league. The team accumulated more wins and points (102) than any Wolves team to come before or since. Forwards like Alex McKendry, Hector Marini, Wes Jarvis, and John Walker, plus rookies Mike Foligno, Dave Hunter, and Dan McCarthy, added plenty of secondary scoring. Randy Carlyle and Dave Farrish headlined a back-end that was complemented by Mike Gazdic, Kevin Howe, and Sudbury local Brian McDavid. Management executed trades during the season to add forward Randy Pierce from the 67's and defenceman John Baby, another Sudburian, from the Rangers. Jim Bedard played 58 regular season games in net and posted a 3.15 goals-against average, earning him the Dave Pinkney Trophy for lowest goals-against average in the league.[76]

All these years later, many are still in awe of the raw talent that this particular pack of Wolves possessed. "That team was outstanding," says Ken Campbell of the 1975-76 Wolves.[77] Joe Bowen remembers the play of a young Mike Foligno in particular. "He was always going one hundred miles an hour ... You got him playing on the third or fourth line? Wow. That team had a lot of depth, it really did."[78] Although he said that the group did not enter the season fully aware of their capabilities, Randy Carlyle admits that once the season got underway the Wolves felt they could beat just about any team they went up against. "You never think you're that good until you go out and you got to prove it ... We weren't intimidated by going in to any of the buildings that we went in to."[79] In an interview with Ben Leeson of *The Sudbury Star* about forty years later, Dave Farrish, who went on to play over 400 NHL games and work as an assistant coach with the Colorado Avalanche, remembered the group as having "great chemistry. Everybody got along extremely well," while John Baby, who saw some NHL action with the Cleveland Barons and Minnesota North Stars, stated that they simply "jelled, we believed in each other."[80]

The Wolves cruised to the 1976 OMJHL playoffs, where they met the rival Soo Greyhounds in the opening round. "Sault Ste. Marie and us fought every game, tooth and nail," Carlyle says, who also remembers the series as having a "circus-type atmosphere."[81] In Game 3 in Sudbury on March 28, with the series tied, the Wolves pummeled the Greyhounds by a score of 11-2, but things went off the rails in the third period when the Soo turned to intimidation and aggressive play. Even Duguay dropped the gloves after Greyhounds defenceman Tony Horvath blindsided him with a punch at centre ice. "Where ability ends, violence begins. That was disgraceful," said coach Toppazzini afterwards.[82]

Matters only escalated as the series progressed. After the Greyhounds evened the series in Game 4, Soo coach Murray "Muzz" MacPherson, serving a one-game suspension for failing to control his players in Game 3, suggested that Wolves ownership and management did not "know how to spell the word class."[83] The Wolves won Game 5 by a score of 8-0, with three goals coming from 15-year-old local forward Jim Fox, who had been called up to fill in for an injured Randy Pierce. After Game 6 in the Soo ended in a tie, Sudbury wrapped things up in Game 7 with a 5-2 win before a sold-out home crowd. When it was all said and done, the mutual respect that underlined the historic rivalry between these two Northern Ontario hockey clubs shone through. "We beat a club that really worked. That's a hockey club that has soul," said Toppazzini.[84]

Next in line for the Wolves were the familiar red, white, and black striped jerseys of the Ottawa 67's, the third time in four seasons the two teams had met in the postseason. The 67's and Wolves split the first two games of the series in Sudbury before heading to Ottawa. In Game 3 on April 11 at the Ottawa Civic Centre, Duguay rattled off four goals to lead his team to a 5-3 win.[85] After earning another decisive 6-3 win two nights later, the Wolves returned home to the Nickel City with the chance to wrap up the series in Game 5. Tied by a score of 1-1 in the second period, the Wolves pulled away with goals by Jarvis, Walker, Foligno, Duguay, and Schutt, skating toward a convincing 6-1 win and capturing the Leyden Division title. The team was bound for the OMJHL finals against the Hamilton Fincups, champions of the Emms Division. "No doubt about it, it'll be a whale of a series," 67's coach Brian Kilrea predicted of the clash between Sudbury and Hamilton. "Wolves are an awesome team ... and have the best goalie in the league in Bedard."[86]

The Wolves knew that the Hamilton Fincups were a force to be reckoned with. Hamilton had lost the 1975 league finals in seven games to the Toronto Marlies and were determined to be crowned champions the second time around.[87] The Fincups—which derived its peculiar name by combining the surnames of its owners, Joe Finochio and brothers Ron and Mario Cupido—had won 43 regular season games before making short work of the Kitchener Rangers and Toronto Marlboros in the first two rounds of the 1976 playoffs. "They had a big, physical team. They had some creative kids ... but the rest of their team was a bunch of pluggers and tough guys," says Joe Bowen.[88] Randy Carlyle concurs, calling the Fincups "a big, rough-and-tumble team."[89] Hamilton was led behind the bench by head coach Bert Templeton and on the ice by none other than Sudbury boy and team captain Dale McCourt, who had developed into one of the league's premier scorers since his cup of coffee with the Wolves years earlier. In December 1975, the Fincups had brought an end to the Wolves twelve-game unbeaten streak with a 7-3 win at the Barton Street Arena in Hamilton.[90] That game was an unfortunate harbinger of what was to come for the Wolves.

The Fincups wasted no time showing the Wolves they meant business. The city of Sudbury hosted its first ever OMJHL finals game on April 19, 1976 when the Fincups travelled north for Game 1 of the series. Hamilton went up 2-0 in the first two minutes of play, but then Carlyle scored two goals along with another by Jarvis to give Sudbury a 3-2 lead entering the second frame. Starting with McCourt, the Fincups then scored six unanswered goals to trounce the Wolves by a final score of 8-3 to take the first lead of the series.[91] Sudbury lost Game 2 on the road by a score of 6-5. The third game was hectic as the 6,000 fans at the Sudbury Arena watched the Wolves and Fincups wrack up numerous of penalties and fighting majors; the Wolves won the game 7-5. That would be Sudbury's only victory of the series, however, as Hamilton won the next meeting at home before finishing the Wolves off in Game 5 in the Nickel City by a score of 5-4 on a winning goal by centreman Ed Smith. "The crowd of 5,893 sat in stunned silence when Smith netted what proved to be the deciding goal of the game," wrote *The Sudbury Star*.[92] "I was heartbroken, I was absolutely heartbroken," reflects Ken Campbell, who passionately followed the Wolves' run to the finals as a youngster.[93] The OMJHL champion Hamilton Fincups went on to win the 1976 Memorial Cup, with McCourt taking home the Stafford Smythe Memorial Trophy as the tournament's most valuable player.

What had gone wrong for the seemingly unbeatable Sudbury Wolves? A few factors appear to have spelled the team's demise. The most obvious was McCourt's exceptional play. "They ran in to a wrecking ball of Dale McCourt, who basically carried the Hamilton Fincups on his back," says Campbell.[94] McCourt, coming off a 55-goal, 139-point regular season campaign, scored two goals in all five games of the championship series to lead Hamilton past his hometown club. Another element that worked against the Wolves was the nearly 70-year-old Barton Street Arena in Hamilton, an unusually small ice surface that had contributed to the home team's advantage all year long.

There were some off-ice distractions, too, that seemed to have held Sudbury back from matching Hamilton's physicality. Rod Schutt once stated that there were some "agents hanging around and telling players … play hard, but don't get hurt, and those sort of things got in the way of winning."[95] Joe Bowen also remembers hearing from various sources that some risk-averse agents dissuaded certain players from banging and crashing against Hamilton. "'Hey, don't get hurt. Hey, this doesn't mean anything. You're going on to play professional hockey next year.' And we really, really needed … the counterforce to what was going on as far as the Fincups were concerned, and it really never happened."[96] In retrospect, Randy Carlyle thinks the warlike series against the Soo Greyhounds hurt the Wolves in the long run: "They took a pound of flesh from us."[97]

The 1975-76 Sudbury Wolves nonetheless had a profound impact on the city of Sudbury and instilled a sense of pride in the community that can still be felt nearly fifty years later. "The excitement in the building was just electric … That would've been probably our first experience of that type of atmosphere," says Randy Carlyle of the Sudbury Arena in those years.

"There will be people, you can walk down the street today, and they'll stop me and … they'll still talk about the teams from '75-76 [and] '74-75 [and] how great the hockey was at the Sudbury Arena."[98] Along with the host of statistical franchise records that the 1975-76 Wolves put together, various members of that team have been immortalized as franchise legends. Jerry Toppazzini was awarded the Matt Leyden Trophy as coach of the year for the 1975-76 season, a feat which none of his successors have managed to duplicate.[99] Four players from the team have since had their numbers retired by the organization: Randy Carlyle (No. 6), Rod Schutt (No. 8), Ron Duguay (No. 10), and Mike Foligno (No. 17). "It's the memories of those years that bring everybody together," Rod Schutt once said of his teammates in an interview with *The Sudbury Star*, though it could just as well be applied to the wider Wolves fanbase. "When you rehash some of those times, whether good or bad, it brings that closeness back."[100]

By 1976, the Sudbury Wolves organization had laid the foundation for what was to become one of the most cherished junior hockey franchises in North America. Even in defeat, the club had established itself as a legitimate contender and proven that it had the community support it needed to continue producing positive results. In the days following the Wolves' loss to the Fincups, reporter Jack Falldien wrote that it was already "time to recollect what the Sudbury Wolves did for hockey in Northern Ontario over the past year."[101] Indeed, having proven itself as a worthy member of one of the world's top junior hockey leagues, the Sudbury Wolves organization had passed through its trial by ice and emerged stronger than ever.

CHAPTER 3:

REBUILD AND REBOUND, 1976-1980

In the aftermath of the franchise having the J. Ross Robertson Cup slip from its fingers, the Sudbury Wolves, along with the city of Sudbury itself, had to deal with some adversity and rapid change. The Regional Municipality of Sudbury was formed in 1973 through an amalgamation of various local communities surrounding Sudbury, propelling its total population to over 160,000 residents.[1] Mining remained Sudbury's economic driver, but in the late 1970s the Nickel City was faced with large-scale layoffs and one of the longest strikes in Canadian history. The city's re-greening effort also began in earnest as the people of Sudbury sought to distance themselves from the city's environmentally unfriendly reputation.

The Wolves, meanwhile, had to come to terms with the reality that a lot can change in a short period of time in the world of junior hockey. Today, the OHL allows each of its teams a maximum of three 20-year-old players on their roster, referred to as overage players, who in some cases turn 21-years-old before the end of the season. While the rules were slightly different in the 1970s, within a couple of seasons most of the core members of the Leyden Division champion Wolves had either moved on to the professional ranks or simply aged themselves out of junior altogether. Combined with a revolving door of coaching staff and rumours of ownership change, at times it seemed as though the franchise was on rocky footing. Ironically, what emerged was the last era of reliably competitive Wolves hockey that fans would get to experience for over a decade.

HANGOVER

The 1976-77 Sudbury Wolves obviously had a difficult act to follow. "The 1975-76 season was the best in Wolves' Major 'A' history," aptly declared *The Sudbury Star* in September 1976.[2] "It's going to be a tough record to beat. Last year, we had an exceptionally good team," coach Jerry Toppazzini said days before the start of the new season.[3] Jim Bedard, Rod Schutt, Randy Carlyle, Dave Farrish, and Alex McKendry had all played their final junior hockey games against the Hamilton Fincups the previous April, but the Wolves had more than a few returnees to count on. Ron Duguay, Mike Foligno, John Baby, Dave Hunter, John Walker, and a handful of others came back to play in Sudbury, with the only real concern lying between the pipes. As executive Joe Drago put it, "a team is only as good as its goaltending," and the Wolves were looking for answers in that regard.[4] With no clear-cut starter emerging by the end of training camp, in late September, the team decided to sign a trio of goalies to give Toppazzini some options: Ken Kirby, who had backed-up Bedard the year before, former Peterborough Pete Howie Murney, and local product Lou Malbeuf.[5]

The Wolves did not exactly get off to a spectacular start. In the team's season opener at the Sudbury Arena against the Kingston Canadians, the Wolves blew a three-goal lead with less than seven minutes left in the game and lost by a score of 5-4.[6] In early October, the team acquired rookie netminder Jack Shaw from the Oshawa Generals to rectify the team's goaltending woes. On November 7, starting in his tenth consecutive game for the Wolves, Shaw led his team to a crushing 10-1 victory over the Ottawa

67's. Management decided to further stabilize the Wolves' crease by trading a draft pick in the 1977 OMJHL draft to Ottawa in exchange for veteran goalie Jack Fraser. "I don't think I'll be getting much ice now ... I wish I could give you my honest opinion," Shaw was quoted as telling sportswriter Danny Gallagher after the Fraser deal.[7] Other players began to voice their displeasure as the Wolves mostly underachieved. Veteran defenceman Kevin Howe told *The Star* that he was dissatisfied with the amount of ice-time he was receiving, while Ron Duguay was stripped of his captaincy in November for breaking team rules regarding curfew and other matters. While the star centre said that management was "making a fuss over nothing," he actually welcomed the decision, stating that "I just want to play hockey" in his final year of junior.[8] Days later he was replaced as captain by forward John Walker, who was playing in his fourth season with the Wolves.[9]

The Wolves' difficulties did not end there, even if statistically the season was going quite well. By late November Bud Burke had once more suspended *The Star* from communicating with the team after it published both Howe and Shaw's comments, prompting the newspaper to ramp up its critique of the Wolves' owner.[10] Then, in January, with the Wolves tied for first place in the Leyden Division, Jerry Toppazzini abruptly resigned from his position as head coach due to what he felt was the team's insufficient confidence in him. He decided to remain in Sudbury to focus on his family life and work at a local insurance and real estate firm. In 1977, Toppazzini purchased the Belvedere Hotel, eventually transforming it into a bar known today as the Beef 'n Bird. This family-owned tavern is famous in Sudbury and beyond for hosting "porketta bingo"—a card game played for Italian-style pork roast—nearly every Saturday afternoon from October to April, with proceeds generally going toward supporting minor hockey in the area. The Beef 'n Bird and its often rowdy porketta bingo events have become unique cornerstones of Sudbury culture.[11] After Toppazzini left the Wolves, the team hired Noel Price, a former NHL defenceman who grew up in Coniston and had worked as an NHL and American Hockey League (AHL) assistant coach.[12]

The city of Sudbury was in the junior hockey spotlight in the winter of 1977 for another reason as well. On February 2, the Nickel City hosted the OMJHL all-star game, the league's first such event in twelve years. Duguay served as the captain of the Leyden Division squad, alongside teammates Randy Pierce, Hunter, and Baby, while Dale McCourt—playing for the temporarily relocated St. Catharines Fincups—captained the Emms Division group. The Emms all-stars defeated the Leyden all-stars in a 5-4 overtime match at the Sudbury Arena. McCourt put on another show in his hometown, netting his third goal of the night in overtime and receiving honours as the game's top forward and most outstanding player.[13]

In addition, before the puck dropped for the all-star match, Sudbury mayor Jim Gordon delivered exciting news to the 3,500 fans in attendance. The cities of Sudbury and Sault Ste. Marie, Gordon proudly announced, had officially been named co-hosts of the 1978 Memorial Cup. Four games, including the finals, were set to be played at the Sudbury Arena, while another three would take place at the Sault Memorial Gardens. Unlike the present-day Memorial Cup format whereby the host automatically earns a spot in the tournament, only three teams—the champions of Ontario, Quebec and Western Canada—would be playing in Sudbury and the Soo in May 1978. Still, the upcoming opportunity to host this historic sporting event was one that Northern Ontario warmly embraced.[14]

The Wolves' regular season was still a success despite all the off-ice distractions. The Wolves won 38 regular season games and finished behind only Ottawa in the Leyden Division while setting a franchise record for most goals scored at home (226). Ron Duguay led the team in scoring with 109 points but expressed frustration with his scoring regression in what was his NHL draft year. "I just don't know what is going wrong this season," the young centreman said in March.[15] Perhaps the most impressive performance from a Wolf that season came from defenceman John Baby. The Sudbury-born blueliner broke Randy Carlyle's single season scoring record for a Wolves defenceman and finished with 93 points. While that record has since been surpassed, Baby's 32 goals in a season has yet to be eclipsed by a Wolves' defenceman.[16] Both Duguay and Baby had their names called at the 1977 NHL draft that June, with Duguay going in the first round to the New York Rangers and Baby in the fourth round to the Cleveland Barons. Fellow Wolves Randy Pierce and Hector Marini were also selected by the Colorado Rockies and New York Islanders, respectively.

The 1977 postseason was a far cry from the previous year for the Pack. Taking on the Kingston Canadians, the Wolves lost Game 1 at the Sudbury Arena by a score of 6-4, with Duguay scoring a hat trick and winning a fight against Brian Whitwell. Sudbury then lost the next two meetings before eking out a 1-1 tie in Game 4 on the road to keep the series going. With the point total for the series now 7-1 in favour of Kingston, the Wolves could not settle for anything less than a win moving forward. On Sunday March 27, the Canadians were up by a score of 3-0 in Game 5 entering the third period, all but guaranteeing the Wolves would be eliminated in front of 4,200 fans. But the hometown team pulled off a tremendous third period comeback, with goals from Pierce, Jarvis and Hunter evening the score. Then, with only 1:30 left in regulation, the Wolves pulled Shaw in favour of the extra attacker. The gamble paid off as Pierce scored his second of the night with 44 seconds remaining in the game to give Sudbury a 4-3 win. "I was so excited I just shot," said Pierce of the game-winning goal that elicited a thunderous applause from the Sudbury crowd. The Canadians came back with a vengeance in Game 6, though, and handed the Wolves a 7-2 loss to end the series.[17] With the spring thaw barely beginning in Sudbury, the Wolves' season was already over.

NOT-SO-SWEET SIXTEEN

It did not take very long to realize that 1977-78 was going to be one of the more challenging seasons in the Wolves' franchise short history. "What the future holds in store for the 1977-78 edition of the Sudbury Wolves is still a big question mark, but one thing is certain, the talent on the present squad is inferior to that connected with the '74-'75, '75-'76, and '76-'77 clubs," wrote sports reporter Jack Fallidien in the midst of the team's preseason.[18] This was evidenced in part by the Wolves' four consecutive preseason losses to the Soo Greyhounds, the first of which took place at the Sudbury Arena on September 6. The visiting Greyhounds cruised to an 8-3 victory while giving Sudburians their first opportunity to watch the Soo's phenom rookie centreman, Wayne Gretzky, in action. Selected third overall by the club in the draft that June, the teenage Gretzky terrorized the Wolves with a goal and five assists.[19] The hype around Gretzky was not lost on the hockey mad fans of the Nickel City, even if he was playing for the Wolves' oldest rival. "I remember as a kid, everyone was talking about this guy that played for Sault Ste. Marie," says current Wolves' owner Dario Zulich. "And I convinced my dad, a Croatian-Italian immigrant, to take me and my two younger brothers at the time to the hockey game. And I remember walking in, and there's this 16-year-old kid on the Soo Greyhounds, which was Wayne Gretzky. I hardly remember seeing him play, but all I know is it was standing room only."[20]

While the Wolves could hardly be blamed for not having a player of Gretzky's calibre to call their own, the team's roster was nevertheless not quite up to snuff. The presence of veterans like Mike Foligno, Dave Hunter, John Walker, and Dan McCarthy could not fully compensate for a fairly shallow depth chart following the departure of so many key players from the previous season. Aside from local boys Brian McDavid and Mike Gazdic, the Wolves' defence generally lacked experience, while in goal the club was left with sophomore Jack Shaw and rookie Jim Sidwell. The Wolves did win their first two games of the 1977-78 OMJHL season, including a 7-5 home win over the Greyhounds in which they held Gretzky to a single assist.[21] Before long the team owned a 5-10-5 record, however, and in November coach Noel Price was axed.[22] To try to give the team a new lease on life, the Wolves hired Armand "Bep" Guidolin, a former head coach of the Boston Bruins who in 1942 had become the youngest player to skate in an NHL game at 16-years-old.[23]

Guidolin's hiring did not improve the Wolves' fortunes, and by season's end they had mustered only 16 wins. The 52-year-old Guidolin was also let go in February 1978 and replaced by former NOHA Wolves coach Marcel Clements.[24] Management unloaded multiple players before the trade deadline, sending Jarvis and Shaw to the Windsor Spitfires and Walker to the Kitchener Rangers.[25] Fans were predictably less inclined to fill the Sudbury Arena to watch the struggling Wolves, a situation which was probably made worse by the shock to the local economy caused by INCO's unexpected announcement of 3,000 layoffs in 1977.[26]

Throughout the history of the Sudbury Wolves, the stuffed wolf on the wire that descends from the rafters of the Sudbury Arena after every home team goal has mysteriously disappeared several times, only to resurface later or be replaced by a new wolf entirely. One such episode took place during the 1977-1978 season. Having apparently gone missing in 1968, the piece of taxidermy was recovered in December 1977 when Mike Spratt, the son-in-law of local politician Mike Solski, reportedly discovered it in the Toronto home of an unnamed former Laurentian University student. Solski returned the iconic wolf to the club in mid-January, nearly ten years after it had mysteriously vanished. He told *The Northern Life* that he thought "It might be a good omen. I hope it can improve the fortunes of the arena and the Wolves."[27] Over the years, other fans and even opposing teams such as Kingston Frontenacs, London Knights and Oshawa Generals have allegedly taken the stuffed wolf for a brief period before returning it to its rightful owner. The Wolves eventually installed a latch and lock to prevent future theft.[28]

Those who did go watch the Wolves occasionally had the pleasure of seeing some memorable feats. On January 15, for instance, Mike Foligno, who scored a team-high 47 goals that season and was named captain after Walker was traded, tallied five goals against the Peterborough Petes in an 8-6 Wolves home win. In doing so, he tied the franchise record set by Rod Schutt in 1976 for most goals in a single game and was met with a lengthy ovation from the crowd upon netting his fifth of the night. The Wolves sealed their fate as a non-playoff team on March 7 with a 6-5 loss to the Soo, signalling the first time in franchise history the club did not qualify for the postseason. The Wolves ultimately finished last in the OMJHL.[29]

The Wolves poor performance coincided with changes to its ownership group. In January, Burke indicated he was looking to pull out of the franchise. "For 30 years, I've honestly worked seven days a week and 16 hours a day. I am generally retiring this year and hockey is one of those things," the majority owner told *The Sudbury Star*. Burke owned four of the club's seven shares, with Bill Plaunt of CKSO owning two and Barry Mackenzie holding one. Mackenzie was now playing for a hockey club in Japan and wanted to sell his single share, too.[30] Mackenzie eventually found a buyer in local Gord Ewin. A retired educator and the franchise's first-ever season ticket holder, today Ewin serves as the Wolves' director of education, where he is responsible for ensuring that the players stay on track academically while pursuing their OHL careers. "When Barry Mackenzie moved … Bud Burke said I had first chance to buy a share, so I did," remembered Gord Ewin in a 2011 interview with *The Star*. "That cost $25,000 in '77-'78, and there were seven shares at the time. Bud had four, Bill Plaunt had two and I had one."[31] Burke began publicly advertising that his stake in the team was up for sale, but for the time being he decided to wait until the right deal materialized.[32]

The 1978 Memorial Cup threw salt in the wound for the Wolves and their fans. Within a week of tickets going on sale in November 1977, half of the 5,020 available seats at the Sudbury Arena had sold, with single games tickets going for five to six dollars and packages from sixteen to twenty dollars. By the spring of 1978, the landmark event for Northern Ontario had been dampened by the fact that neither Sudbury nor Sault Ste. Marie had even come close to seeing their home teams in the tournament, as the Wolves missed the OMJHL postseason and the Greyhounds lost in the quarterfinals to the Ottawa 67's. In May the crowds at the Sudbury Arena and Sault Memorial Gardens watched as the Peterborough Petes, Trois-Rivières Draveurs, and New Westminster Bruins battled for the CHL championship. The Bruins defeated the Petes in the finals in Sudbury to capture their second consecutive Memorial Cup.[33]

The people of Sudbury still found a way to celebrate their role in the most recent Memorial Cup by assembling the surviving members of the 1932 Cub Wolves for an honorary banquet dinner a few days before the championship finals. Among the attendees from the former team were Sam Rothschild, Toe Blake, Red Porter, and Nakina Smith, who travelled all the way from California for the occasion. Dignitaries and fans gathered at a local hall on a Thursday evening to commemorate the Cub Wolves' Memorial Cup run some 46 years earlier. Mayor Jim Gordon presented each of the men with a gold medallion on behalf of the citizens of Sudbury. "These gentlemen represent the guts, determination, and drive that makes this community what it is today," Gordon expounded in his presentation speech. Captain Red Porter reminisced that "The team had inner faith, and they knew that if they did their best, nobody could beat them." Jim Nichol, *The Sudbury Star* reporter who broadcast the championship game live from Winnipeg, reminded everyone that the Cub Wolves' title in 1932 helped thousands of Sudburians take their minds off "the throes of the

Great Depression … layoffs, soup lines and relief cheques" and allowed them to "revel in the new found glory brought to them by a memorable Memorial Cup series."[34]

THE FANTASTIC FOLIGNO

Bud Burke, Joe Drago, and the Wolves top brass undertook their first real rebuild during the 1978 offseason. With the first pick in the OMJHL draft, the Wolves selected Mike Allison from the Kenora Thistles. A six-foot-three, 202-pound centreman, the rookie Allison was expected to make an immediate impact on Sudbury's lineup. Management orchestrated some key trades as well before the season got started, acquiring forwards Dave MacQueen from the Ottawa 67's and Dale Hunter, the younger brother of former Wolves forward Dave Hunter, from the Kitchener Rangers. The team's coaching carousel went round once more as the Wolves brought in another new face behind the bench. Andy Laing had been coaching the Rochester Monarchs of the New York-Pennsylvania Junior Hockey League when he was offered the chance to come to Sudbury and turn the floundering Wolves around. Laing entered the season fairly optimistic about the Wolves' future, predicting that the team's offence in particular "should be strong."[35] Captain Mike Foligno was ready to lead the charge in that regard, with *The Sudbury Star* dubbing him "the only Sudbury Wolves' player who is the epitome of the superstar image."[36]

The 1978-79 season witnessed a marked improvement for Sudbury, though it took some time for the team to realize its full potential. After getting off to a decent start, the Wolves found themselves near the basement of the Leyden Division by December.[37] The group hit rock bottom following a 6-0 road loss to the 67's in January, marking the first time the team had been shut-out since 1974.[38] The Wolves started to pull it together thereafter, however, and were soon neck-and-neck with the Oshawa Generals for second place in the Leyden Division. Wolves' supporters were no doubt enthused by the upward trend, and the Sudbury Arena was once more attracting large crowds of hockey fans to watch the locals make a return to the OMJHL playoffs. At the same time, Sudbury was dealing with unprecedented labour strife when workers at INCO voted to strike in September 1978. It would take eight-and-a-half months to resolve the industrial dispute, making it one of the longest strikes in Canadian labour history.[39] Months later, Drago commended Wolves fans for their "excellent" support in the face of all the tumultuousness and uncertainty facing the city. "The fan support here is better than in three-quarters of the league," he surmised.[40]

The Wolves' rebound season was truly a team effort. The team won 40 regular season games, finished second in their division, and scored 397 goals during the regular season, which remains a franchise record. Coach Laing received accolades for reinvigorating the group in such a short time. "It's really not that hard to explain the sudden change in the team," Foligno said in March 1979. "Andy provided the leadership and the players just picked it up from there."[41] MacQueen and Hunter each accumulated over 100 points on the season. Forwards Scott Gruhl and Bob Lekun, a Sudbury native playing in his third season with the team, were other important offensive weapons. Allison posted a respectable 24 goals in his rookie year. Rookie netminder Don Beaupre, selected by the club in the 1978 draft, was a workhorse in goal, posting a 4.78 goals-against-average in 55 games played. When the Wolves defeated the Kitchener Rangers by a score of 5-0 on November 13, 1978, he became the first Sudbury goaltender to post a shutout since Jim Bedard had done so in March 1976. He also finished second in voting for OMJHL rookie of the year.[42]

It should come as no surprise that the OMJHL's highest-scoring team was led by the league's top-scorer. Mike Foligno put on an amazing display in his final season in a Wolves uniform, racking up 65 goals and 150 points in 68 games. No member of the Sudbury Wolves before or after has registered more points in a single regular season.[43] The six-foot-two, 190-pound right winger led the OMJHL in scoring that year to become the first player in Sudbury Wolves history to win the Eddie Powers Memorial Trophy as the league's leading scorer. He incidentally won the Jim Mahon Memorial Trophy as the OMJHL's highest-scoring right winger, too. After securing the titles in Sudbury's last regular season game on March 11 in a 7-3 home victory over the London Knights, Foligno stated that "It's really great to win the scoring title but that's not the most important thing to me. After last year and the poor season the team had I was determined to help out any way

I could."[44] He was also later awarded the 1978-79 Red Tilson Trophy as the OMJHL's most outstanding player. That summer Foligno was selected third overall by the Detroit Red Wings in the 1979 NHL Entry Draft.

The Wolves played the Oshawa Generals in the opening round of the 1979 OMJHL playoffs. Two-goal efforts by both Foligno and Gruhl elevated the Wolves over the Generals by a score of 7-4 in Game 1 at the Sudbury Arena. In Game 4 in Oshawa, with Sudbury up two games to one in the series, the Wolves and Generals engaged in a bench-clearing brawl in the first period after Oshawa player Diego Odino took a run at Wolves forward Frank Perkins. Odino was likely seeking retribution against Perkins for having sidelined Tom McCarthy for the remainder of the playoffs following a scrap between the two earlier in the series. Gord Ewin still remembers the tilt between Perkins and McCarthy well: "McCarthy takes his gloves … and throws them in the air to fight. Before his gloves hit the ice, Perkins had decked him."[45] The melee in Game 4 seemingly shifted the game in the Wolves' favour as they emerged with another 7-4 victory. "I just can't believe how one team can change so quickly when so much is at stake," said Laing after the match. "Away from Oshawa that club (Generals) is like pussycats but here in Oshawa all of a sudden they get tough."[46] The Wolves sent the Generals packing in Game 5, winning it by a score of 4-2 in front of over 5,500 spectators. "Super, just super, we knew we had to work to win the series and here we are," exclaimed Hunter, who scored the series-winning goal.[47]

The Wolves next travelled to Central Ontario for Game 1 of the best-of-seven Leyden Division finals against the Peterborough Petes. The Pack had won five of eight regular season meetings against the Petes but lost the first two games of the playoff series. Bob Lekun scored three goals in Game 3 on April 8 at the Peterborough Memorial Arena as the Wolves thrust themselves back into the series with a 5-2 win. In the long run Peterborough was too much to handle and the Wolves were eliminated in five games. The triumphant Petes went on to win their second consecutive J. Ross Robertson Cup and the 1979 Memorial Cup. Laing said his Wolves had "certainly nothing to apologize for … we were just up against a stronger team."[48]

FOR PETE'S SAKE

The Sudbury Wolves franchise underwent its first major ownership change in the months leading up to the 1979-80 OMJHL season. Bud Burke finally decided he was ready to sell the team and presented Joe Drago with the opportunity to buy it. "Well, being a teacher, I didn't have that kind of money to buy the hockey team," Drago recalls. "So, he gave me two weeks." Drago proceeded to canvas far and wide for potential partners in the enterprise, and eventually brought together a group of investors interested in buying the Wolves.[49] Over the summer, Burke officially sold his shares in the club to Drago and nine others, including former Wolves defenceman Randy Carlyle, now playing for the Pittsburgh Penguins, while Bill Plaunt and Gord Ewin retained their respective stakes in the team.[50]

After the transaction was finalized, Burke was presented with a plaque from the organization as a token of appreciation for his role in founding and directing the club during its first seven seasons.[51] "I had a couple of businesses running, and I just was short of time," is how Burke explains the rationale behind his decision over forty years later. He considers the sale of the team as the closing of yet another chapter in his long life and business career, but to this day affirms that "I have not a sad or a bad thought about the Sudbury Wolves."[52] The franchise continues to honour its founding owner at their annual year-end banquet by recognizing its most outstanding rookie each season with the Bud Burke Top Rookie award.

Some other changes followed. In 1979, Joe Bowen left Sudbury for Halifax where he found work as a play-by-play sportscaster with the Nova Scotia Voyageurs of the AHL, bringing an end to his five-year career covering the Wolves at CKSO.[53] Notwithstanding swirling rumours that he was in the running for an AHL coaching job, Andy Laing returned as Sudbury's bench boss for the 1979-80 OMJHL season. Despite the loss of players like Mike Foligno, Scott Gruhl, Bob Lekun, and Dave MacQueen, he boldly predicted that the Wolves "could go all the way" that season. The depletion of its high-flying offensive ranks naturally led Laing to reconsider the team's game strategy. "There's no doubt, we're concentrating on keeping the puck out since it is our strong point. It's almost impossible to do what some of our guys did last year." Frank Perkins was named captain, a player who Gord

Ewin describes as "probably the best fighter ever to be in a Sudbury Wolves uniform."[54] Shane Swan, a Vancouver Canucks prospect, and third-year defenceman Randy Hillier highlighted the Wolves' blueline. With other exciting pieces such as Mike Allison, Don Beaupre, and Dale Hunter, drafted by the Quebec Nordiques in the 1979 NHL draft, it seemed a pretty safe bet that the team would prove Laing right and make another postseason appearance.[55]

As is so often the case in the world of sports, things did not exactly play out according to plan for Laing and his crew. Injuries plagued the Wolves all season, with key players like defenceman Swan missing much of the year with a knee injury. In another telling example of the team's misfortune, in December third-year forward Norm Stefan, one of Sudbury's leading scorers, fractured his wrist in his first game back after being out for almost a month with an ankle injury.[56] The Wolves clung to the final playoff spot in the Leyden Division in large part due to Beaupre's solid goaltending and Allison's offensive prowess, who broke out with a team-leading 95 points, and Hunter, who tallied 34 goals. Management did not bother trying to address its injury bug through trades because, in the words of Laing, "We need bodies to trade. Nobody trades injured players, besides, if we have a full team for the playoffs, we have as good a chance as any to win."[57] The Pack did finally find themselves at full strength near the end of the season and won four of their final five regular season games to finish with a record of 33-33-2.[58]

The Wolves played the Kingston Canadians in a best-of-five series in the first round of the playoffs, with the winner set to move on to the Leyden Division quarterfinals. Kingston held home-ice advantage in the series, and had won four of six regular season meetings with the Wolves, but come playoff time the game script was flipped. The Wolves won Game 1 in the Limestone City handily by a score of 5-1 as Beaupre stopped 33 shots, followed by another big 5-2 win at the Sudbury Arena on March 18. Back in Kingston for Game 3, the Wolves found themselves in a tie game with twelve minutes of play remaining. Goals by John Kirk and Wayne Groleau, both acquired by the Wolves earlier in the season through trades, lifted Sudbury over Kingston by a final score of 7-5. The Wolves had stunned everyone, except perhaps themselves, with a clean sweep of the series in three consecutive games.[59]

A familiar foe awaited in the quarterfinals in the form of the Peterborough Petes. The reigning Memorial Cup champions, coached by Mike Keenan and led by defenceman Larry Murphy, had finished with the best regular season record and had won all six meetings with the Wolves that year. The opening match of the seven-game series took place on March 27 in Peterborough, the evening before Mike Allison's nineteenth birthday. The Wolves' star centreman celebrated a bit early by scoring four goals that night, including the overtime winner, to lead his team to a come-from-behind 4-3 win over the Petes. Beaupre also made 49 saves for the Wolves.[60] "It was sure a great feeling to see the goal light go on," said Allison.[61] After the Petes won Game 2 at the Sudbury Arena, the Wolves returned to Peterborough and pulled off another nail-biting victory. Frank "Captain Colorado" Perkins—a reference to the American captain's home state—scored in sudden-death overtime to record a hat trick on the night and give the Wolves a 6-5 victory.[62]

Up two games to one in the series, the Wolves were unable to contain the persistent Petes. In Game 4, Sudbury found itself on the wrong side of a controversial double overtime goal when Peterborough's Carmine Cirella ended the match by a score of 5-4. The Wolves protested that Cirella had kicked the puck into the net, but the call on the ice stood.[63] The Petes bested the Wolves in the following two meetings, ending the series in Game 6 by a score of 5-3 before a standing room only crowd at the Sudbury Arena. "In retrospect the entire series turned around in favour of them (Petes) when we lost the double overtime game," stated Laing upon his team's playoff elimination. "Losing hurts like hell but the kids (Wolves) have nothing to be ashamed of."[64] The Peterborough Petes proceeded to win their third straight OMJHL title.

The 1970s had been an eventful time for Sudbury and the city's junior hockey team. Reflecting on the decade, the *INCO Triangle*, a monthly publication produced by INCO for its employees from the 1930s to the late 1990s, asserted that in "the last few years Sudbury has flourished into a proud city with a clean cosmopolitan look." It also commended Sudbury's "tradition of athletic excellence," and referenced multiple former Wolves who had since gone on to play professionally, among them Eric Vail, winner of the Calder Memorial Trophy in the 1974-75 NHL season with the Atlanta

Flames as the league's best rookie.[65] Seven playoff appearances in the Wolves' first eight seasons—not to mention making it all the way to the league finals—was an impressive track record for the upstart Northern Ontario franchise. The Soo Greyhounds, by comparison, had qualified for the postseason on only three occasions, and by the late 1970s were dealing with financial difficulties and an organizational restructuring.[66] Unbeknownst to the Sudbury Wolves, the tables would soon turn and the club would find itself in the midst of the most difficult period in its history.

CHAPTER 4:

GREEN, WHITE, AND RED, 1980-1985

At the turn of the decade the resilience of Sudburians, as residents of the Nickel City and as supporters of the Sudbury Wolves, was once again put to the test, though this time on a scale of another magnitude. "Nothing in Sudbury's history compares to the gloom and despair of the early 1980s," wrote one local historian. It was certainly a concerning time for Sudbury. The decline of the area's stranglehold over the international nickel market, another mining strike, and extended shutdowns at both INCO and Falconbridge contributed to Sudbury's rising unemployment and declining population. By September 1982, over one quarter of Sudbury's workforce was out of a job, and by 1986 the city's total population had dropped to under 89,000. Citizens, business leaders, and government officials alike were compelled to rethink Sudbury's economic future as its dependence on nickel became more and more unsustainable.[1]

The Sudbury Wolves were coincidentally the worst performing team in the CHL throughout the 1980s, and especially so during the first half of the decade.[2] The losses piled up, a multitude of head coaches were either fired or quit, dozens of players donned and shed the green and white, and fans listened anxiously as rumours swirled that the franchise was either going to fold or relocate. The ownership group was quite open about its finances sliding into the red as it grappled with dwindling numbers coming through the gate of the Sudbury Arena. "Not the most decorated days of the franchise, but they did what they could to keep things going in very lean times," explains former Wolves captain Craig Duncanson.[3] Only in hindsight did this period prove that the city of Sudbury in general and the Sudbury Wolves organization in particular could overcome almost anything if they could weather the storm of the early 1980s.

BIRTH OF THE OHL

The 1980-81 season was the first in modern OHL history and it did not play out favourably for the Wolves. Known today by hockey fans across the globe as arguably the top producer of professional hockey players, the OMJHL re-branded itself as the OHL under the umbrella of the CHL (known as the Canadian Major Junior Hockey League until 1987).[4] In his third year as the Wolves' head coach, Andy Laing was tasked with molding a contending squad from a young talent pool. The anticipated loss of veterans like Dale Hunter and Frank Perkins was worsened by the departure of Mike Allison, drafted by the New York Rangers in the second round of the 1980 NHL Entry Draft, and goaltender Don Beaupre, selected by the Minnesota North Stars two picks later, both of whom had been expected to return to Sudbury for another season.[5] Laing hoped for big things from Mike Hickey, a late round pick by the Wolves back in 1978, and veteran forward Rob Motz, both of whom he projected to score at least 40 goals during the season. Forward Chris Kontos and goaltender Mike Sands were thrown into important roles only months after getting selected by the Wolves in the 1980 OHL Draft.[6]

Preseason projections that the Pack could compete for the top spot in the Leyden Division proved to be overly optimistic. The Soo Greyhounds visited the Sudbury Arena for the Wolves' home opener and skated away with a convincing 7-4 win.[7] By November, with his team having only four wins through eighteen games, there were rumours that Laing's job was on thin ice. The coach's frustration may have gotten the best of him on November 21 when the Oshawa Generals visited the Nickel City. In a fight-filled affair, which the Generals won by a score of 7-4, Laing lost his cool and verbally blasted a referee. He was subsequently fined and suspended by OHL commissioner David Branch for three games. Joe Drago filled in as coach during Laing's absence, something he had done in the past when called upon.[8]

The Wolves tumbled down the standings and stayed there for the bulk of the season. Perhaps things would have been different if the team had been part of the Emms Division. After beating the Toronto Marlies at Maple Leaf Gardens by a score of 4-1 on February 15, the Wolves earned their seventeenth win of the season up to that point, thirteen of which had come against Emms Division opponents. "We're obviously playing in the tougher bracket," said Laing.[9] Even Woofer—the Wolves' mascot today known as Howler—took a beating when a player from Niagara Falls Flyers (a second incarnation of the team after the St. Catharines Black Hawks were sold and relocated in 1976) struck the teenager in a wolf costume with his stick for heckling him while in the penalty box. The incident, which occurred during a game that saw the Wolves end a nine-game losing streak, prompted the league to forbid mascots from going near players' benches or penalty boxes.[10]

The Wolves ended the 1980-81 OHL season with a record of 20-45-3, and it put them ahead of only the London Knights in the OHL standings. Captain Mike Hickey led the team with 90 points and tied Motz with 41 goals, fulfilling Laing's preseason goal-scoring projections for the two forwards. Sophomore defenceman Rob Mazzuca, from the railway town of Capreol outside Sudbury, also had a solid season by recording 59 points and 162 penalty minutes. "It's been a long, frustrating year and I'm certainly glad it's over," Laing admitted at the conclusion of the regular season.[11]

WHAT'S WRONG WITH THE SUDBURY WOLVES?

In the spring of 1981, the Wolves made the first of a long list of coaching changes that would characterize the team's management style throughout the decade. Former part-owner Gord Ewin once recalled that the big ownership group "was our downfall. There were too many people. Somebody always wanted to fire the coach."[12] Andy Laing was dismissed in April with one year left on his contract and was replaced by Joe Drago. The Wolves' long-time executive and team shareholder was granted a one-year leave of absence from his job as a Sudbury district high school principal to serve as head coach for the 1981-82 OHL season. "My owner friends, they got disenchanted and upset because we weren't winning," explains Drago. "But we fired so many damn coaches, so I … decided I would take a leave of absence from my principal's job and I would go and coach the team."[13]

The OHL underwent a realignment in 1981 that directly affected the Wolves. The expansion franchise Belleville Bulls was added to the league, while at the same time the back-to-back defending Memorial Cup champion Cornwall Royals were transferred from the QMJHL to the OHL. To balance out the standings of the now fourteen-team OHL, the Wolves and Soo Greyhounds were moved to the Emms Division alongside the London Knights, Windsor Spitfires, Brantford Alexanders, Kitchener Rangers, and Niagara Falls Flyers. Furthermore, the Bulls were automatically granted the first overall selection in the 1981 OHL Draft, pushing both London and Sudbury to the second and third picks, respectively.

Gord Ewin remembers the 1981 draft well because of the difficult decision management had to make regarding the third overall selection. "We had a choice between two guys: Pat Verbeek or Steve Yzerman," he explains. Ewin adds that Yzerman had notified the Wolves that he was interested in coming to Sudbury, but at the time the club felt they needed someone more physically mature than the undersized centreman from the Nepean Raiders. "Verbeek was as if you had cut him out of rock. And so, we decided—we had missed the playoffs, obviously—we needed somebody a little tougher than Yzerman."[14] After much deliberation, the conflicted Wolves used their first-round selection to take Petrolia Jets' forward Pat Verbeek.[15] The Peterborough Petes next used the fourth overall pick to take Steve Yzerman, the future captain of the Detroit Red Wings and member of the Hockey Hall of Fame.[16]

Drago and his team soon found out that competing in the Emms Division was no less gruelling than its Leyden counterpart. "What's wrong with the Sudbury Wolves?" asked *The Star* on Halloween as the Wolves sat with a 3-12-0 record. Their head coach was just as perplexed: "I don't know whether it's a lack of coaching ability on my part but I do know one thing—this team has the talent to win … it's just that I can't seem to keep them up mentally for three periods of hockey." The team sought to shake things up through some trades, notably sending Chris Kontos to the Toronto Marlies in exchange for centre Keith Knight.[17]

From a business standpoint the Wolves' losing ways could not be tolerated. It was no secret that the franchise was struggling financially because of a sharp decline in attendance over the previous few seasons, a trend that was strongly linked to Sudbury's economic woes as the world nickel market softened. Several Wolves' games at the Sudbury Arena had drawn fewer than 500 attendees during the season. Drago did not mince words when probed about the situation only days into the New Year. "There's only so much cash available and we can only borrow so much before we have to take steps to determine the future of the hockey club. I really can't say if the team will be in Sudbury next season," he told one Toronto newspaper. "The situation at INCO doesn't help."[18] Within about one month's time, however, the Wolves organization was able to confirm that it would not be folding or moving anytime soon. "We're going to be back in Sudbury next year," Drago said firmly in February 1982. "This is only the second bad year we've had, fan-support wise. Let's face it, nobody likes a loser. For seven or eight years, the Soo Greyhounds were starving at the gate financially, but now that they're winning, the club is doing well. The same will happen here."[19]

Perhaps the team's modest uptick in play had temporarily given fans and ownership a renewed sense of hope. The Wolves ended a 10-game winless streak on February 10 by beating the Brantford Alexanders 6-5, and following another win over the Flyers by a score of 9-7 days later, the club was suddenly within two points of the Spitfires for the sixth and final playoff spots in the Emms Division standings.[20] The string of losses that followed stamped out any chance of a postseason appearance; the team finished last in the OHL. The Wolves' final game of the regular season was a 6-5 loss to the visiting Greyhounds on a Friday evening in March, leaving the club with 48 defeats against 19 wins and a single tie. It was the last game in the green and white for players like captain Rob Mazzuca and leading-scorer Rob Motz, the latter of whom managed to set a franchise record by potting seven short-handed goals during the regular season.[21]

One of the few positive takeaways from the season was the play of Pat Verbeek. In his first OHL season, the young forward scored 37 goals and 88 points, along with 180 penalty minutes, to earn the Emms Family Award as the league's rookie of the year. He was the first player in Wolves' history to accomplish the feat, and did so even while his team struggled on the ice. "It was tough winning for whatever reason. We had some good players. Just not enough good ones to win," Verbeek remembered of his rookie year in an interview with Mike Commito years later.[22] As *Sudbury Star* sportswriter Jack Falldien put it at the conclusion of the Sudbury Wolves' 1981-82 campaign, "Nothing could be worse than the season which came to an end last night."[23] It was, in retrospect, a premature declaration.

THE LAST HURRAH?

The Sudbury Wolves organization entered its ten-year anniversary and eleventh season of play determined to make a return to the OHL playoffs. The team was set to dress several NHL prospects for the 1982-83 OHL season. Pat Verbeek had been selected by the New Jersey Devils in the 1982 NHL Draft, while Jim Koudys (New York Islanders), Tim Hrynewich (Pittsburgh Penguins), Sudbury native Mike Savage (Winnipeg Jets) and goaltender Mike Sands (Minnesota North Stars) all returned for another year of junior hockey. Having fulfilled his one-year commitment as the Wolves' caretaker coach, Joe Drago returned to his job as a high school principal and role as the leader of the ownership group. His first task was to find a replacement behind the bench. Sudbury ultimately decided on Ken Gratton, a former player with the Kitchener Rangers who had previously coached the Brantford Alexanders. In addition, while the club was technically entitled to the first overall pick in the 1982 OHL Draft, the arrival of another expansion franchise, the Guelph Platers, again nudged the Wolves down a spot. After Guelph chose Kingston native Kirk Muller first overall, the Wolves selected defenceman Jeff Brown from the Hawkesbury Hawks. The 16-year-old was already being touted as the next great junior defenceman, comparable to the likes of NHL blueliners Craig Hartsburg (Soo Greyhounds) and Denis Potvin (Ottawa 67's).[24]

The 1982-83 OHL season was the most taxing in the Wolves' decade-long history. The team opened the year with seven straight losses. In mid-December, having lost eleven of their previous twelve contests and owning a 9-23-0 record, Ken Gratton resigned and Marcel Clements stepped in for another stint as the Wolves' head coach. On January 20, Clements guided the Wolves to their first road win of the season over the Cornwall Royals by a score of 8-7, defeating a club which featured OHL leading scorer Doug Gilmour.[25] By February, Sudbury had made yet another coaching change by bringing in Billy Harris, a former player who won a Memorial Cup with the Toronto Marlboros in 1955 and three consecutive Stanley Cups with the Toronto Maple Leafs in the early 1960s. He had been an assistant coach with the Edmonton Oilers for the previous two seasons before joining the Wolves.[26] It was too late for Harris to salvage the season, though, and the Wolves were eliminated from the playoff hunt by early March. Team captain Pat Verbeek led the team in scoring with 40 goals and 107 points. Unfortunately, his team won just fifteen games all season—a new franchise low—and finished ahead of only the Guelph Platers in the OHL standings.[27]

From 1982 to 1983, the people of Sudbury were dealing with problems that extended far beyond the Elgin Street rink, and this had implications that called the very fate of the Wolves franchise into question. In June 1982, workers at INCO voted to strike, whereupon the company suspended operations indefinitely due to a shrinking worldwide nickel market. Falconbridge ceased production as well. By September, almost 27 percent of Sudbury's workforce was unemployed, leading some to label the city the "Unemployment capital of Canada." The extended layoffs for thousands of Sudburians and their families only ended in the spring of 1983 with both Falconbridge and INCO resuming production, but the latest downswing made clear that the local economy could no longer count on the mining industry alone for prosperity.[28]

The ripple effects of Sudbury's latest economic blows meant fewer and fewer fans had the money or desire to watch the Wolves toil in the OHL's basement. Ownership was still scoping the market for potential buyers, but Bud Burke held right of first refusal under the terms of the 1979 sales agreement. Burke offered to take another look at the books to see if he would be interested in reacquiring the club. He voiced the concerns of the community at large regarding the possibility of an out-of-town investor swooping in instead and moving the team elsewhere. "Should Sudbury lose the Wolves now, it would be a death blow for hockey in this community at the OHL level," he told *The Globe and Mail* in February 1983.[29]

The Wolves' devoted fanbase listened anxiously for news of an impending deal. An informal *Sudbury Star* survey conducted in the latter half of the 1982-83 season implied that the majority of citizens would be saddened if the team left town. "Yes, I'd be upset. I think they're a vital part of the community, despite the fact they're losing right now," stated one Sudbury man.[30] Following the Wolves' final home game of the year, a 5-1 loss to Brantford, *The Sudbury Star* solemnly reported that the "Sudbury Wolves' hardcore fans bid adieu to their team, perhaps for the season and maybe forever last night." The newspaper further explained that the "Wolves' fate ... has to do with the roll of the dice, as to who might buy the Wolves and whether the club stays in the Nickel Capital." In the interim, everyone sat and pondered whether this season had it really been the team's "last hurrah."[31]

SPRUCING THINGS UP

The Sudbury Wolves, of course, did not leave town, but that did not mean the club's financial troubles were a work of fiction. "We were losing money," says Gord Ewin. "I remember sitting at the game one night and the people in front of me said, 'Every game it costs us $4 a ticket.' I said, 'You're lucky, it costs me $800 a game!'[32] Both Ewin and Joe Drago attest that the large ownership group, despite some of its pitfalls, provided the organization with deeper pockets than it might have had with a single shareholder, and this allowed them to keep things afloat. At a certain point, however, Drago notes that "the guys weren't prepared to put more money in ... so it looked like this could be a disaster."[33]

For the time being, the club continued to push ahead toward a better tomorrow by replenishing its stock of prospects. With the second overall selection in the 1983 OHL Draft, the Wolves chose left winger Craig Duncanson from the St. Michael's Buzzers. Although Duncanson grew up in the town of Walden (now part of Greater Sudbury) he had moved to Toronto to play junior 'B' hockey for the Buzzers during his draft year. Duncanson remembers getting selected by his hometown club at the annual draft at the North York Centennial Arena in Toronto. "It wasn't much of a surprise," says Duncanson. "Mr. Drago at the time had called me and told me they were interested." He was particularly grateful for the opportunity to work with head coach Billy Harris. "That was a big part of me coming here, and being excited about coming here, because Billy was just a legendary guy and a real gentleman."[34] Duncanson remains the highest local player ever drafted to the Wolves. Other Sudbury picks from the 1983 draft class included goaltender Sean Evoy from the Don Mills Flyers and forward Brian Verbeek, the younger brother of Pat Verbeek, from the Petrolia Jets, the Wolves' junior 'B' affiliate.

The 1983-84 OHL season followed a familiar storyline for the troubled Wolves. By the time team captain Ken Minello had returned to the lineup after missing the first twenty games of the season due to a bad knee and a bout of mononucleosis, the team was 5-14-1. In January 1984, tied for last place in the OHL after an 8-7 overtime loss to the Guelph Platers, Billy Harris was relieved of his duties. Days later, the 29-year-old Andy Spruce, coach of the Petrolia Jets, was promoted and became Sudbury's sixth coach since 1980. The young bench boss had played professionally with the Colorado Rockies and Vancouver Canucks before retiring in 1982.[35] His debut was spoiled by the Kitchener Rangers, who rallied from a 3-1 deficit in the second period to win the game by a score of 7-4. "From what I've seen from this contest, I find the players are not in shape to play a full 60 minutes of hockey," Spruce concluded.[36]

The Wolves and their newest coach finished in last place in the OHL with only 19 wins through 70 games. The team struggled defensively all year-long. A telling example came on January 14 when the Wolves blew a 4-0 lead against the Rangers and lost the game by a score of 13-8.[37] The Pack allowed its opponents to collectively score 425 goals during the 1983-84 season, setting a franchise record for most goals against in a single season. The goaltending tandem of rookie Sean Evoy and Danny Long, a veteran netminder acquired from the Windsor Spitfires the previous offseason, were not entirely to blame. "It was a real eye-opener and a frustrating year," says Duncanson, who led the Wolves in penalty minutes while notching 38 goals and 76 points in his rookie season. "It was still the back end of a somewhat less attractive brand of hockey. It was very tough. It was very dirty. It was ugly … it wasn't as nice a brand of hockey as we watch today," he explains. "I was just happy to be in the league and happy to be playing and optimistic about a brighter future."[38]

The Wolves and their fans wondered how much longer they would have to wait for this brighter future after missing the postseason for the fourth consecutive year. Locking up the first overall pick in the upcoming 1984 OHL Draft was a good starting point for a team which, in the words of coach Spruce, was "short of talent" and set to lose leading scorer Jim Koudys, captain Minello, and other important veterans. "My top two priorities are to reduce the goals against and win home games," said Spruce at the end of the regular season in March. "And to put a style of hockey on the ice that the people of Sudbury will want to watch."[39]

MAKE IT FIVE

In the winter of 1984, officials from the CHL were set to meet with NHL general managers in Phoenix, Arizona, to discuss a three-year-old junior hockey entry draft agreement that was set to expire in June of that year. The agreement was widely unpopular amongst players, agents, owners and fans alike, with Alan Eagleson, the infamous hockey agent and first executive director of the National Hockey League Players' Association, stating that "Anything would be better than the present system. It has had a devastating effect on the NHL, on the junior teams and on the players." The point of contention stemmed from the lowering of the NHL draft age from 20 to 18-years-old in 1979, prompting an exodus of elite talent from junior clubs to the professional ranks. "Without the big drawing cards, attendance at junior games has fallen and some franchises have come dangerously close to folding," read *The Globe and Mail* in January 1984. "Especially near the brink are the Sudbury Wolves of the OHL."[40]

With the team's misfortunes well-known in the hockey world, the Sudbury Wolves looked to the 1984-85 OHL season as another chance to redeem themselves. A mixture of grizzled veterans and promising youngsters shouldered that responsibility. The team fulfilled Andy Spruce's desire to recruit more "physical defenceman" by selecting blueliner Dave Moylan first overall in the 1984 OHL Draft. The 17-year-old Moylan was hailed for his skating, size, and overall potential. Sudbury used its second-round choice on Max Middendorf, a big forward from the state of New Jersey.[41] "That draft … was instrumental," says Craig Duncanson, who was named captain of the Wolves for the 1984-85 season. "We had Dave Moylan, Max Middendorf, Warren Rychel, Brad Belland, Brent Daugherty … Mario Chitaroni. There was a number of guys in that draft that contributed."[42] Defenceman Jeff Brown returned to the Wolves after getting selected by the Quebec Nordiques in the second round of the 1984 NHL Draft, as did forward Glenn Greenough, a Sudbury native, after getting chosen by the Chicago Black Hawks. Another local, forward Jamie Nadjiwan of the Nickel Centre Native Sons of the NOHA, cracked the lineup as an undrafted training camp invitee.

The Wolves start to the season gave the impression that things might finally be different. Despite losing Duncanson to a knee injury in their season opener, the team won four of their first six games of the year, including three consecutive road meetings against Windsor, London, and Guelph. The Wolves even played to a tie against the defending Memorial Cup champion Ottawa 67's at the Sudbury Arena during that span. The exceptional play of second-year goaltender Sean Evoy and the injection of new blood into the roster seemed to be launching the group down the right path. Since Andy Spruce had taken over, indicated *The Star*, "the mood had changed" in Sudbury. "Now the desire to end the cellar doldrums—in which attendance has hit record lows—is somewhat [brighter] in this the Wolves' 13th season in the OHL."[43]

Only weeks later the mood had again changed entirely and precipitated a merry-go-round of roster changes. Following back-to-back losses to the Platers and Toronto Marlies at the end of October, Spruce lamented the Wolves' lack of scoring, particularly on the powerplay. In an effort to shake things up the club traded away multiple players during the 1984-85 season, including sending veteran left winger Chris McRae to the Oshawa Generals and Brian Verbeek to the Kingston Canadians. A few players, like former Cornwall Royals goaltender Paul Kenny, were acquired and then flipped again after only a handful of games in Sudbury.[44] On December 9 the Wolves lost their eighth game in a row in a 12-4 beatdown by the rival North Bay Centennials, leaving them with an abysmal 8-21-2 record.[45]

The second half of the season offered little cause for hope. The Wolves did not win their first game of 1985 until January 25 when they defeated Windsor by a score of 3-2 on a game-winner by Nadjiwan; it also marked their first victory in eleven games. On March 1, the Wolves were mathematically eliminated from playoff contention following a 4-1 loss to the Soo Greyhounds at the Sudbury Arena.[46] The rival Greyhounds had a polar opposite season from the Wolves, setting an OHL record by winning all 33 of their regular season home games and ultimately capturing the franchise's first J. Ross Robertson Cup that spring.[47] Sudbury's seventeen regular season wins put them second from last in the OHL standings. Brown became the first defenceman in Wolves' history to lead the team in scoring with 64 points in 56 games played. Captain Duncanson recovered from his early season injury to score a team-high 35 goals.

By the mid-1980s the Sudbury Wolves organization was hanging by a thread, but thankfully another poor season for the team did not deter NHL clubs from plucking several members of the Sudbury Wolves in the 1985 NHL Entry Draft hosted in Toronto. Duncanson was selected ninth overall by the Los Angeles Kings. "Obviously I was very excited," he says thirty-five years later. "That was the first televised draft, actually, in 1985 … It was on TSN."[48] Duncanson's selection was followed by teammates Middendorf (Quebec Nordiques, 54th overall), Moylan (Buffalo Sabres, 77th overall), Belland (Chicago Black Hawks, 95th overall), and Nadjiwan (Washington Capitals, 145th overall). Nevertheless, five straight seasons without a playoff appearance for the Sudbury Wolves had put the future of the green and white in serious jeopardy. The franchise could not afford to continue taking such heavy losses at the box office. Something needed to change—and quickly.

CHAPTER 5:

ROAD TO REDEMPTION, 1985-1989

From a purely statistical standpoint, the Sudbury Wolves did not radically improve in the latter half of the 1980s, but in a broader sense the organization was trending in the right direction, and in many ways its host city was, too. Investment and job growth in the medical, educational, and public sectors in Sudbury began to bear fruit through the efforts of local leaders in partnership with the provincial and federal governments, lessening the city's dependence on the mining industry. New housing subdivisions were being built in districts across the city and facilities like the J.N. Desmarais Library at Laurentian University and the Science North museum on Lake Ramsey had been erected. Along with the ongoing re-greening of Sudbury's once devastated landscape, a highly conspicuous transformation was gradually taking place in the Northern Ontario community.[1]

For the Wolves, a lone and very brief playoff appearance was the first real flicker of light in what had been a dark decade. A bigger spark was ignited in 1986 when the team's ownership group at last decided to sell its shares to a single stakeholder with a refreshing and energized plan of action. The transaction was crucial to saving a franchise in crisis, providing a sense of stability that would eventually propel the Sudbury Wolves back into the spotlight.

THE PACK STRIKES BACK

It was a busy offseason in 1985. Using the second overall pick in the OHL Draft, the Sudbury Wolves selected Hawkesbury Hawks forward Ken McRae, and then used its second-round selection to take local forward Todd Lalonde.[2] The organization also hired another coach before the start of the new season; in fact, it hired two. Andy Spruce's contract was not renewed after one and a half seasons behind the bench, and in May the club recruited Bob Strumm, former coach and general manager of the Regina Pats of the WHL, as his successor. About two months later, however, Strumm advised the team that he would not be taking the opportunity in Sudbury "due to personal reasons." With training camp and the preseason only weeks away, the 42-year-old Wayne Maxner was then hired as the Wolves' coach and general manager. A former player with the Boston Bruins in the mid-1960s, Maxner had over 300 games of OHL coaching experience with the Windsor Spitfires and even a stint behind the bench of the Detroit Red Wings from 1980 to 1982.[3]

The Wolves' start to the 1985-86 OHL season was the team's best since the 1970s. Maxner made his debut with the club on September 27 (coincidentally his birthday) and guided the Wolves to a win in their season opener by topping the Spitfires by a score of 4-1 at the Sudbury Arena. Sudbury stayed hot and manhandled the defending champion Soo Greyhounds 9-3 in the first meeting between the two rivals that season, and by mid-November owned a strong 14-4-1 record.[4] Max Middendorf, Mario Chitaroni, Glenn Greenough, and Craig Duncanson provided veteran firepower, while rookies Lalonde and McRae had noticeable impacts virtually right away. Defenceman Jeff Brown and Dave Moylan provided stability on the backend in front of a solid Sean Evoy.[5]

As the team battled for top spot in the Emms Division, management made multiple alterations to the lineup, some of which made more sense than others. Forward Mike Hudson was obtained from the Hamilton Steelhawks in October and by season's end emerged as one of the Wolves' scoring leaders, notching 35 goals and 77 points in 59 games played. The most unexpected and controversial move came in December when Maxner shipped Duncanson and Evoy to the Cornwall Royals in exchange for goalie Mike Patrick, centre Jeff Smith and defenceman Mike Rouleau.[6] "It was a total surprise," remembers Duncanson of the deal. "We had a lot of fun. That was an exciting year. I was excited about the upswing and I was disappointed with the trade."[7] Duncanson returned to the Sudbury Arena just a few days later, scoring a goal and an assist against his former team to pace the Royals to a 7-4 victory. "I had some butterflies throughout the game … I will always have some fond memories playing here, but I guess it was time for a change," the young Kings' prospect told *The Sudbury Star* after the match. Duncanson finished among the top ten of OHL scorers that season with 110 points.[8] Thirty-five years later, Gord Ewin calls the Duncanson deal "probably … the worst trade in the history of the team."[9]

The Wolves collapsed in the second half of the season, yet lucked out and clung to a playoff position. Sitting second in the division before Christmas, by the end of February the team had slipped to fourth place. On March 7, with only six regular season games remaining, the Wolves lost by a score of 8-6 to the Kitchener Rangers, but it was the outcome of another OHL game that same night that caught the attention of the team and its fans. After the Steelhawks were eliminated from the playoff picture following an 8-6 loss to the London Knights, the Wolves officially clinched their first playoff berth in six years. "There was a lot of pressure on us … But now, the monkey's finally off our backs," said Maxner. The Wolves still ended the season with nine straight losses on the road and finished with a 29-33-4 record. This all occurred despite the contributions of Middendorf, who led the Wolves in scoring with 82 points, and Brown, whose 22 goals and 50 points in 45 games helped earn him the Max Kaminsky Trophy as the OHL's most outstanding defenceman, the first player in franchise history to receive this honour.[10]

The fifth place Sudbury Wolves were paired against the second place Guelph Platers in the 1986 Emms Division quarterfinals. It was both the Wolves' first playoff appearance since 1980 and the Platers' first time qualifying for the postseason since joining the league in 1982. The series commenced at Guelph Memorial Gardens on March 23, with the Platers earning a 5-3 victory. In Game 2 in the Nickel City, the Wolves were behind 6-1 by the midway point of the game. Back-to-back goals by Middendorf and tallies by Smith and defenceman Brad Walcot brought the Wolves within one goal of tying it up, but the Platers held on for a 6-5 win. Guelph thrashed Sudbury in the following two matches by scores of 8-1 and 6-3 to sweep the series in four straight games. It was a demoralizing end to a rollercoaster season for the Wolves; the team had started off as a contender only to tailspin into mediocrity.[11] The Guelph Platers, led by coach Jacques Martin and a young power forward named Gary Roberts, went on to win the 1986 Memorial Cup.

SAVING THE SUDBURY WOLVES

"The Sudbury Wolves will be trying to avoid the dreaded black hole again this season," relayed *The Sudbury Star* on the eve of the team's 1986-87 opener. With the status of NHL prospects like Max Middendorf and Mike Hudson—the latter drafted by the Chicago Blackhawks in 1986—still up in the air, the club was not sure exactly what its roster would look like, but the recent taste of the playoffs kept the group motivated to improve. At the 1986 OHL Draft the Wolves picked outside the top three for the first time since 1980, selecting Mississauga-born forward Wayne Doucet seventh overall. In the fourth round of the draft, Sudbury management looked westward and drafted Paul DiPietro, an undersized but highly skilled centreman from Sault Ste. Marie.[12]

The franchise also partook in what began to feel like an annual offseason tradition of firing its head coach. Even though Wayne Maxner had led the Wolves to their first postseason appearance in six years, Joe Drago explained that ownership felt the club "could do much better. Had the regular season gone another week we would not have made the playoffs."[13] Many fans also attributed the team's late season struggles to Maxner's decision to trade

Craig Duncanson and Sean Evoy midway through the year, and resented the deal even more when none of the three players he got in return from the Cornwall Royals were back for the start of the 1986-87 OHL season. The Wolves hired Guy Blanchard as Maxner's replacement, a Sudbury local who had formerly served as an assistant coach with the North Bay Centennials.[14]

The Wolves had a terrible start to the season under Blanchard. The team opened the season on the road for only the fourth time in franchise history, travelling about 130 kilometres east down Highway 17 to North Bay and falling in defeat to the Centennials by a score of 5-1. The Wolves proceeded to tie a franchise record set in 1982-83 by dropping the first seven games of the season before finally registering a 7-3 victory over the Royals on October 17.[15] Only sixteen games into the season, sports reporter Norm Mayer wrote that "the Wolves are going nowhere fast – again," and decried that the team was "nothing more than a comic act on ice." Fans seemed to agree; barely over 1,000 patrons came to the Sudbury Arena to watch the Wolves take on the Greyhounds for a mid-November matchup that saw the home team lose 9-5.[16] Shortly thereafter, former first overall selection Dave Moylan, who had succeeded Duncanson as team captain, was dealt to the Kitchener Rangers in exchange for defenceman Ken Alexander. Mike Hudson was next to have the 'C' stitched onto his Wolves sweater.[17]

The shuffling of Moylan was indicative of what was to come for the Wolves throughout the course of the 1986-87 OHL season. Max Middendorf and Ken McRae were among other high-profile pieces that were moved during a year that saw the team dress roughly 50 different players and start seven goalies. "It was just a mess," remembers Ken Campbell. After graduating from Carleton University, Campbell returned home to Sudbury to cover the Wolves as a reporter with *The Northern Life* from 1986 to 1988. "Guys would come, guys would go … They were just terrible."[18] The team had just four wins through the first twenty games of the season.

The Sudbury Wolves franchise had reached a tipping point. Nearly thirty-five years later, Joe Drago remembers how he orchestrated the sale of the entire team to local businessman Kenneth "Ken" Murray Burgess through a chance encounter. "I was at the bank, and when I came out Ken Burgess was in the parking lot," recalls Joe Drago. "So, we ended up chatting, and he said that he wouldn't mind getting involved in the Sudbury Wolves … So, I said 'Ken, how would you like to buy the entire group?' He said, 'Well, I never thought of that.'" After meeting and reviewing the relevant business information, Drago and Burgess came to an agreement. "This was just me doing this. I was the president of the organization. The guys gave me total control of the team and I could make decisions, so I sold the team to him," explains Drago. "And then I called all the guys together and divvied up the monies that were available, and that was the end of our organization."[19]

On November 21, 1986, Drago formally resigned as president and part-owner of the OHL club he had helped pioneer. "This is by far the toughest day of my life," he told those in attendance at a press conference. "You just can't run a hockey club with 14 owners involved. I figured it was [as] good a time as any to part company. I have very mixed emotions about this. It's going to be a big change for me and my family," a solemn Drago added in his public statement.[20] Years later, he still feels the same way. "It was very, very hard," Drago states. "Because, even though I was a principal, my heart and soul was in the game of hockey." After selling the Sudbury Wolves, Drago continued to embrace his love of the sport in various ways, most notably serving as the chair of the board of directors of Hockey Canada.[21]

Ken Burgess, who passed away in 1998, was now the sole owner of the Sudbury Wolves. Originally from Nova Scotia, he eventually settled in Sudbury and founded a mining equipment company called Burgess Power Train and Manufacturing Ltd. When he acquired the Wolves, he was already the owner of the Nickel Centre Power Trains of the NOHA Junior 'A' League and sponsored the Burgess Power Train Major Midgets of the Great North Midget League. "There have been some tough negotiations the past 24 hours. But in the end, everyone knew it had to happen," Burgess said upon announcing the deal. The new owner advised that Blanchard would remain as coach but would be replaced as general manager by Marcel Bedard, who at the time was serving as the manager of the Nickel Centre Power Trains. "Ken has complete control now … it's something that will surely help the hockey club in the long run," predicted Blanchard.[22]

Burgess's acquisition of the franchise appeared to pay dividends early on. "Things got better almost immediately," recalled former Wolves forward Mario "Tiger" Chitaroni in an interview with *The Sudbury Star*.[23] The fanbase, too, seemed keen to see where the new owner would steer the team. "I mean, actually, for a team that was that bad, they actually had pretty decent fan support," acknowledges Ken Campbell.[24] The "Wolfpak" booster club, for instance, received a noticeable uptick in support in the months following the franchise changing hands. This volunteer group of avid Wolves' supporters handled 50-50 draws and organized community activities like public skates and social events with players and management. The Wolfpak booster club had existed in the club's past only to disband for a number of years before getting revived in the fall of 1985. "We're getting better communication and more cooperation thanks to Marcel Bedard and Ken Burgess," said one Wolfpak committee member. "Our goal is simple: we want to become the best booster club in the OHL."[25]

The 1986-87 season was nevertheless another discouraging campaign for the Wolves. The team won only twenty games and finished last overall in the OHL standings. Sudbury closed the year on March 20 with a 9-3 loss to North Bay at the Sudbury Arena and watched as its northern rival, coached by Bert Templeton, secured first place in the Emms Division. "My nightmare started from that opening game," said coach Blanchard at the season's conclusion. "Right from the start, we had a bad attitude and some didn't care ... it was every man for himself."[26]

One player who did receive accolades for his efforts and determination throughout that troublesome season was Mario Chitaroni. Playing half the season with a broken wrist, the Cobalt native tallied 54 goals and 102 points in 63 games to lead the squad in scoring and was recognized by the team as the most improved player. "That was one of the all-time great individual performances I've ever seen," asserts Ken Campbell. "Just a really heart and soul guy that I thought was just an amazing character player ... I never once ever heard him complain." Chitaroni was not drafted to the NHL, but he went on to have an excellent career overseas that included playing on the Italian men's national ice hockey team at both the Winter Olympics and Ice Hockey World Championships.[27]

WAR STORIES

In May 1987, Ken Burgess and the Sudbury Wolves made a sequence of consequential moves to help try to lift the team out of the bottom of the OHL. The Wolves sent forward Mark Turner and a fourth-round pick in the 1987 OHL Draft to the Kingston Canadians in exchange for two siblings from Sudbury, veteran defenceman Marc Laforge and his younger brother Alain, a left winger. The elder Laforge was the centrepiece of the deal, having been drafted by the Hartford Whalers in the 1986 NHL Draft and widely regarded as one of the toughest players in the OHL. Burgess soon thereafter announced that Guy Blanchard's coaching contract would not be renewed, but did not immediately name a replacement.[28] The following week, for the second time since 1984, the club was tasked with making the first overall selection in the OHL Draft. Just as the organization had done three years earlier with Dave Moylan, it used the pick to take a defenceman. It was an emotional day for John Uniac, a right-shot blueliner from Stratford, who referenced his late father upon being selected first overall. "My father died two summers ago. I tried so hard for him. He made me what I am today."[29]

In June, the Wolves hired John Wallin as their next coach. A native of Chicago, Wallin had been a scout for the Calgary Flames from 1979 to 1983 and coached at Kent State University in Ohio. He was also a veteran of the Vietnam War. Wallin embraced the challenge of taking over a last-place team and building it into a winner. "You have to have patience and you have to be a teacher if you want to coach junior hockey," he stated. "My job is to try and develop their confidence." The recruitment of the Wolves' seventeenth coach in seventeen seasons had become almost laughable for the team's fans. By that time, for example, the Frood Hotel, a Sudbury tavern owned by Larry Rubic, had a portrait of every Wolves' coach since 1972 hung on one of its walls. "It got to be a joke," Rubic told *The Globe and Mail*. "They were changing so fast ... But the new owners are trying hard now. And it looks like they'll have a winner." Rubic had himself helmed the team in the early 1970s, serving as only the second coach in franchise history.[30] The Wolves also chose veteran defenceman Jordan Fois, acquired from Hamilton the previous season, as the next team captain.

At first it appeared that Wallin might have cooked up a recipe for success. The team opened the year with a 4-1 win over North Bay as rookie goalie Ted Mielczarek earned first star honours with 31 saves.[31] Wallin appeared to bring structure to the junior organization, going so far as to send one player home and suspend three others for breaking curfew not even ten games into the season. "I'm not asking for much. All I ask is to follow a few simple rules," the head coach reasoned to *The Sudbury Star*.[32] By the end of October, the Wolves were 6-6-0, an encouraging start given the results of years past, and attendance figures were on the rise at the Sudbury Arena. Ken Burgess was, so far, impressed with Wallin's coaching abilities. "He's always doing something different, something new," the Wolves' owner said. "The players never get bored."[33]

It was far from a boring season for the Sudbury Wolves, but for all the wrong reasons. The rest of the 1987-88 OHL campaign was in fact one of the more dramatic in the team's history. One of the lowlights came on November 6 when the Guelph Platers, the worst defensive crew in the OHL, visited the Sudbury Arena. The match ended in a 5-4 loss for the Wolves and a bench-clearing postgame brawl. During the ten-minute melee, Sudbury's hulking Marc Laforge went on a rampage and threw punches at eight different Platers who were engaged in separate fights and thereby defenceless. He was also reported to have slammed Guelph goaltender Andy Helmuth's head against the ice several times. Three of Laforge's targets suffered broken noses. The Wolves defenceman received a match penalty on the spot which carried an automatic five-game suspension.[34]

Laforge was later slapped with one of the most severe punishments in OHL history. On November 17, league commissioner Dave Branch announced that Laforge would be suspended for the remainder of the current season plus the entire 1988-89 season. This decision put an end to the 19-year-old's junior hockey career. "It's a message to players and fans that we don't condone this type of activity," Branch affirmed. Laforge had already been suspended a number of times for various incidents during his OHL career.[35] "It was obviously the dumbest thing I've ever done. I have no excuses," Laforge told *The Toronto Star* years later. The Sudbury-born defenceman went on to appear in a total of fourteen NHL games with Hartford and the

Edmonton Oilers, though he spent most of his time as an enforcer in the minor leagues before retiring in the early 2000s.[36]

Another piece of scandalous news out of Sudbury made headlines across the hockey world in the months following the Laforge suspension. With only 10 games left in the regular season, the Wolves were 12 points out of a playoff spot.[37] On February 15, *The Hockey News* printed an article, written by journalist Jim Cressman, which recounted head coach John Wallin's military service in Vietnam in 1969. The piece was based on interviews with former and current Wolves players who stated that Wallin had shared stories with the team that involved him biting off a rat's head, being held as a prisoner-of-war for two years, and carrying a fellow soldier on his back for almost 100 kilometres after escaping capture. About one week after the story was released, Wallin admitted that he had embellished his exploits in Southeast Asia. "Yes, I'll admit those things didn't happen to me personally," the 38-year-old told *The Sudbury Star*. "Those things happened to other people there. I was there (in Vietnam) and I saw a lot of it. I exaggerated about being a prisoner of war and about the rat incident." He later explained that he told "those stories in a joking way, just like you would over beers" and did not intend for them to be taken seriously.[38]

The fallout from Wallin's tall tales was swift. Three days after owning up to his misleading heroic anecdotes, he resigned as head coach at the request of Ken Burgess.[39] The bizarre incident was widely covered by media outlets across Canada.[40] *The Hockey News* ran a follow-up article in early March that quoted its editor-in-chief, Bob McKenzie, who stated that "We didn't check out the facts and we misled our readers." Cressman, too, owned up to the misrepresentation, though he did point out that he had given Wallin the chance to comment on the matter and at no time did the head coach deny telling the stories or provide proper context: "I definitely made a mistake. But what really gets me is that Wallin didn't point out the stuff was false when given the opportunity."[41] It was later reported that Wallin had provided evidence to clarify aspects of his claims in the weeks following his firing, supposedly demonstrating that he had been a prisoner-of-war for 47 days; that the rat-biting episode was true, but had happened to another soldier; and that Wallin, with the help of several others, had carried a wounded comrade to safety.[42]

Whatever the case, Burgess apologized to the people of Sudbury and the team's fanbase for all the controversy and distractions, and indicated that the Wolves were going to refocus on building a winning club. The team was 16-40-1 when assistant coach Ken MacKenzie, a native of Sudbury, took the lead behind the bench. His first win as an OHL head coach came on March 4 with a 5-4 Wolves win over the Kitchener Rangers, halting a ten-game losing streak in the process.[43] It was Sudbury's final win of the 1987-88 season, however, as it finished with a record of 17-48-1, ahead of only Kingston in the OHL standings. Forward Todd Lalonde of Garson, drafted by the Boston Bruins in 1987, led the Wolves with 70 points. Sophomore Paul DiPietro followed close behind, notching 25 goals and 67 points in 63 contests.[44]

WHO EVER HEARD OF A GREEN WOLF?

In the spring of 1988, the Wolves organization made its biggest splash in a decade by hiring Sam McMaster as its new general manager. Originally hailing from Vancouver, McMaster came to Sudbury with a wealth of junior and professional hockey management experience. He had previously served as the top executive for the Soo Greyhounds, capturing two Emms Division titles and the 1985 OHL championship along the way. McMaster then worked as the assistant director of player personnel and recruiting with the Washington Capitals before returning to the OHL. "The fans here have had it with promises, they want results," he proclaimed upon arriving in Sudbury. "Our first challenge is to become credible so that they'll listen when you tell them something." McMaster's first draft with the Wolves took place that May, selecting Adam Bennett, a six-foot-four defenceman from the Georgetown Geminis, with the second overall pick, followed by forward Terry Chitaroni, cousin of Mario Chitaroni, in the second round. In the fourth round the Wolves selected another sturdy blueliner by the name of Sean O'Donnell.[45]

Ken Burgess further crafted his vision for the Sudbury Wolves by introducing a completely new colour scheme for the team's jerseys in 1988-89. The traditional green and white, which had been in place for over 60 years, was replaced with a combination of blue, white, and grey, although the appearance of the iconic wolf logo itself remained relatively unchanged.[46] "When Ken Burgess … took over, I remember his famous quote was, 'Who ever heard of a green wolf?'" recounted Blaine Smith, the Wolves' marketing director, about one year after the makeover. "And so, the idea was set that we should look at a grey wolf, and what better colour to go with grey [than] blue, which happened to be also the corporate colours of Mr. Burgess's international corporation that he owns. And so, the blue and grey came to be."[47] Some fans criticized the colour change for breaking with tradition, but Burgess maintained that the "Wolves will win their next championship with these colours." The decision was indicative of a larger culture change that was underway in the organization.[48]

The 1988-89 season was indeed a transformative one for the Sudbury Wolves, but at the time it may not have been readily apparent. In retrospect, this was the year that Burgess laid the groundwork for the organization's future success by hiring McMaster and giving Mackenzie his first full season behind the bench. "Ken [Burgess] came in and he began to run it like a professional organization," credits Ken Campbell. "I think the biggest thing was bringing in Sam McMaster … Sam was the one that, I think, really rebuilt that whole program, and the reason why they were able to get him is because Ken was willing to spend the money."[49] The Wolves started the year at the Sudbury Arena in front of 4,361 fans with a thrilling 4-3 overtime win against the defending OHL champion Windsor Compuware Spitfires. The group soon fell into a gruelling nine-game winless streak, however, which was finally snapped in late October when captain Jordan Fois netted the game-winning goal over the Belleville Bulls.[50]

McMaster moulded the roster through various trades in his first year at the Wolves' helm. In the early weeks of November, he acquired five players from the Spitfires, including goaltender David Goverde and two cousins from Sudbury, forward Tyler Pella and defenceman Dean Pella. Within a matter of months Goverde had emerged as the Wolves' starting goalie and as a frontrunner for the team's most valuable player. McMaster then sent former first overall pick John Uniac to the Kitchener Rangers in a package deal that included Calgary Flames' draft pick Kevin Grant. Another key acquisition was veteran forward John Andersen from the Niagara Falls Thunder, who eventually found himself playing with top-scorers Todd Lalonde and Paul DiPietro to form the so-called "Dirty Dozen" line.[51]

McMaster's mastery of deal-making was not enough to get his team into the 1989 OHL playoffs, however. The Wolves had gone through several multi-game winless slumps, yet the equally poor play of teams like Windsor, North Bay, and the Soo managed to keep the Pack in the hunt almost right until the end. Sudbury was mathematically eliminated from postseason contention only on March 16 when the Spitfires defeated the London Knights. The Wolves finished one point behind the rival Centennials for the final spot in the Emms Division. "It's been nine years and counting since the Sudbury Wolves last won a playoff game," lamented *The Sudbury Star*. "Pierre Trudeau was prime minister of Canada then. Jimmy Carter was still president of the United States. And Wayne Gretzky was in his first National Hockey League season with the Edmonton Oilers."[52]

Indeed, a lot had changed for the Sudbury Wolves organization since its last playoff win nearly a decade earlier. From the 1979-80 to the 1988-89 seasons, the club had compiled a regular season record of 212-438-24 and accumulated zero playoff victories. It was a far cry from the winning ways of the 1970s, but ever since Ken Burgess had assumed control of the club something felt different. Ownership and management were restoring a connection with the team's fans by demonstrating they had a serious strategy to put together a winning product and by engaging more with the Sudbury community at large. In March 1989, for instance, the Wolves hosted their first annual charity benefit game with the Sudbury Regional Police, raising $5,000 towards the Laurentian Hospital cancer treatment centre.[53] The Wolves were heading down the road to redemption thanks to their new owners' leadership and formation of a knowledgeable, unified front office. It would not be much longer before this approach finally paid off.

CHAPTER 6:

SUDBURY'S RENAISSANCE, 1989-1994

In April 1991, renowned Canadian writer Peter C. Newman authored a piece in *Maclean's* magazine about the city of Sudbury. His choice of words was not always particularly flattering, but the message was clear: Sudbury had undergone dramatic change over the previous two decades. "Once the armpit of Northern Ontario," wrote Newman, "the city's life is far from perfect now, but if it can revive itself, maybe the country will follow." Newman was referring to Sudbury's economic diversification efforts, which had succeeded in attracting investment and creating jobs in retail, tourism, scientific and medical research, and the public sector. In the mid-1970s, INCO and Falconbridge accounted for about 35 percent of Sudbury's employment; by 1990 that number had dropped to about 15 percent. In 1992 the city also received an award from the United Nations for its environmental reclamation efforts, which had resulted in the planting of millions of trees, a decrease in air pollution, and an overall healthier local landscape.[1] Taken as a whole, Newman referred to this transformation as "Sudbury's sunny renaissance."[2]

The Sudbury Wolves organization experienced a rebirth of its own during the early 1990s. The team kicked off the decade with a string of consecutive postseason appearances, swiftly re-establishing the Sudbury Community Arena as one of the best-attended barns in the CHL. Led by top executive Sam McMaster, head coach Ken MacKenzie, and a fresh crop of dynamic young players, the Wolves lifted themselves up from the drudgery of the 1980s and turned into a relevant force for much of the late twentieth century. In 1990, Bob McKenzie, a hockey commentator with TSN, called the team's turnaround a "real genesis junior hockey story."[3] The Wolves newfound success incidentally occurred in tandem with the city of Sudbury's overall revitalization, together breathing new life into a community that had for too long been waiting for something to cheer about.

PRIDE: A WINNING FORMULA

The 1989 OHL Priority Selection in May was one of the more controversial in the league's history, but for the Sudbury Wolves it was quite a success. The draft was highlighted by the unanimous first overall pick Eric Lindros, a 16-year-old centre from Toronto who had for years garnered national attention for his rare blend of size, physicality, and scoring ability. The Sault Ste. Marie Greyhounds owned the first choice, and used it to select the six-foot-four generational talent despite the fact that he and his family had repeatedly advised that he would not report to the team. Lindros faced the wrath of Greyhounds fans when he stuck to his word and refused to head to the Soo. Eventually, in December, they announced that his rights had been traded to the Oshawa Generals in a blockbuster deal that included $80,000 cash going to the Greyhounds. The Wolves were in the shadow of all this chaos because they happened to have the second overall pick. With that selection the team chose Jamie Matthews, a forward from Nova Scotia, and in the second round took Glenn Murray, a right winger from the same province. The Wolves stuck closer to home later in the draft by picking up local forward Jason Young.[4]

The 1989-90 OHL season showcased the Wolves' rebirth under Ken Burgess and Sam McMaster. The club opened the year with a forgettable

5-5 tie against Windsor at the Sudbury Arena on September 22, but from then on remained among the top teams in the Emms Division. Following a 9-7 win over North Bay on New Year's Eve, Sudbury had a 20-15-5 record that left coach Ken MacKenzie confident that the group would make the postseason.[5] A telling example of the Wolves' newfound success came in January 1990 when the team travelled to London to take on the Knights. A standing-room only crowd of 5,531 at the London Gardens set a new record for attendance at that arena for an OHL game as the hometown Knights edged the visiting Wolves by a score of 7-6.[6]

"Pride in the community, pride in the team," explained Sam McMaster when asked about the factors that contributed to the Wolves' winning ways. "And getting everybody believing we can win ... I think that was the number one thing that I wanted to change." The strategies of Ken Burgess and his marketing staff, led by Blaine Smith, also helped instill this sense of pride, extending well beyond just a change in jersey style. The Wolves placed a greater emphasis on community involvement, partaking in charity and fundraising events for organizations like the Kidney Foundation in order to build a stronger relationship with the people of Sudbury. "This isn't my team, or our coach's team, this is their team," McMaster said of the Wolves' fanbase. "And they come out and cheer their team on, and I think they're having a lot of fun doing that."[7]

The players themselves, of course, were the ones making it all happen on the ice, and their performances did not go unnoticed. Fan favourite and team captain Paul DiPietro, playing in his fourth and final OHL season, more than fulfilled his leadership role. On October 3, he scored five goals against the Greyhounds to tie Mike Foligno and Rod Schutt for the franchise record for the most goals in a single game. Months later, the 19-year-old forward became the sixth player in franchise history and the first since Mario Chitaroni to score 50 goals. DiPietro ultimately finished the year second in goals (56) and points (119) in the entire league. In January, McMaster acquired centre Darcy Cahill from the Cornwall Royals in exchange for two players and a draft pick. Cahill was the OHL's leading scorer at the time of the trade, ending the year with 109 points. The Wolves also had one of the OHL's top defenceman in Adam Bennett, drafted sixth overall by the

Chicago Blackhawks in the 1989 NHL Entry Draft, and received secondary scoring from players like rookie Jason Young, who finished second on the team with 73 points. Goalie David Goverde posted an impressive 28-12-7 record, the second-most wins amongst OHL goaltenders that season.[8]

Coach Ken MacKenzie likewise received praise for his tutelage of the young Pack. His stable tenure behind the bench was a refreshing change from the hiring-and-firing of the 1980s. "I think they should have had Ken MacKenzie when I first came here, because I think he's done a great job and I think he's a great coach," said DiPietro. MacKenzie knew he had entered a pressure cooker when he first took over, but as the team's fortunes improved, he saw firsthand just how devoted Wolves fans were in spite of the years of mediocrity. "They went through so many lean years here in Sudbury that my first season here, when we started to lose, they let you know what was going on," MacKenzie explained. "I think once we started putting a few games together, they started believing in us."[9]

As the season drew to a close the Wolves' long-awaited rebuild had fully captivated observers across the CHL. "The Sudbury Wolves have been transformed from disaster of the decade to Ontario Hockey League contender in less than two seasons," read *The Ottawa Citizen*.[10] The Wolves established a franchise record by winning eleven straight home games before finally losing to the Knights at the Sudbury Arena by a score of 3-0 in a late February match that was featured as the CHL game of the week on TSN. Predictably, the Sudbury Arena saw its best attendance numbers in ten years; in fact, the Wolves averaged 3,204 fans per home game, the second-highest in the OHL behind only the Kitchener Rangers.[11]

The Wolves finished third in the Emms Division with a record of 36-23-7—only the sixth winning season since the club had joined the OHL in 1972-73—and were matched with the Owen Sound Platers (a franchise that had just relocated from Guelph) in the opening round of the playoffs.[12] On March 18, a crowd of over 4,200 fans showed up to watch the first postseason game in the Nickel City since 1986. It was a high-scoring, physical game that saw the Wolves go down by four goals before tying things up at 6-6 as both teams entered the third period. Owen Sound's captain Mike Speer buried the game-winner in the final frame as the Platers took Game 1 by a score of 8-7. "They (Owen Sound) are one of the dirtiest teams in the league," an angry Ken MacKenzie said in a postgame interview.[13] In Game 2 in Owen Sound, the Wolves responded with the franchise's first playoff game win since March 1980. Terry Chitaroni scored twice and Goverde made 48 saves as the Wolves edged the Platers by a score of 3-2. Although it took the Wolves ten years to win that one playoff game, it took them only two days to win another as Sudbury again beat Owen Sound by a score of 4-2 in Game 3 at the Sudbury Arena. A crowd of over 5,100 fans watched as the Wolves and Platers racked up 124 minutes in penalties, including four fights. The temperature in the series was heating up fast. MacKenzie openly stated he was "losing more respect" for Owen Sound coach Len McNamara as the series progressed. "I noticed he laughs every time there's a fight on the ice," the Wolves' coach noted.[14]

The rest of the Emms division quarterfinals did not play out as the Wolves and their fans had hoped. After taking a 3-1 series in Game 4 on a huge overtime goal by Sean O'Donnell, Sudbury dropped the following two matches by scores of 5-1 and 3-2. The Platers kept up their aggressive play, with Wolves defenceman Wade Bartley getting cross-checked head-first into the boards by forward Kirk Maltby in the dying seconds of Game 6. McMaster blasted the Platers in-person and in the press for the incident.[15] Tensions were high entering Game 7 on March 28. The Sudbury Arena was filled to the brim with nearly 6,000 spectators as the Wolves dominated play for most of the game. Tied up at 3-3 at the end of regulation, the match rolled into sudden-death overtime. Within the first minute or so of play in the extra frame, the Wolves had two goals recalled: one by DiPietro due to referee Paul Coleman blowing the whistle before the puck crossed the line and another by Chitaroni because of an offside call by the linesman. These bad breaks cost the Wolves dearly, as forward Jeff Perry scored minutes later to take the game and the best-of-seven series for the Platers. Wolves' fans were so infuriated that Coleman required a police escort out of the Sudbury Arena. A disappointed Sudbury team continued to protest that they had been robbed of the win, but eventually accepted that they had no other option except to look toward next year. "This is only the beginning for this franchise," said Goverde after the loss.[16]

In the months following the heartbreaking defeat, several Wolves were recognized for their contributions to the franchise's best season since the golden years of the 1970s. Both Goverde and DiPietro were drafted in the fifth round of the 1990 NHL Entry Draft by the Los Angeles Kings and Montreal Canadiens, respectively. DiPietro went on to win the Stanley Cup with Montreal in 1993, scoring two goals in the final game of the championship series over Wayne Gretzky and the Kings.[17] Sam McMaster, meanwhile, was recognized as OHL Executive of the Year for the 1989-90 season. Months before he was honoured with the award, McMaster outlined the core tenet of his management philosophy. "I'm a believer that junior hockey has a turnaround every year. We only have players for three, maximum four years … Therefore, there is absolutely no reason in the world why you can't be competitive every year," he explained.[18] Over the next few seasons, McMaster would demonstrate that he knew how to put his theories into practice.

BATTLING THE NEXT ONE

For the first time in recent memory the Sudbury Wolves entered the new season touted as one of junior hockey's top teams. In a preseason poll prior to the start of the 1990-91 campaign, the club was rated the top junior team in the entire CHL, outranking 41 other competitors across North America. The loss of leading-scorer Paul DiPietro and starting goaltender David Goverde to the professional circuit apparently did not dissuade analysts from thinking highly of the Wolves, with multiple returnees such as Terry Chitaroni, Glenn Murray, Jason Young, and Jamie Matthews expected to steer the ship. Veteran defencemen Adam Bennett, who signed an NHL contract with the Chicago Blackhawks in the offseason, and Wade Bartley served as the team's co-captains. At the 1990 OHL Draft, the Wolves used the eleventh overall selection to take forward Michael Peca. The Wolves, along with the North Bay Centennials, were shuffled into the Leyden Division as part of a league realignment triggered by the granting of an expansion franchise to the Detroit Compuware Ambassadors, bringing the OHL to a total of sixteen clubs.[19]

From practically the drop of the first puck it was evident that pollsters had overestimated the Pack. The Wolves lost their home opener to the

Windsor Spitfires by a score of 6-4 and by late November were second last in the Leyden Division with a brutal 3-12-0 road record. Management reacted with numerous trades. In early October, the offensively gifted but troublesome Darcy Cahill was sent to the Dukes of Hamilton; before the end of the year Cahill's new team waived his rights entirely and the 20-year-old headed overseas to play professionally in Scotland. In return, the team re-acquired Dan Ryder, a veteran netminder whom Sudbury had traded to Hamilton the season previous.[20] In December, the Wolves further addressed its goaltending gap by acquiring John Tanner from the London Knights, a 19-year-old Quebec Nordiques prospect who had generated controversy during his OHL career for making insulting comments about opposing players, his teammates, and coaches.[21]

A nasty incident involving forward Jason Young on December 4 added strain to an already shaky beginning to the season. In a game at the Sudbury Arena versus the Ottawa 67's, Young, who at the time was the OHL's third-leading scorer with 21 goals and 59 points in 37 games, checked rookie defenceman Grant Marshall from behind into the boards as they raced for the puck. Marshall suffered a broken neck on the play and Young was handed a major penalty and an automatic one-game suspension. Young played another six games until, on December 20, OHL commissioner David Branch suspended him for the remainder of the season, citing the need to eliminate hitting-from-behind from the game. While no one questioned the seriousness of Young's actions and the need for him to be held accountable, many were shocked by the severity of the punishment given the star player's clean record and reputation. Even Don Cherry weighed in during one of his *Hockey Night in Canada* broadcasts, suggesting that Branch had over-reacted. Sam McMaster and the Wolves successfully appealed the decision and Young, who had expressed remorse from the beginning, was reinstated by the league in March after missing 28 games. Most importantly, Grant Marshall thankfully made a full recovery and went on to have a long NHL career that included two Stanley Cup championships.[22]

The Wolves managed to lock up a consecutive playoff appearance for the first time in over ten years and did so without the help of their top-scorer. Young's temporary absence presented more chances for players like Murray,

Matthews, and Peca to cut their teeth. The Wolves rolled three well-balanced lines. Backed by an experienced blueline and good goaltending from Ryder and Tanner, at times the Wolves demonstrated exactly why they had been so highly regarded entering the year. At the end of the regular season, McMaster attributed the Wolves underperformance to a range of factors, including injuries, the Young suspension, and a lack of steady goaltending at the start of the year, but suggested the Wolves were "the best sixth place team in the history of junior hockey."[23] The fanbase seemed to agree. Spectators flocked to the Sudbury Arena in greater numbers than any other OHL rink that season, averaging over 4,100 attendees each home game and about 400 more fans-per-game than the next closest club, the Kitchener Rangers.[24]

The relief of securing the sixth and final playoff spot in the Leyden Division came with strings attached. The Wolves were matched with the Oshawa Generals, the defending Memorial Cup champions and the winners of the 1990-91 Hamilton Spectator Trophy as the team with the best regular season record in the OHL. Eric Lindros was the Generals' crown jewel. The consensus first overall pick in the upcoming 1991 NHL Draft had led the league in goals (71) and points (149) and was later awarded the Red Tilson Trophy as the OHL's most outstanding player as well as CHL Player of the Year. Lindros' resume had earned him the moniker "The Next One" in reference to Wayne "The Great One" Gretzky. The Wolves were not without hope, however. In eight regular season contests against Oshawa, the Wolves had gone 3-4-1 and shown that they would not just roll over. "I think we can play with anybody in this league with our scoring balance," said overage Wolves' forward Bob Berg after Sudbury defeated Oshawa by a score of 4-3 in early March. "Who do you check and focus on? You can't do that with our team."[25]

The Wolves were unable to contain the domineering Lindros and the Generals come playoff time, however. In Game 1 in Oshawa on St. Patrick's Day, the Next One recorded four points in a 4-2 win for the Generals. Down two games to none entering Game 3, the Wolves handed Oshawa its first playoff defeat in ten games dating back to the previous postseason. Glenn Murray ripped a natural hat trick in the first period, Jamie Matthews scored twice, defenceman Shawn Rivers recorded four assists, and John Tanner earned the win in goal as Sudbury whipped Oshawa 8-2. This was as close as the Wolves got to tilting the series in their favour. An absolute capacity crowd at the Sudbury Arena showed up for Game 4, which the Generals won by a score of 7-6. The Generals finished things off with a 6-4 win over the Wolves in Game 5, ending the first round series four games to one.[26]

The series concluded on a sour note after Lindros, who scored 5 goals and 12 points in the five games against Sudbury, made a taunting gesture at Tanner upon tallying the series-clinching empty net goal with just 13 seconds left in play. Tanner lost his cool and went after the Generals' phenom before being escorted off the ice. Although the majority of the Wolves engaged in the traditional post-series playoff handshake, several team members skated directly off the ice, prompting Oshawa coach Rick Cornacchia to label Sudbury "a classless organization." Both Ken MacKenzie and Sam McMaster fired back and defended their team, with the latter asserting that "sportsmanship has always been something I take pride in. I've yet to run into a coach as classless as Cornacchia."[27] The Generals made their way to the OHL Finals for the second straight year, this time losing the series in six games to the Sault Ste. Marie Greyhounds, the club that Lindros had snubbed two years earlier.[28]

THE RETURN OF WOLVES-MANIA

The Sudbury Wolves twentieth OHL regular season followed a similar storyline to the one preceding it. Rated as the number one junior hockey team in the country by *The Hockey News*, the Wolves had had eight players selected in the 1991 NHL Entry Draft, more than any other team in North America: Glenn Murray (Boston Bruins, 18th overall), Jamie Matthews (Chicago Blackhawks, 44th overall), Jason Young (Buffalo Sabres, 57th overall), Terry Chitaroni (Toronto Maple Leafs, 69th overall), Dan Ryder (San Jose Sharks, 89th overall), Sean O'Donnell (Buffalo Sabres, 123rd overall), Barry Young (New York Rangers, 128th overall), and Bill Kovacs (Washington Capitals, 256th overall). Remarkably, all these NHL prospects returned for the 1991-92 season, except for O'Donnell, who immediately made the jump to the AHL.[29] Sudbury used its first-round pick in the 1991 OHL Draft to select defenceman Jamie Rivers of Ottawa, the younger brother of veteran

Wolves' blueliner Shawn Rivers. For Jamie, it was the beginning of, in his own words, "the four best years of my life."[30]

The Wolves were an offensive juggernaut with an arsenal of weapons at their disposal. Co-captain Terry Chitaroni scored three goals and added an assist in the team's 7-2 season opener win against the London Knights at the Sudbury Arena, setting the tone for the season to come.[31] Eight different Sudbury players scored at least 26 goals, with sophomore centre Brandon Convery, the Wolves' third round selection in the 1990 draft, leading the way with 40 markers. Seasoned players like Matthews, who registered a team-high 95 points, Murray, Young, and Shawn Rivers—who also wore the 'C' during the season—were predictable contributors, but lesser-known skaters, like forwards Derek Armstrong and Rod Hinks, both chosen among the final picks in the 1990 OHL draft, broke out with surprising offensive numbers of their own.

The Wolves scored the second-most goals in the OHL during the 1991-92 season, trailing the reigning-OHL champion Soo Greyhounds by a total of only four goals on the year.[32] Even rookies like Jamie Rivers got in on the action. He scored a goal in his very first game with Sudbury. "I'll never forget it. It was a one-timer slap shot pass from Michael Peca, and I thought this league's easy. I went on to find out that it wasn't so easy," Rivers recalled of the milestone in an interview with Mike Commito years later.[33] The Wolves' high-flying offence helped the Sudbury Arena again lead the OHL in average attendance with about 4,262 fans showing up to each game.[34]

Defensively things were less rosy. The Wolves had the third-worst goals-against total in the OHL by the end of the season despite McMaster's attempts to grease the team's squeaky wheels through trades. A few days before the trade deadline, Sudbury sent Dan Ryder and Michael Peca to the Ottawa 67's in exchange for goaltender Mike Lenarduzzi and a fifth-round draft pick. McMaster also swapped two draft picks with the Guelph Storm in return for 18-year-old Kayle Short, a six-foot-two, 197-pound defenceman. The loss of Peca was difficult—he had recorded 50 points in 39 games before he was traded—but both Lenarduzzi and Short were certainly valuable additions to the squad. The Wolves secured fourth place in the Leyden Division with a record (33-27-6) that was nearly identical to the previous season (33-28-5).[35]

Sudbury and Oshawa were paired in the first round of the OHL play-offs for the second year in a row. There was certainly no love lost between the two clubs from their showdown twelve months earlier. On March 13, with their postseason matchup already confirmed, the Generals visited the Sudbury Arena for a regular season game against the Wolves just before the postseason. Although Eric Lindros had been selected first overall by the Quebec Nordiques in the 1991 NHL Draft the previous June, he had once again refused to report to the team that had chosen him. While awaiting a trade (he was eventually dealt to the Philadelphia Flyers), he played a handful of contests with the Generals during the 1991-92 season, and actually skated in his final junior hockey game that evening in the Nickel City. More than 6,000 Sudbury fans booed the Next One incessantly as the Wolves won by a score of 5-4. A homemade banner reading "Don't send me to Quebec mommy" was briefly hung over the Oshawa entrance to the ice surface to taunt Lindros before it was removed by arena staff.[36]

The Wolves were bent on revenge and were expected to benefit from having home ice advantage in the series, having gone 22-7-4 at the Sudbury Arena during the regular season, and knowing that Lindros would not be suiting up for the Generals in the postseason. It was Oshawa that took control early, however, stealing Game 1 on an outstanding 40-save night by goaltender Mike Fountain and then winning 6-3 in Oshawa the following night. The Wolves pulled up their socks at home in Game 3 as Young netted two shorthanded goals in a 5-2 win. The Wolves and Generals fought hard in Game 4 and forced overtime with the score tied at 3-3 at the end of regulation played. Oshawa's Stephane Yelle received credit for the game-winner after Sudbury's Barry Young inadvertently fired the puck into his own net behind Lenarduzzi. The favoured Wolves were suddenly down 3-1 in the series and poised to again get bounced by the Generals in five games.[37]

Coach Ken MacKenzie and his team dug deep in hopes of pulling off a seemingly insurmountable comeback. The result of Game 5 was both encouraging and worrisome for the Wolves. While the home team won the match by a score of 5-2, Convery suffered a fractured ankle and Armstrong broke a bone in his neck. Both top forwards were expected to miss six to eight weeks. "It's a terrible blow to the team losing two players like Convery and Armstrong … Even with our backs against the wall, we're still giving everything we've got," said MacKenzie after the big win. Sudbury's other offensive leaders then stepped up to the plate. Murray scored four goals in Game 6 at the Oshawa Civic Auditorium as the Wolves won 5-1 and forced a seventh and deciding game.[38]

The match was set for Friday, March 27 at the Sudbury Arena, and was one of the most anticipated Wolves' games since the mid-1970s. By 6 a.m. on Wednesday people were lining up at the box office and within three hours the line had stretched as far as the Ledo Hotel down the road; by noon the game was entirely sold out. Fans prayed that the Wolves would finally end their twelve-year playoff series win drought.[39] Fountain was spectacular for the Generals, making 48 saves in the game and protecting his team's 1-0 lead until the second period when forward Mike Yeo tied things up for the Wolves. The score remained deadlocked after three periods. At the 6:17 mark of overtime, Chitaroni—who had signed a three-year contract with the Leafs earlier that week—scored the series-winning goal and at long last ended Sudbury's painful playoff losing streak. "I couldn't believe it at first," the Haileybury native said after the biggest goal of his young career. "When the crowd started to cheer, then I realized I had scored." The players and management applauded the fanbase for standing behind the team during the come-from-behind series win. "You, the fans of Sudbury deserved it," said Sam McMaster. "In Oshawa for game six, (the Generals) only had 2,200 fans to support them. Here they wait in line for tickets and then jam the arena."[40]

A feeling of Wolves-mania returned to Sudbury for the first time in years as the hometown team prepared to take on the rival North Bay Centennials in the second round of the playoffs. The morning after the Wolves had eliminated the Generals, the team's box office was flooded with calls from fans, businesses, and the media enquiring about tickets and other promotional material to support the local team.[41] Dubbed the "Highway 17 Series," the Wolves were totally outplayed by the Cents and were swept in four straight games. Only Game 2 was decided by a one-goal margin. Injuries hurt the Wolves as players like Armstrong, Convery, and Short were either out of the lineup or hurt.[42] North Bay ultimately met Sault Ste. Marie in the 1992 J. Ross Robertson Cup championship series, which remains the only time in modern OHL history that two teams from Northern Ontario have played in the league finals. The Greyhounds beat the Centennials in seven games to win their second consecutive OHL title.[43] Wolves fans, as disappointed as they were with the loss to North Bay, understood that this year's playoffs had solidified a culture shift in the organization. Their team was officially a competitor again.

ANOTHER CLOSE CALL

Practically as soon as the 1992 playoffs were over for Sudbury, rumours began to crop up that Ken MacKenzie would not be returning as the Wolves' head coach.[44] By May the speculation was put to rest as MacKenzie announced his resignation. While the Wolves organization had offered MacKenzie a three-year contract, he cited his desire to focus on his family as the primary reason behind his departure. His regular season coaching record of 125-114-25 was the best of any Wolves' coach in the past decade, and made him the longest-serving and winningest coach in franchise history. "I'm going to miss it, especially the players ... They become like one of your kids," MacKenzie stated upon the announcement.[45]

Three weeks later, the Wolves hired 32-year-old former NHL player Glenn Merkosky as MacKenzie's successor. Merkosky had served as an assistant coach with the Adirondack Red Wings of the AHL before joining the Wolves organization as head coach. "I'm excited about it. I've been looking to step out on my own and this will be a good challenge," the Edmonton native told *The Sudbury Star*.[46] The Wolves further solidified their leadership group in September by naming veteran defenceman Kayle Short as the new team captain, with Jamie Rivers and Jamie Matthews serving as assistants.[47]

The Wolves had a relatively average regular season in Merkosky's first year behind the bench. The team started the 1992-93 campaign, which marked exactly twenty years since the organization joined the province's top junior league, with two big wins over the North Bay Centennials in what was developing into an intensely bitter rivalry. In October, Sam McMaster made a critical trade by sending Brandon Convery, who had been selected eighth overall by the Toronto Maple Leafs in June 1992, to the Niagara Falls Thunder in exchange for left winger Dennis Maxwell and defenceman

Steve Staios.[48] Although the Wolves finished only one game above the .500 mark, the club sat fourth place in the Leyden Division entering the postseason.[49] Derek Armstrong, drafted by the New York Islanders in the 1992 NHL Entry Draft, and Rod Hinks, who ended up being chosen by that same organization in 1993, both registered over 100 points to lead the team in scoring. This marked the first time since 1978-79, when Mike Foligno, Dave MacQueen, and Dale Hunter each surpassed the triple-digit plateau, that more than one Wolves player recorded 100 or more points in a season.[50]

The season revealed just how much the Sudbury Wolves as a brand outperformed most of its competitors. In January 1993, it was reported that the Wolves were the number one seller of souvenir items in the 44-team CHL. At the previous year's Memorial Cup in Seattle, a tournament in which the Wolves were not even participating, the blue, grey, and white sweaters of Sudbury had sold out within two days.[51] So dramatic was the Wolves' transformation that *The Toronto Star* published an entire article covering the team's evolution from "a struggling franchise into an entertaining, competitive team." The newspaper specifically cited Sudbury's signature howling stuffed wolf that descends from the rafters when the team scores as a unique aspect of the Wolves' fan experience, and also noted that enticing ticket packages, an expansion of corporate sponsorships and advertising, and enhanced community and customer involvement were all part of the organization's successful marketing strategy. Marketing director Blaine Smith advised that the players collectively put in around 1,000 hours of community work over a six-month season. Sam McMaster explained that a junior hockey club "can't really succeed today without good marketing ... We're just a little bigger than most."[52]

Unsurprisingly, then, the Wolves were easily able to draw fans to their first-round playoff series against the Newmarket Royals, a franchise that had just relocated from Cornwall. The Wolves pounced in Game 1 at the Sudbury Arena, with Armstrong setting a new franchise record for goals in a single playoff game. The Islanders prospect lit the lamp and beckoned the wolf down from the wire five times—four on the powerplay and one empty netter—as the Wolves won 7-5. Despite Sudbury going up 3-1 in the series, the Royals proved difficult to dethrone. In Game 6 in Newmarket, the Royals humiliated the visiting Sudbury squad with an 11-0 beatdown. To make matters worse, the Royals, along with a host of other gimmicks, had hung a stuffed wolf with a noose around its neck from the roof of the Newmarket Recreation Complex. When the Royals would score, the wolf was lowered while a recording of a wolf howl and two gunshots echoed from the public address system.[53]

Infuriated by the loss and the spectacle that came with it—Merkosky called it a "tasteless act"—the Wolves were amped up entering Game 7 in the Nickel City. Sudbury and its fans got the last laugh as they routed the Royals by a score of 6-1 to take the game and the series. Staios scored three goals, while Jamie Matthews collected five assists, one helper shy of a club playoff record set by Wes Jarvis exactly 17 years earlier to the day.[54] The team later cited the wolf-hanging incident in Newmarket as a motivating factor entering the match. "We take a lot of pride at showing off the wolf symbol on our sweaters," defenceman Jamie Rivers, who scored the game-winner in Game 7, told *The Sudbury Star*. "We were upset at how they made fun of us in Newmarket with the stuffed wolf and all. That not only embarrassed us, it brought us closer together and made us more determined to show them who was the best team."[55]

The OHL-leading Peterborough Petes and their star defenceman Chris Pronger, along with forward and future Wolves' head coach Cory Stillman, awaited Sudbury in the Leyden Division semi-finals. The Pack captured the opening game of the series 5-1 on an acrobatic 34-save performance by goaltender Greg Dreveny. The following two games in Peterborough were disastrous for the Wolves as they were soundly defeated by scores of 9-0 and 9-4. The clubs then traded wins back-and-forth until a Game 7 was required. The series-deciding match was held at the Peterborough Memorial Centre on April 15. The Wolves had not won in Peterborough since November 1990, a winless stretch of thirteen games; the trend continued as the Petes took Game 7 by a score of 7-3. "It's harder every year to lose like this. This is a frustrating end to a frustrating season," expressed Sudbury forward and future NHL coach Mike Yeo.[56] Peterborough later won the J. Ross Robertson Cup after defeating the Soo Greyhounds, who were making their third consecutive appearance in the OHL Finals, in five games. The city of Sault Ste.

Marie still played host to the Memorial Cup that year, and the Greyhounds captured their first Memorial Cup by defeating the Petes in the championship game in front of their home crowd at the Sault Memorial Gardens.[57]

A TALE OF TWO JAMIES

The Sudbury Wolves were well-represented at the 1993 NHL Entry Draft held at the Quebec Coliseum in Quebec City, and this translated into another solid year for the team when most of these players came back to junior for the 1993-94 OHL season. Ten Wolves were chosen that day in June, starting with defenceman Mike Wilson by the Vancouver Canucks in the first round and ending with Jamie Matthews, who had re-entered the draft after not signing a contract with the Chicago Blackhawks, in the eleventh round by the San Jose Sharks. Local sportswriter Norm Mayer projected that the Wolves would finish in second place in their division for the first time since the 1977-78 season.[58]

The Wolves strength proved to be their veteran presence and strong blueline. Defencemen Jamie Rivers, drafted by the St. Louis Blues, and American Rory Fitzpatrick, the Wolves' first-rounder in 1992 and a Montreal Canadiens' prospect, anchored a backend that also included the steady presence of Wilson and veteran Bob MacIsaac.[59] Czech forward Zdenek Nedved had a breakout season, scoring 50 goals (the first Wolf to do so since Paul DiPietro) and 100 points in 60 games. He also set a Wolves franchise record for powerplay goals in a season by tallying 26 markers with the man-advantage. Nedved, a Maple Leafs draft pick, had been the fifth overall selection by Sudbury in 1992 in the first ever CHL Import Draft, which gives CHL teams the opportunity to select players from outside Canada and the United States, but had missed most of the 1992-93 OHL season with a shoulder injury.[60] Sam McMaster once more addressed the team's goaltending gaps through a trade, sending netminder Shawn Silver and forward Joel Poirier to the Windsor Spitfires in exchange for goalie Matt Mullin and centre Colin Wilson. The 19-year-old Mullin thrived in Sudbury, registering a 23-9-3 record and earning recognition as the most valuable player during the regular season and playoffs at the Wolves' end-of-the year banquet.[61]

It was Jamie Rivers and Jamie Matthews who had the greatest impact on the franchise that season. Matthews, who served as captain of the team later in the year after MacIsaac had started off with the 'C,' reached 301 regular season games played in a Sudbury Wolves' uniform. This set a club record for all-time games played that would stand for the next twenty-five years. After putting up 97 points in only 46 games in his final year of junior hockey, Matthews also became (and still remains) the team's all-time leader in assists (249) and points (369).[62] "I kind of had mixed emotions," he recalled in an interview in 2000 when asked about becoming the Wolves' leading scorer. "I was glad I did it, but to think of myself being up with guys like [Mike] Foligno and [Ron] Duguay, guys that were pros, was kind of funny." Matthews himself never played in the NHL and later returned to his home province of Nova Scotia to pursue other interests.[63]

Jamie Rivers, meanwhile, put on one of the most awe-inspiring performances by a defenceman in OHL history. In February alone, he recorded 37 points in 13 games and was named CHL Player of the Month.[64] That same month, in a game versus his hometown Ottawa 67's at the Sudbury Arena, Rivers racked up three goals and three assists to set a new franchise record for points by a defenceman in a season. "It's an unbelievable feeling," he said upon surpassing John Baby's points record. "It's nice to be recognized … The main thing is that I want this team to be successful."[65] In total, Rivers ended up scoring 32 goals and 121 points in 65 regular season games, the third-highest point total ever by an OHL defencemen at that time. He also tied Baby's record for goals by a Wolves' defencemen in a single season. As one might expect, that year Rivers was awarded the Max Kaminsky Trophy as the OHL's most outstanding defenceman.[66]

With a 34-26-6 record, the Wolves finished in third place in the Leyden Division and earned a playoff spot for the fifth consecutive season. The team had played especially well from Christmas onward, including setting a new club record on March 4 by winning eight games in a row. For the third time in four seasons, the team was matched against the Oshawa Generals in the OHL playoff quarterfinals.[67] The Wolves and Generals split the first two games of the series before Sudbury started to pull ahead. Mullin was incredible in goal throughout, especially his 45-save night in Game 4 at the

Oshawa Civic Centre. Local rookie forward Sean Venedam scored two goals in that game as the Wolves won by a score of 3-2 and took a 3-1 lead in the best-of-seven matchup. In Game 5 in Sudbury, the Wolves and Generals found themselves all tied up at 4-4 after three periods of play. At the 9:09 mark of overtime, veteran forward Steve Potvin beat Oshawa goaltender Ken Shepard to end the game and the series in favour of the Wolves.[68]

The Wolves moved on to face the Ottawa 67's in the division semi-finals, a team led by Michael Peca. In 55 games with Ottawa that season, Peca, who had since been drafted into the NHL by the Vancouver Canucks, had amassed 50 goals and 113 points, and was set to showcase the offensive prowess he had developed against his old team since McMaster had traded him two years earlier.[69] Game 1 in Sudbury was chaotic as the Wolves and 67's combined for thirteen goals, 115 shots on net, and four hours of hockey before it was settled. Matthews tucked the game-winner in double overtime to win the match for the Wolves by a score of 7-6, but this turned out to be Sudbury's only win of the series. Ottawa won the next four games in a row, including another double-overtime decision in Game 3. Peca had scored five goals and seven points against the Wolves and was the OHL's leading playoff scorer as the 67's advanced to the next round.[70]

This postseason exit had left a sour taste in the mouths of the organization and its fans that had not been felt for some time. Rumours quickly began to swirl about whether both Glenn Merkosky and Sam McMaster were on the chopping block as the Wolves had again failed to advance further than the second round of the playoffs. "I wish I had the answers to what happened in this series. Our season had some highs, but in the end it was another disappointing season," said Merkosky after the loss to Ottawa.[71] With the disappointment of the 1980s now but a distant memory, the Wolves were no longer content with simply qualifying for the postseason. The expectation of a championship run was once again the new benchmark.

CHAPTER 7:

HOWLING ALONG, 1994-1999

BACK IN THE HUNT

The 1994 offseason brought organizational changes to the OHL in general and the Sudbury Wolves in particular. In June, the OHL governors approved the realignment of the league's sixteen teams into three new divisions: Central, East, and West. The Wolves were slotted into the Central Division alongside Guelph, Owen Sound, Niagara Falls, and Kitchener, with the expansion Barrie Colts penciled into the Central once the franchise officially began playing in 1995-96. Sudbury and the league's other northern clubs—the Soo Greyhounds and defending-OHL champion North Bay Centennials—were not pleased with the fact that they were all now in separate divisions, putting a damper on rivalries that dated back decades. Wolves president Mark Burgess, the son of Ken Burgess, openly criticized the shuffling, stating that "The north has had all the success, but the south runs the league."[1]

Weeks earlier, the Wolves experienced an even bigger upheaval when Sam McMaster resigned from his position as general manager. Only five days after the team was eliminated by the Ottawa 67's in the Leyden Division semi-finals, the 50-year-old McMaster announced that effective June 30 he would be ending his six-year stint with Sudbury, staying on long enough to direct the team through that year's OHL Priority Selection hosted in Belleville. "It may be a corny statement, but it was time to move on," he said at a press conference at the Sudbury Arena. "I'm proud of how the fans support this team. I wish I could have done more for the Sudbury fans."[2] About one month later, McMaster was hired as the general manager of the Los Angeles Kings, infamously trading Wayne Gretzky from the Kings to the St. Louis Blues in February 1996 before being axed in 1997.[3]

The Wolves were expected to make some noise during the 1994-95 season even without McMaster leading the front office. Glenn Merkosky took over as the general manager while maintaining his duties as head coach. He received support in both roles from Todd Lalonde, a former Wolves player who had been serving as an assistant coach with the team since 1992 after an injury ended his own professional playing career. Captain Rory Fitzpatrick, Zdenek Nedved, Jamie Rivers, Mike Wilson, and Matt Mullin all came back for another season of junior hockey, with other veterans such as Sean Venedam and Andrew Dale, the latter having been drafted by the Los Angeles Kings, filling out what was projected to be one of the OHL's deadliest rosters.[4]

Starting the year with five 19-year-old defenceman, the Wolves' blueline was practically impenetrable. "The biggest part of this defence is its depth," Merkosky said in mid-October as his team sat fourth overall in the national rankings. "Our strength will be our ability to keep the puck out of the net."[5] The coach's prediction was spot on as Sudbury allowed the second-fewest goals in the OHL that year. Mullin received credit as one of the league's elite starting netminders, while his backup, David MacDonald, earned the F.W. "Dinty" Moore Trophy for having the best goals-against average (3.07) amongst first-year OHL goaltenders. With assets to spare on the backend, the club pulled off a blockbuster deal in January by trading defender Jay

McKee, the Wolves' first round pick in 1993, along with forward Chester Gallant and two draft picks to the Niagara Falls Thunder in return for American centre Jason Bonsignore and left winger Ethan Moreau. Both Bonsignore and Moreau were chosen in the first round of the 1994 NHL Entry Draft by the Edmonton Oilers and Chicago Blackhawks, respectively, and gave Sudbury added threats up-front.[6]

The Wolves skated to one of the most successful seasons in team history. Aside from an ugly stick-swinging incident against the Guelph Storm in November that saw enforcer Gary Coupal get suspended for the remainder of the year, it was largely all-smiles for the team and their fans from September onward.[7] The Pack again set a new franchise winning streak, capturing eleven games in a row until they were beaten by the Centennials 5-4 in North Bay on March 12.[8] The Wolves won 43 games in total, the second best record (43-17-6) in franchise history and the first time the club had reached the 40-win mark since 1978-79.[9] Veteran forwards Nedved and Barrie Moore, a Buffalo Sabres' prospect, each netted 47 goals. Rookie centre Richard Rochefort impressed with 65 points. The dynamic Jamie Rivers, too, registered 65 points, nearly half his total from the previous year, albeit in only 46 games played due to a knee injury. Rivers also played in the World Junior Ice Hockey Championships in Red Deer, Alberta, where he helped Team Canada capture a third straight gold medal. The Wolves finished second in the Central Division behind the OHL-leading Guelph Storm, a team that happened to feature star power forward and Sudbury native Todd Bertuzzi.[10]

The OHL's divisional realignment exposed the Wolves and their fans to some unfamiliar playoff opponents in the spring of 1995, beginning with the Kitchener Rangers. The two teams had not met in the postseason since 1973-74, when the Rangers swept the budding Wolves franchise in four straight games. Twenty years later the outcome was practically reversed as Sudbury, ranked the No. 3 junior team in Canada, was in the driver's seat from the outset of the series against a club that had won only 18 games that season. The Wolves outscored the Rangers 21-6 in the first two meetings. Kitchener earned its only win in Game 3 with a narrow 2-1 victory thanks to a 48-save night by goaltender Dave Belitski. Ahead 3-1 in the series following overtime heroics by Bonsignore in Game 4, the Wolves closed things out in five games with a 6-1 win on home ice on March 26. "I don't doubt our team is going a long way in these playoffs … We're looking forward to the next challenge," said Jamie Rivers after the first-round win.[11]

That next challenge turned out to be the Windsor Spitfires. The Wolves got off to another strong start, in large part to a formidable power-play. After Barrie Moore opened the scoring in Game 1 on a shorthanded penalty shot, the Wolves scored three powerplay goals on four opportunities and cruised to a 6-2 victory. Windsor soon demonstrated that it was a bigger, more physical team than the Kitchener Rangers, however. The Spitfires travelled to Sudbury for Game 2 and intimidated the host Wolves "from start to finish" to secure a 6-1 win. It was a rare loss for the Wolves at home, having gone 24-5-5 at the Sudbury Arena during the regular season and 4-0 in the playoffs.[12]

After the match, *The Windsor Star* printed an article that parodied the classic fairy tale of Little Red Riding Hood, with the titular character representing the hometown Spitfires and the Big Bad Wolf representing their opponents from Sudbury. "The biggest and baddest of the Big Bad Wolves was none other than the Friendly Giant, Jason Bonsignore," read the article. "At which point Little Red decided he'd heard one woof too many. He threw an overhand right, connected, and Bonsignore hit the ground with a thud that was heard as far away as Edmonton."[13] Bonsignore was not impressed with the piece but later claimed it "added a little fire under me" after he scored two goals in Game 3 at the Windsor Arena. The Wolves lost that game 4-3, though, and were now down two games to one in the series.[14]

Sudbury proceeded to buck a couple of negative trends that had plagued the franchise for years. First, the team defeated the Spitfires 5-1 in Game 4 in the Automotive Capital of Canada, signifying the first time since March 30, 1980 that the Wolves had won a second-round playoff road game. The fifth game of the series was the tipping point for Sudbury. "It was electric in the dressing room prior to the game. Then we go out to start the game and the fans are going crazy, even during the singing of the anthem. That really pumped us up even more," Moore later described. The standing-room-only crowd of 5,800 onlookers at the Sudbury Arena celebrated six unanswered goals by the home team in the first nine minutes of play. The Wolves won the game 9-2 to take back the series lead. "I knew we had firepower, but I've never seen anything like this in all my years of playing hockey," admitted Moore, who scored twice that night.[15]

The Wolves were on the verge of extinguishing the Spitfires and advancing past the second round of the postseason for the first time since 1976. Windsor established a 2-0 lead early in Game 6, but Sudbury clawed back and went up 5-4 in the third period, chasing veteran Spitfires netminder Jamie Storr from the crease in the process. Rookie Glenn Crawford tied the game for Windsor with a shorthanded breakaway goal. The two teams remained deadlocked at the end of regulation. The 3,797 fans at the Windsor Arena were treated to less than one minute of overtime action as Jamie Rivers buried his fifth goal of the playoffs early in the extra frame, ending the game and the series. "It's nice to score the winning goal, but I certainly can't take all the credit … We've been playing like brothers since the playoffs began," said Rivers. The Wolves' lethal powerplay was a huge factor in the team's success, scoring at a rate of 41.7 percent in the six-game series. For only the second time in the franchise's 23-year history, the Sudbury Wolves had earned a spot in the third round of the OHL playoffs.[16]

For the first two games of the OHL semi-finals, the Wolves would have to cross the Canada-U.S. border into Michigan. On the other side of the Detroit River and just across from the city of Windsor, the Wolves faced the Detroit Junior Red Wings. Coached by Paul Maurice, the Junior Red Wings were undefeated in the postseason, having swept both the London Knights and the Peterborough Petes, and had not played for nine days when the best-of-seven series against the Wolves opened on April 15 at the now-demolished Joe Louis Arena. The Wings' streak seemed at its end after Sean Venedam scored his first of the playoffs to put Sudbury ahead by a score of 4-3 in the third period, but Detroit stunned the Wolves with two quick goals, including the game-winner by Jeff Mitchell with less than thirty seconds of play remaining, to take the match 5-4. The second game was even closer as Sudbury erased a two-goal deficit before squandering another 4-3 lead in final period. Once again tied at 4-4, the Wolves and Wings settled the score in overtime. Forward Nic Beaudoin slipped a goal passed Matt Mullin in the fourth period to give Detroit a 2-0 series lead.[17]

Nevertheless, the ice tilted in Sudbury's favour once the series shifted to Northern Ontario. "We've developed quite a hate for their hockey club," said Wolves assistant coach Todd Lalonde after Game 2. "The players are down right now, but I expect them to be fired up again when they play at home."[18] Over 5,400 people filled the Sudbury Arena for Game 3. Rookie Richard Rochefort came up clutch for Sudbury, scoring his second of the game on an assist by Nedved early in the third period to put his team up 4-3. The Wolves actually held on to this lead, handing Detroit its first loss in eleven playoff games. Building on the momentum, the Wolves responded two nights later with another 4-3 victory at home, this time on a two-goal game by Jason Bonsignore, who had been benched by Merkosky in the previous contest.[19]

With the series tied at two games apiece, the Wolves made another excursion to Detroit for a Saturday night contest at the Joe Louis Arena, this time joined by two busloads of fans who made the over 700-kilometre trip from the Nickel to the Motor City. In a nail-biting affair, the game was deadlocked at 1-1 after three periods. About seven-and-a-half minutes into overtime, Venedam—playing alongside Rick Bodkin and Ryan Shanahan to form the so-called "Mucker Line"—picked the puck up from behind the net and fired it at Wings' netminder Jason Saal. The shot deflected off Saal's arm and bounced into the net, securing a 2-1 win for the Wolves. "It was a fluky one," is how Venedam described the biggest goal of his young career. Matt Mullin, who made 33 saves that night, was named the game's first star. It also happened to be the Wolves' first ever playoff win on American soil.[20]

Only one win away from the OHL finals, the Wolves could not finish off the tenacious Red Wings. In Game 6 in Sudbury, Detroit earned a hard-fought 2-1 victory to send the series to a seventh game. "That was a heartbreaker," remembered Jamie Rivers in an interview over twenty years later. "We should have closed it out. We had opportunities, we had powerplays, we had chances, especially in our barn to at least send it to overtime. That was our chance to win."[21] Given that every game of the series had been decided by one goal, it was reasonable to expect that Game 7 would be the tightest match of them all. It was, in fact, the complete opposite, as the Red Wings delivered a "Massacre in Motown" on April

26, levelling the Wolves by a score of 11-4. "This is a devastated hockey club, but we're not going to make excuses. It's just one of those things that happen," conceded Merkosky after the loss.[22]

It had been a disappointing but unforgettable playoff run for the Wolves and their fans, especially for players like Rivers who had played in their final OHL game. "It was an electric atmosphere. Honestly, it's the closest you can get to playing in the Stanley Cup Playoffs, is having played playoff hockey in Sudbury in that era," recollected Rivers, who went on to play over 450 NHL games before retiring from professional hockey in 2011. After beating Sudbury, Detroit advanced to the 1995 OHL championship finals, defeating Guelph in six games to win the J. Ross Robertson Cup.[23]

FIRST TIME SINCE '89

The departure of several veterans naturally suggested that the Sudbury Wolves would take a step backwards, but it still had plenty of talent on its roster. The steady presence of Matt Mullin in net was replaced by the tandem of New York Islanders draft pick Dave MacDonald and the towering Steve Valiquette. Local forward Sean Venedam was named captain of a roster that featured several products of the Sudbury area, including Andrew Dale, Neal Martin, Luc Gagne, and Darryl Moxam. Richard Rochefort, a New Jersey Devils prospect, and Ryan Shanahan, a Detroit Red Wings draft pick who was in his fourth and final season in a Wolves uniform, were both given an elevated offensive role. On September 22, Sudbury travelled to Sault Ste. Marie to open the 1995-96 OHL season and lost by a score of 7-4, an outcome that proved to be an early indicator of the road that lay ahead.[24]

The Wolves' relative inexperience shone through as the season progressed. Clinging to the second to last spot in the Central Division at the end of the calendar year, the team went on a losing skid in early January and soon found itself on the outside looking in on playoff contention. "Our biggest challenge now is to try to stop this bleeding," said assistant coach Todd Lalonde after the Wolves' fifth consecutive loss, an 8-4 drubbing by the Greyhounds that saw rookie centre Joe Thornton, chosen second overall by the Soo in the 1995 OHL Priority Selection, post a goal and four assists.[25] On January 15, just days after trading Andrew Dale to the Kitchener

Rangers, the Wolves dismissed head coach and general manager Glenn Merkosky and handed both roles to Lalonde. "It's going to be an easy transition," the 27-year-old Lalonde confidently stated upon his promotion. "The biggest thing now is to instill enthusiasm in the players again." Merkosky departed the organization tied with Ken MacKenzie for most regular season career coaching wins (126) in franchise history.[26]

Time was running out for Lalonde to instill much of anything in the Pack as the postseason rapidly approached. The Wolves succeeded in Lalonde's coaching debut on January 19 by defeating the Owen Sound Platers by a score of 2-1 at the Sudbury Arena, but the season did not begin following an upward trajectory under his watch. The team had to win its final two games of the regular season—which happened to be against Sault Ste. Marie and then North Bay—in order to clinch a playoff spot. Those hopes were dashed on March 12 when the Greyhounds once more beat the Wolves 8-3 in the Soo. Statistically eliminated from postseason contention, the Wolves won their last game of the year against the Centennials by a score of 8-6. Shanahan collected six points, including a hat trick, in what was his final game of major junior hockey.[27]

Sudbury had failed to qualify for the playoffs for the first time since the 1988-89 season. The team had finished dead last in the Central Division behind even the Barrie Colts, an expansion franchise captained by former Wolves defenceman Shawn Frappier, whom Merkosky had traded before the season started. While captain Sean Venedam's 47-goal campaign had been something to admire for Wolves' fans, for the most part it was a season worth forgetting. Assessing the club's lacklustre year, Norm Mayer of *The Sudbury Star* remarked that "Local hockey fans are denied OHL playoffs for the first time since 1989. And that shouldn't have happened. Hopefully, the Wolves have learned from their mistakes. Time will tell."[28]

CAPTAIN COMEBACK

The 1996-97 season was a commemorative one for the Sudbury Wolves. Not only did the franchise celebrate its twenty-fifth season in the OHL, but it also retired the jersey number of one of its most beloved players for the very first time. In a pregame ceremony on September 20 prior to the team's season opener versus the Erie Otters, the Sudbury Wolves officially raised former captain Mike Foligno's No. 17 to the rafters of the Sudbury Arena. *The Sudbury Star* also reported that Foligno had earlier been voted by Wolves fans as the greatest player in franchise history. Over 4,500 attendees watched as Foligno received praise from the likes of Mark Burgess—who had since taken over the organizational reigns from his father Ken—OHL commissioner David Branch, and city councillor Gerry McIntaggart, the latter of whom, on behalf of Sudbury mayor Jim Gordon, declared September 20 "Mike Foligno day."[29]

Foligno, who had retired from professional hockey in the early 1990s after playing over 1,000 NHL games, was presented with a Wolves jersey bearing his name and retired number. Upon donning the sweater, the Wolves' all-time leading goal-scorer pumped his fist in the air and gave one of his trademark leaps, a goal-scoring celebration he had made famous during his career. "I had the best time of my life playing for the Sudbury Wolves," Foligno told the Sudbury crowd. Unfortunately, the Wolves disappointed Foligno and their fans by blowing a 5-2 lead against the Otters that night and losing by a score of 7-6.[30]

The Wolves produced another subpar campaign despite ample excitement surrounding some of its rookie talent. Selected third overall by Sudbury in the 1996 OHL draft, forward Norm Milley was expected to inject an immediate offensive spark into the lineup, while fourth-round choice Paul Mara, an American defenceman projected as a first-round pick in the 1997 NHL draft, was boldly described by *The Star* as "the most anticipated rookie ever in Sudbury."[31] Milley wound up scoring 30 goals in his rookie year, while Mara was indeed drafted seventh overall by the Tampa Bay Lightning in June 1997 after putting up nearly a point-per-game with the Wolves. "It was the best decision of my life, to go up to Sudbury," Mara later remarked, referencing the fact that he had considered returning to play high school hockey in his home state of Massachusetts that season.[32] Collectively, however, the Wolves finished in last place in the Central Division with only 21 wins on the year, and for the second straight season missed the playoffs.[33]

The Wolves front office had tried to remedy the situation by making another change behind the bench in the midst of the season. In February, after weeks of scrutiny from fans and the media for the team's poor performance, general manager Todd Lalonde decided to step down from his position as head coach after going 15-27-4 to start the season. It had been a frustrating year for Lalonde; after a 5-4 overtime loss against the North Bay Centennials earlier in the season, he tossed a water bottle in the direction of a referee and was subsequently suspended for one game and fined $250. "I think that this move is in the best interest of the Sudbury Wolves. Something had to be done to give the club the spark it needs to get into the playoffs," Lalonde said upon announcing the decision. Despite bringing in over a dozen new players, Lalonde had failed to rebuild the team as quickly as he had hoped, but felt confident that delegating head coaching duties to assistant coach Murray Nystrom could help turn things around. Nystrom had previously coached the London Knights before coming to Sudbury to work alongside Lalonde. Although the Wolves defeated the Guelph Storm 7-6 in Murray's debut, the team went 6-10-4 under his watch to finish the season.[34]

It was an underwhelming way for team captain Sean Venedam to end his OHL career, but in the years that followed the Sudbury local underwent a journey that would have seemed unimaginable years earlier. After registering 91 points in 66 games to lead Sudbury in scoring during his final year of major junior hockey, Venedam went on to play professionally for nearly a decade, mostly in the East Coast Hockey League (ECHL). He continued to display the scoring prowess that made him a fan favourite while playing for the Wolves, netting 258 goals during his professional career. Then, in February 2008, while playing with the Bakersfield Condors of the ECHL, Venedam suffered a serious injury, shattering the tibia and fibula in his right leg. He was expected to make a full recovery and be back on the ice within six weeks after undergoing surgery to repair the broken bones. However, it was not long before the doctor's assessment proved far from guaranteed. "Shortly after surgery that's when I had some complications and things went a little sideways," Venedam recalled to Mike Commito in an interview ten years after the initial procedure took place.[35]

The next three-and-a-half years were a challenging time for Venedam to say the least. Unable to walk without crutches, he attended countless physiotherapy sessions and endured other forms of treatments and surgeries in an effort to rehabilitate the severe nerve damage in his leg. Setbacks came in the form of repeated infections and leg fractures. "Unless you've gone through something like that, people don't understand the magnitude of it," Venedam explained. "There are so many things you can't do. The simple task of going to the store to get groceries. You can't do it." Finally, after years of procedures and medical treatments, Venedam found himself at a crossroads. Upon suffering another break to his leg while out running routine errands in Ottawa, he consulted an orthopaedic surgeon at St. Michael's Hospital in Toronto. The doctor informed Venedam that amputation might be the only way to allow him to move on from the injury for good. "At that point, amputation had always been brought up to me in the past that it might be an option, but obviously you want to exhaust all options before going down that road," said Venedam.[36]

Faced with the possibility of this life-altering surgery, Venedam ultimately found a renewed sense of determination and achieved an amazing personal comeback story. After reaching out to several people who had undergone similar procedures, during which time he was presented with the opportunity to represent Canada at the International Standing Amputee Ice Hockey world championship in Finland the following year, he decided that he would undergo the operation and begin working toward his new goal. At 35-years-old, Venedam's right leg below his knee was amputated, but as soon as he could he set out to learn how to skate using a prosthetic. "It was one of the most frustrating things I had to do," he explained. "It was almost like starting from scratch." The former Wolves captain refused to quit, however, and one year later successfully qualified for the national team, where he helped Canada win its sixth consecutive world championship. "One of the closest groups I ever played with because we were all in the same boat. Especially when you're representing your country," he proudly recalled. While the tournament has not been held since 2012, Venedam still hopes to return to the ice again one day and represent Canada.[37]

YOUNG GUNS

The 1997-98 season marked the rise of a handful of young Wolves players who would go on to have successful careers in Sudbury and eventually make a name for themselves in the NHL. In the 1997 OHL Priority Selection, the Wolves used their first and second round picks to select left winger Taylor Pyatt and centre Mike Fisher, respectively. Later in the draft, the club also nabbed centre Derek MacKenzie (the son of Ken MacKenzie) and goaltender Andrew Raycroft from the Wellington Dukes. A few other selections, such as forward Ryan Barnes, had very successful tenures in the OHL, leading some to suggest later that the Wolves' 1997 draft class was perhaps the best in franchise history. Regardless, Sudbury's roster on September 19, 1997 sported eight rookies in total when the team started the season at home against the Erie Otters for the second consecutive year. The Otters won by a score of 5-2, leading Sudbury captain and Buffalo Sabres prospect Jeremy Adduono to remark that "We have a lot of young players and there's lots of pressure … But there's no excuses, we didn't play our best as a team."[38]

Todd Lalonde made yet another coaching change less than a year after he had stepped down from the role. Murray Nystrom was abruptly dismissed in early October after the Wolves compiled a 2-5-0 record and he was promptly replaced with Tom Watt, a former NHL coach whose resume included the Jack Adams Award as NHL coach of the year in 1981-82 and a Stanley Cup as an assistant coach with the Calgary Flames in 1989. "What I wanted was someone who could come in to be a teacher of the game of hockey. He's got a tremendous winning background," explained Lalonde. Watt immediately set out to work; one player called the first practice under his direction "the toughest … we've had all year." The Wolves appeared to respond to the change, defeating the Owen Sound Platers by a score of 7-5 in Watt's debut. "I saw a lot of positive things out there. Everybody worked hard," said the 62-year-old former teacher following the win.[39]

Watt's hiring did not magically fix the Wolves' woes, however. At one point, president Mark Burgess had instituted a self-imposed 16-game deadline for a change in the team's performance, but within a couple of weeks publicly called it off and instead indicated that he sought a period of stability within the organization. Expressing full support in Lalonde and the rest of his staff in spite of the continued on-ice struggles, Burgess advised that "Everybody's job is secure at this point … No more nonsense, just play hockey." He also denied any rumours he was considering selling the franchise to a group of investors that allegedly included Sudbury local and Montreal Canadiens forward Brian Savage. "This whole season has been fueled by rumors and hearsay and it's time for everyone to come to the rink and have some fun," Burgess stated. At least one of the rumours that was swirling around the Sudbury Arena proved to be legitimate when, just days before Christmas, the Wolves executed a blockbuster trade involving four teams, twelve players, and three draft picks. In the end, Sudbury dealt Paul Mara and Steve Valiquette and acquired centre Glenn Crawford, defence-men Kip Brennan, and a fourth-round selection. The new acquisitions made their debut with the Wolves on December 19 in a 4-1 loss to the Barrie Colts, dropping the team's record to 13-18-4 on the year.[40]

The Wolves' considerable improvement in the second half of the season was partly overshadowed by the passing of Ken Burgess from cancer on February 23, 1998. He was remembered for his implementation of "a business-like approach into the day-to-day operations of the hockey club … that helped transform the Sudbury Wolves into one of the top-rated OHL franchises both on and off the ice." He had also been a prominent figure in Sudbury's minor hockey scene, earning the 1991 Canadian Amateur Hockey Association Award for his financial contributions and service to youth hockey. Although Burgess had been less involved with the daily operations of the club in recent seasons, he had remained proud of his role as owner and still had a vested interest in the Wolves' progress. As expected, Mark Burgess was set to continue carrying the family's ownership torch moving forward. A few days after Ken Burgess's passing, the Wolves faced off against the Sault Ste. Marie Greyhounds at the Sudbury Arena in a game dedicated to their late owner. Not only did the Wolves win the game by a score of 4-1, but they simultaneously clinched a playoff spot for the first time in three years.[41]

As the final playoff seed in the Central Division, the Wolves were the clear underdogs in the opening round against the Barrie Colts and their decorated head coach, Bert Templeton. All hope was not lost, however. Sudbury's rookies had proven themselves to be key contributors to the team's late-season charge to the postseason, and Adduono had finished the year with 106 points, good for second overall in the league behind only

Peter Sarno of the Windsor Spitfires. The best-of-seven series did not get off to a great start for the Pack. The Colts edged the Wolves in Game 1 by a score of 4-3—Sudbury had what looked to be the tying goal waved off with just over a minute in regulation—and then again in Game 2 with a 4-3 victory in overtime. The Wolves finally responded in Game 3 by besting the Colts 6-3 at the Barrie Molson Centre. Sudbury goaltender Kory Cooper made 43 stops in the match, while veteran forward Konstantin Kalmikov—a Wolves import draft pick and a Toronto Maple Leafs prospect—scored two goals.[42]

From there on it was a whole new series. Rookie forward Taylor Pyatt was the overtime hero in Game 4 when he deflected a shot from the point past the Colts' netminder to give his team a huge 4-3 win. "The goal against Barrie was by far the biggest goal I've ever scored," the Thunder Bay native said.[43] Following a third consecutive win in Game 5, the Wolves entered Game 6 determined to eliminate the Colts and advance to the OHL quarterfinals. The Sudbury Arena housed 5,300 fans on March 24 in anticipation of the potential series-win. Peter Campbell scored his fifth goal in four contests to open the scoring for the Wolves, who went on to win the game by a score of 4-1 and close out a series that was called the "biggest upset of the 1997-98 OHL playoffs." Wolves defenceman Brad Morgan, who had been acquired from Barrie in a trade earlier in the season, stated that "It's an incredible feeling, something I can't describe. To come back like that and put them away in the first round … it was amazing."[44]

The Guelph Storm were an even larger hurdle than the Barrie Colts, however, and one that the Wolves in the end could not overcome. Having won the Hamilton Spectator Trophy for finishing with the best regular season record in 1997-98, the Storm completely overwhelmed the Wolves. After winning Game 1 by a score of 6-3, Guelph rolled out another three consecutive victories, sweeping the series in four games. The Storm advanced all the way to the Memorial Cup tournament held in Spokane, Washington, losing the championship game in overtime to the Portland Winter Hawks of the WHL. "I hate to admit it, but, in the end, we basically came up against a better hockey team," said coach Tom Watt after the Wolves were eliminated from playoff contention at the Sudbury Arena in early April. Fans gave the home team a standing ovation as they left the ice. "That was very special … It just proves that this is a great hockey town with great fans," said Adduono.[45]

BULL-DOZED

The Sudbury Wolves organization made some significant front office changes that coincided with another large-scale realignment by the OHL for the 1998-99 season. With the addition of the expansion Brampton Battalion and Mississauga IceDogs, the latter owned by Don Cherry, the league organized itself into two conferences, East and West. Sudbury remained in the Central Division within the Eastern Conference, which also included North Bay, Barrie, Mississauga and the Toronto St. Michael's Majors in what was predicted to be the weakest division in the OHL. The Wolves, meanwhile, parted ways with both head coach Tom Watt and general manager Todd Lalonde. Watt was replaced by Reg Higgs, former head coach of the University of Regina men's hockey team and assistant coach with the New York Rangers. Ken MacKenzie returned to the Wolves franchise as an assistant coach and general manager after having spent the previous two seasons coaching the Rayside-Balfour Sabrecats of the Northern Ontario Junior Hockey Association (NOJHA).[46]

The Wolves' roster boasted a wealth of NHL talent. Captain Mike Fisher, along with teammates Norm Milley, Ryan Barnes, Kip Brennan, and Andrew Raycroft, returned to Sudbury after having been drafted in the 1998 NHL Entry Draft, while Taylor Pyatt and Derek MacKenzie, among others, were expecting to hear their names called at the next draft in June 1999. During an interview on the popular hockey podcast *Spittin' Chiclets* in September 2020, Raycroft, who was selected by the Boston Bruins in 1998, recalled the standout play of Mike Fisher in particular. "Right away, leader," Raycroft said of Fisher, a Peterborough native and second-round choice of the Ottawa Senators. "Fish was great his first year, and then even better that second year … And you knew, he was getting strong, and he was going to the NHL." Fisher did indeed graduate to the professional ranks the following season and went on to play over 1,000 NHL games with the Ottawa Senators and Nashville Predators before retiring in 2018.[47]

Yet, all things considered, the Wolves had a mediocre season in 1998-99, but lucked out by being slotted into the dismal Central Division. The team won only two of its first ten games, including handing the Brampton Battalion its first win in franchise history. On October 14, the Wolves dealt Ryan Barnes to the Guelph Storm in exchange for the six-foot-three, 210-pound right-winger Brian McGrattan, a future NHL enforcer.[48] By the end of the first third of the season, the team was tied for second place in the division despite owning a mediocre 9-12-3 record. A prime example of Sudbury's underlying potential came on December 18 against the Barrie Colts, ranked as the third best junior team in Canada. The Wolves broke the Colts with a 9-4 beatdown, with the explosive top forward line of Fisher, Pyatt, and Milley combining for 17 points on the night. Fisher and Milley each tied franchise records by recording seven points apiece, with Milley concurrently tying the record for most assists in a single game (7). "It's always been a dream to get a team record. I always wanted to be remembered with something like that, and I love the fact I was able to do it in front of the Sudbury fans," Milley beamed after the memorable outing.[49]

The Wolves were fortunate enough to overcome their inconsistencies and secure a playoff spot for the second consecutive season with a record of 25-38-8. Upon defeating the North Bay Centennials by a score of 7-3 in early March, Sudbury locked up second place in the Central Division. About one week later, Milley scored his fiftieth goal of the season in a 6-4 loss to the Oshawa Generals at the Sudbury Arena. He finished second in OHL scoring with 120 points on the season and earned the Jim Mahon Memorial Trophy as the league's top-scoring right winger. Captain Fisher also eclipsed the 100-point mark with 41 goals and 65 assists. Another award-winner on the roster was veteran defenceman and New York Rangers draft pick Ryan McKie, who received the OHL Humanitarian of the Year (now known as the Dan Snyder Memorial Trophy) for serving as a positive role model and making notable contributions to the community.[50] Several other Wolves finished among the OHL's best in various categories, including rookie forward Jason Jaspers, who finished fifth amongst rookies with 61 points, and Derek MacKenzie, who recorded 32 assists on the powerplay, tied for the fourth-highest in the league.[51]

Sudbury's first-round series against the Belleville Bulls was nothing short of a disaster. Coach Higgs turned to goaltender Mike Gorman, acquired from the Kitchener Rangers earlier in the season, for Game 1 of the series. Gorman surrendered seven goals on 54 shots as the Bulls routed the Wolves by a score of 7-2, leading Higgs to give Raycroft, born and raised in Belleville, the nod for Game 2 in his hometown. He fared no better and was pulled by the second period of play as the Bulls won another lopsided 8-3 affair. Defensive holes aside, a major part of the problem was that the trio of Fisher, Pyatt, and Milley had stopped producing, accounting for only one goal in the first two contests. Wolves' fans seemed to have packed it in already as fewer than 2,000 people showed up for Game 3 at the Sudbury Arena on March 23; the Bulls drubbed the home team 8-3, the Wolves' worst playoff loss on home-ice since 1976. The best-of-seven quarterfinal series came to an end in four straight games after the Wolves were defeated 8-5 in Game 4, closing the book on Sudbury's final full season of the decade and the century.[52]

CHAPTER 8:

GREAT EXPECTATIONS, 1999-2003

With the dawn of the new millennium just around the corner, the people of Sudbury and the Sudbury Wolves organization looked toward an uncertain yet intriguing future. Both the city and its hockey team had undergone immense change over the course of the previous century. Sudbury had evolved from a shanty mining town established in the 1880s to one of the premier hubs in all of Northern Ontario. On January 1, 2001, the City of Greater Sudbury officially came into existence through an amalgamation of the Regional Municipality of Sudbury with several nearby communities and townships. The move expanded Sudbury's population and physical boundaries, making it one of the largest communities by land area in the entire country. The "Wolves of the North," meanwhile, had grown from a collection of teams sporadically competing for various hockey titles to one of the most treasured junior clubs in the CHL. The twenty-first century presented the Sudbury Wolves franchise with a chance to build upon its historic past by adding a championship banner to the rafters of the Sudbury Arena, and at first glance this possibility appeared just within reach.

A LEGEND COMES NORTH

The Sudbury Wolves entered the 1999-2000 season with high expectations. In the summer of 1999, *The Sudbury Star* referred excitedly to the upcoming season as one "of the most highly-anticipated" in team history.[1] The hype was entirely warranted. During the previous offseason, five returning players had been selected in the 1999 NHL Entry Draft: Taylor Pyatt (New York Islanders, 8th overall), Alexei Semenov (Edmonton Oilers, 36th overall), Jason Jaspers (Phoenix Coyotes, 71st overall), Brian McGrattan (Los Angeles Kings, 104th overall), and Sudbury native Derek MacKenzie (Atlanta Thrashers, 128th overall). Following the departure of Mike Fisher to the Ottawa Senators, veteran defenceman Brad Morgan was named the team captain, but he was later replaced by Norm Milley. A few months before the season got underway, the Wolves traded goaltender Andrew Raycroft to the Kingston Frontenacs. This left the team with two options in net: Mike Gorman and rookie Miguel Beaudry, a local prospect who was picked by the Wolves in the first round of the 1999 OHL Priority Selection.[2] By September, experts had Sudbury ranked as the second-best team in the OHL, and the fifth in the Canadian Hockey League (CHL).[3]

Perhaps most impressive of all, in May 1999 the Wolves signed Bert Templeton to a five-year deal as its new coach and general manager. The Scottish-born legendary coach came to Sudbury with a world-class resume. He won a Memorial Cup with the Hamilton Fincups in 1976 (after defeating the Wolves in that year's OHA Junior 'A' finals), and another J. Ross Robertson Cup with the North Bay Centennials in 1994. He also had seven division championships under his belt, and at the time of his hiring sat second behind only Brian Kilrea in career OHL coaching wins.[4] Templeton was the recipient of numerous awards, namely OHL Coach of the Year (1975, 1994), OHL Executive of the Year (1992, 1996), and CHL Executive of the Year (1992). Upon his death in 2003, Templeton was the CHL's second-winningest coach of all time, and in 2005 was posthumously recognized with the Bill Long Award for distinguished service to the OHL.[5]

Templeton came to Sudbury with a reputation as a decorated, no-non-sense bench boss who demanded a lot from his players. Sudbury native Bobby Chaumont, who was drafted by the Wolves in 2000 and made his OHL debut under Templeton during the 2001-02 season, remembers that the veteran coach "definitely could be intimidating. He was definitely hard on the guys, but I didn't mind that ... I enjoyed having Bert, and it was a good experience."[6] As his debut with his new team drew near, Templeton told *The Star* "We have quite a bit of work to do, but that's my job. When we get it done, we'll have a hell of a team."[7]

The Wolves were quickly brought down to Earth once the season actually got underway. The team lost its first five games, the first time Templeton had started a season with an 0-5 record. Following an embarrassing 5-2 loss at home to the Sarnia Sting about two weeks before Christmas, Templeton publicly lambasted his players as "brain dead" and "un-coachable." By that point, the Wolves had registered just 10 wins through 28 games. Fans were fed-up as well, which in part contributed to a nearly 10 percent decrease in attendance from the previous year. The team began to play consistently better from mid-December onward. After Sudbury defeated the Soo by a score of 4-3 on January 28, 2000, the team's record sat above the .500 mark for the first time in five seasons.[8]

The Wolves ended the 1999-2000 regular season on a remarkable note. From February 13 to March 17, Sudbury went undefeated over thirteen consecutive games, a franchise record that still stands to this day.[9] The streak began in an unusual fashion as the Wolves defeated the Rouyn-Noranda Huskies of the QMJHL by a score of 4-0 as part of a series of "interlocking" matches scheduled by the CHL that season. Sudbury extended its streak to four games about ten days later by stomping the league-leading Ottawa 67's in a physical 3-1 victory at home. The Wolves kept on going until March 14, when the team had the chance to set a franchise record with a twelfth consecutive victory against the Frontenacs. Sudbury decimated Kingston 7-2 in front of a sold-out home crowd, leading Templeton to note that he could not "remember winning 12 in a row with anybody" despite having coached "some outstanding clubs" over his

23-year career in the OHL. The Wolves padded the streak with a thirteenth straight win versus Mississauga on St. Patrick's Day at the Sudbury Arena.[10] On March 18, the Barrie Colts handed the Wolves a 5-1 loss to bring the run to an end. Milley and Pyatt were both left off the scoresheet versus the Colts, halting 18-game point streaks for each player.[11] Sudbury finished second in the Central Division with a 39-23-5-1 record.

During and immediately following this historic winning streak, Norm Milley again etched his name in the Wolves record book. Not only did the North York native become the first Wolves player to record back-to-back 50-goal seasons, he also became the franchise's all-time leading goal-scorer. On March 19, the Wolves visited Mississauga in the last game of the regular season. While the Wolves won handily by a score of 6-3, it was Milley who stole the headlines. With only twenty-five seconds left in the match, Milley, playing in his final OHL regular season game, potted an empty net goal to surpass Mike Foligno as the highest goal-scorer in Wolves history with 167 career markers. The goal simultaneously placed Milley just one-point shy of tying Jamie Matthews as the Wolves' all-time points scorer. Milley was understandably quite proud of his accomplishment, but he emphasized that "All I want is to do well in the playoffs and bring home a banner to Sudbury. That would mean so much more to me than those records."[12] Milley led the OHL in goals that season (52) and finished second in points (112).

Observers had reason to believe that the Wolves had a serious shot at a championship as the 2000 OHL playoffs kicked off. They had won fourteen of their last fifteen games of the regular season, and the top line of Milley, Jaspers, and Pyatt was considered one of the most explosive in the league. In the opening round, the Wolves faced the Kingston Frontenacs, backstopped by former Sudbury goaltender Andrew Raycroft. The Wolves won the first two games at the Sudbury Arena, during which time fans quickly developed a distaste for Kingston pest Sean Avery.[13] The Frontenacs struggled to contain the trio of Milley, Jaspers, and Pyatt; over the course of the first four games of the series, the big line combined for twelve goals, the same number Kingston had scored as a team to that point. The Wolves eliminated the Frontenacs from the postseason in Game 5 with a 3-1 win.[14]

Sudbury's next opponent, the Barrie Colts, led by the OHL's leading scorer and future Toronto Maple Leafs head coach Sheldon Keefe, posed a much greater challenge. It was a close, back-and-forth series that included some thrilling contests. Although the Wolves dropped the series opener in Barrie, the Wolves responded with a 3-0 win in Game 2 on Gorman's first OHL career playoff shutout. In Game 4, the Wolves floundered at the Sudbury Arena and found themselves down 3-0 late in the second period. What followed was one of the biggest comebacks in team history. Jaspers broke Colts goalie Brian Finley's shutout bid in the dying minutes of the second frame before the Wolves stormed out in the third with consecutive goals from Morgan, MacKenzie, Kyle Dafoe, and Sebastien Savage to take a 5-3 lead. Barrie scored another goal, but the Wolves held off their opponents to secure the unlikely win and tie the series 2-2. Sudbury dropped Game 5 on the road but staved off elimination in Game 6 with a clutch 4-1 victory.[15]

The OHL Eastern Conference semi-final went to Game 7, which was settled on April 20 at the Barrie Molson Centre. The outcome was infuriating for the Wolves faithful. Tied 1-1 with less than two minutes remaining in regulation, MacKenzie was charged with a holding penalty. The Colts wasted no time capitalizing on the powerplay as former Wolves forward Ryan Barnes scored the series-winning goal. Sudbury players and fans were outraged by the late penalty call, with Gorman calling the referee's decision "career suicide."[16] The season of great hope was over for the Sudbury Wolves. The Barrie Colts would go on to win the 2000 OHL championship and eventually reach the Memorial Cup finals where they would lose the trophy to the Rimouski Océanic.

THE MEMORY OF '32

The Wolves entered 2000-01 season with a revamped roster. Many key players from the previous year, namely Norm Milley, Brad Morgan, Mike Gorman, and Taylor Pyatt, had all moved on from the OHL. In an effort to address these gaps, Sudbury selected defenceman Adam Sturgeon with the fifteenth overall selection in the 2000 OHL Draft. Another significant acquisition was Russian left winger Fedor Fedorov, brother of Hockey Hall of Fame member Sergei Fedorov, who joined the Wolves in September through a trade with the Windsor Spitfires. Most surprisingly, sophomore goaltender Miguel Beaudry, who was expected to own the Wolves' crease, was challenged by Mike Smith after Templeton struck a trade deal with Kingston about one month into the season.[17] In October, Derek MacKenzie was named team captain.[18]

A series of rather public conflicts involving the players put a strain on team morale during the first half of the season. First, in early September, Alexei Semenov found himself at the centre of some unflattering media coverage. The 19-year-old defenceman, who at the time was attending the Edmonton Oilers training camp, was quoted by *The Edmonton Sun* as stating that the city of Sudbury "sucks," that the organization was "cheap," and that he wanted a trade to a different OHL team. While the six-foot-six, 220-pound Russian initially denied the comments amidst backlash, he eventually owned up to what he had said. Mark Burgess, as well as Templeton, publicly defended Semenov as a "good kid" who had made a mistake.[19] Shortly thereafter there was another incident surrounding a young defenceman. After discovering he was a healthy scratch for the team's second game of the season, Adam Sturgeon packed his bags and left for his home in southern Ontario. Templeton would not budge on the matter. Sturgeon was traded to the Belleville Bulls the following year, after having played just a single game for the Wolves.[20]

Most serious of all, in November a conflict arose between Dennis Wideman and Templeton. On November 21, Wideman, a talented defenceman who was Sudbury's second round pick in 1999, left the team and demanded a trade after a game versus the London Knights, citing a lack of ice-time and "personal problems" with his coach. Templeton responded by asserting that he "would not trade any player unless they are active members of the Sudbury Wolves."[21] A few days afterwards, however, Templeton informed the media that Wideman had accused him of physical assault while on the bench during a game against Sault Ste. Marie on November 15. Wideman hired a lawyer and approached the police about the alleged assault, which supposedly involved Templeton grabbing him by the back of the neck.[22] Templeton rebuffed the allegations, firmly telling *The Sudbury Star* that "I have nothing to be afraid of or hide from."[23] No charges were

PRE-1972

Max Silverman – Manager, Sudbury Cub Wolves, 1934-35. Greater
Sudbury Heritage Image, Donated by Travaligni. MK0480.

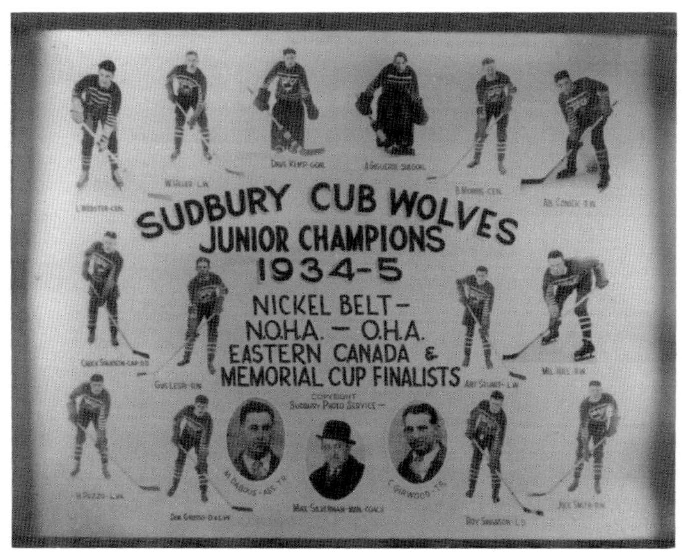

Sudbury Cub Wolves. Junior Champions, 1934-35. Greater Sudbury Heritage Image, Donated by Travaligni. MK0513

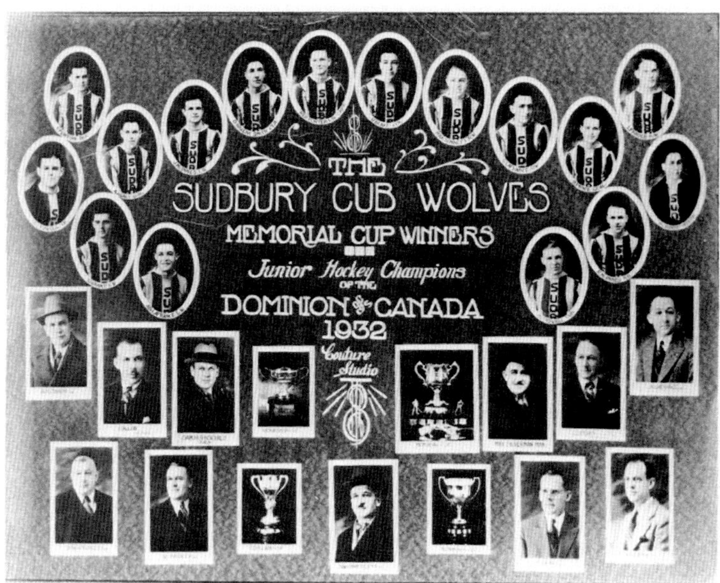

The 1932 Memorial Cup Champion Sudbury Cub Wolves. City of Greater Sudbury Heritage Images, City of Greater Sudbury Heritage Museums Collection. MK0998

ALL ONTARIO CHAMPS 1953-4
First Winners of H. A. HEWITT TROPHY

Sudbury Wolves team, the All Ontario Champs 1953-4 and first
winners of H.A. Hewitt Trophy. Max Silverman was their coach.
Greater Sudbury Heritage Image. K.Z. Postcard collection.
M4758

Don Cherry in his Sudbury Wolves hockey
jersey. Greater Sudbury Heritage Image.
Donated by Robert Keir. MK6341

The famous stuffed wolf on display at the Sudbury Arena.
November 1960. Bob Keir Fonds. City of Greater Sudbury
Archives. 60-732.

Fans waiting in line in front of the Sudbury Arena to buy tickets for the Sudbury
Wolves against the Owen Sound Mercury's. The Canadian Pacific Railway (CPR)
Train Station at 1 Elgin Street can be seen in the background. March 29, 1954.
Sudbury Star Fonds. City of Greater Sudbury Archives. 1185-29.

Pierre Pichette, Andy Voykin, and Yacker Flynn
posing on the ice at the Sudbury Arena. November
1957. Sudbury Star Fonds. City of Greater Sudbury
Archives. 57-11-313.

1970s

Mike Foligno in his playing days with the Wolves (1974-79). In 1978-79, he set the franchise record for most points in a regular season (150), a benchmark which still remains unmatched. Provided courtesy of the Sudbury Wolves.

1973-74 Sudbury Wolves. Provided courtesy of the
Sudbury Wolves organization.

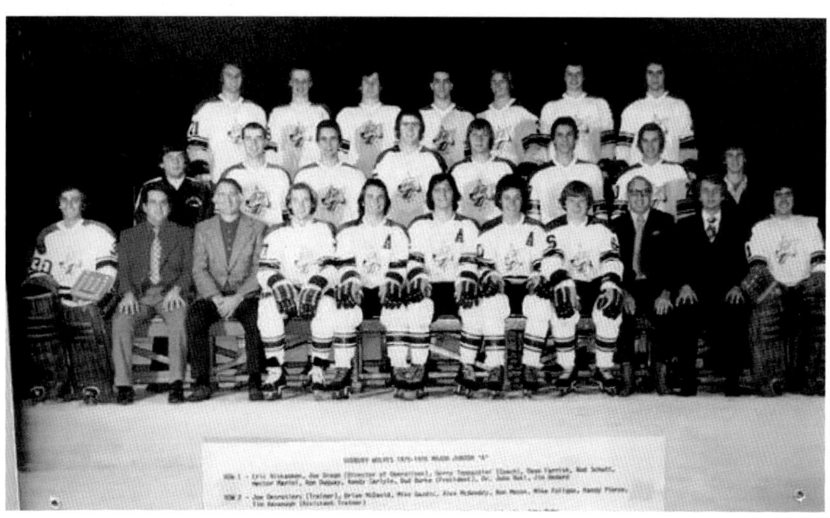

1975-76 Sudbury Wolves. Provided courtesy of the Sudbury Wolves
organization.

1980s

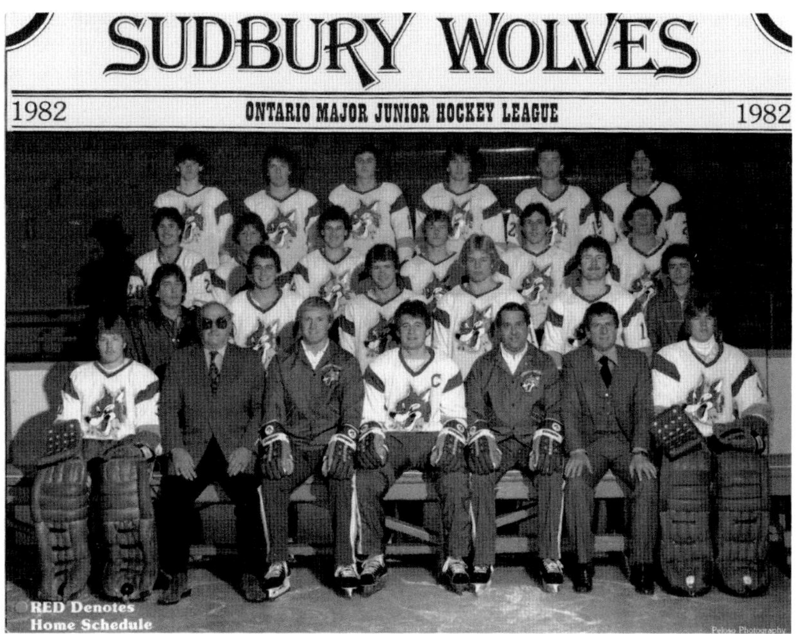

Sudbury Wolves. Ontario junior hockey league, 1982. Greater
Sudbury Heritage Image. Library collection. MK1446

Paul DiPietro in his playing days with the Wolves (1986-90). His five-goal performance against the Soo Greyhounds in October 1989 tied a franchise record also held by Mike Foligno and Rod Schutt. Provided courtesy of the Sudbury Wolves.

1990s

1989-90 Sudbury Wolves. Provided courtesy of the Sudbury Wolves.

2000s

Bert Templeton (left) with captain Zack Stortini. Templeton finished his illustrious junior hockey coaching career with the Wolves before passing away in 2003. Stortini credits Templeton with having a positive impact on his own playing and coaching career. Provided courtesy of the Sudbury Wolves.

The Foligno family. From left to right: Cara, Lisa, Nick, Janice, Mike, and Marcus. Provided courtesy of the Sudbury Wolves.

The Wolves celebrate hometown product Bobby Chaumont for setting the
OHL record for most consecutive regular season games played in March 2005,
a record which still stands (272). Provided courtesy of the Sudbury Wolves.

Sebastian Dahm with a big save against the Belleville Bulls in the 2007
Eastern Conference Finals. Provided courtesy of the Sudbury Wolves.

Matt Dias scored in triple overtime in Game 6 of the 2007 Eastern Conference Finals to propel the Wolves to the J. Ross Robertson Cup for the first time since 1976. Nick Foligno celebrated with the signature jump that his father Mike made famous during his own playing career. Provided courtesy of the Sudbury Wolves.

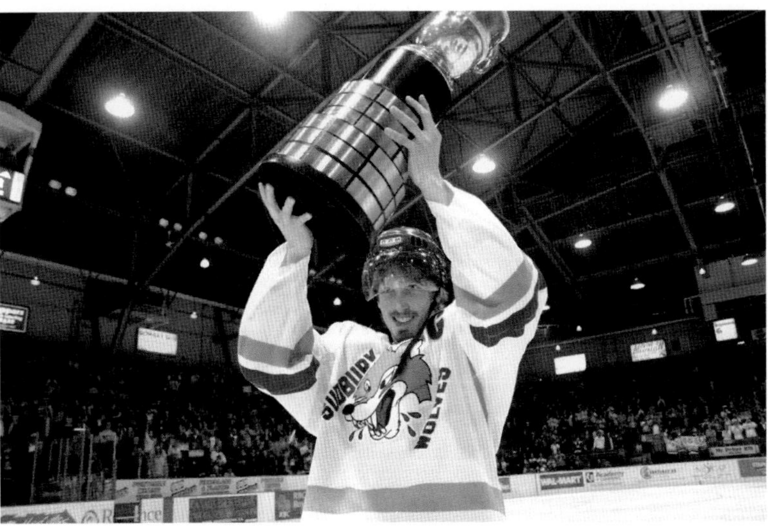

Captain Marc Staal hoists the Bobby Orr Trophy as the Wolves were crowned champions of the Eastern conference in 2007. Provided courtesy of the Sudbury Wolves.

Nick Foligno celebrates a goal against the Belleville Bulls in the 2007 Eastern Conference Finals. Provided courtesy of the Sudbury Wolves.

The Sudbury Community Arena in the early 2000s. It was constructed in 1951. Provided courtesy of the Sudbury Wolves.

This inflatable wolf head is often put on display during the lead up to puck drop at Wolves home games. Provided courtesy of the Sudbury Wolves.

2006-07 Sudbury Wolves. Provided courtesy of the Sudbury Wolves.

Howler, the Sudbury Wolves mascot. Provided courtesy of the
Sudbury Wolves.

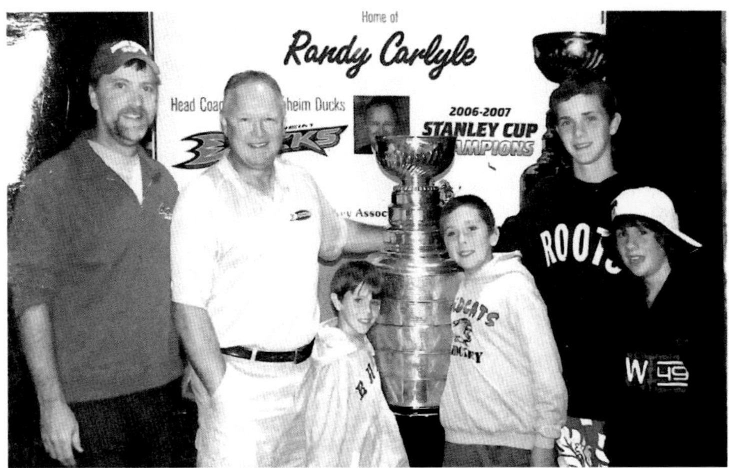

Former Wolves star defenceman Randy Carlyle (second from the left) brought the Stanley Cup back to his hometown of Azilda, Ontario in August 2007 after he coached the Anaheim Ducks to victory. The author can be seen standing second from the right. Provided by the author.

Gord Ewin (right) and captain Zack Stortini. Ewin was the Wolves' first season ticket holder and was later a part-owner of the franchise. Stortini, now assistant coach with his former team, is the longest-serving captain in Wolves history and the franchise leader in penalty minutes. Provided courtesy of the Sudbury Wolves.

2010s

Quinton Byfield was chosen first overall by the Wolves in the 2018 OHL Draft before being selected second overall by the Los Angeles Kings in the 2020 NHL Draft. Provided courtesy of the Sudbury Wolves.

Berk Keaney (left) and Mike Foligno. Keaney was the public address announcer and "Voice of the Sudbury Wolves" from 1953 until his retirement in 2011. Provided courtesy of the Keaney family.

The 2011-12 Sudbury Wolves in throwback jerseys in celebration of the franchise's fortieth anniversary season. Provided courtesy of the Sudbury Wolves.

In 2011-12, Michael Sgarbossa became the first Wolves player since Mike Foligno to lead the OHL in points. Provided courtesy of the Sudbury Wolves.

Former NHL player and Wolves head coach Jerry Toppazzini drops the ceremonial puck during a pregame ceremony during the team's fortieth anniversary season in 2011-12. Toppazzini is the only bench boss in franchise history to have won the league's coach of the year award (1975-76). Provided courtesy of the Sudbury Wolves.

In 2018-19, Ukko-Pekka Luukkonen became the first member of the Wolves to win OHL goaltender of the year and the first European player to win the Red Tilson Trophy as the league's most valuable player. Provided courtesy of the Sudbury Wolves.

The famous wolf on the wire that descends from the rafters of the Sudbury Arena after every Wolves goal. The tradition dates back well over fifty years. Provided courtesy of the Sudbury Wolves.

2020s

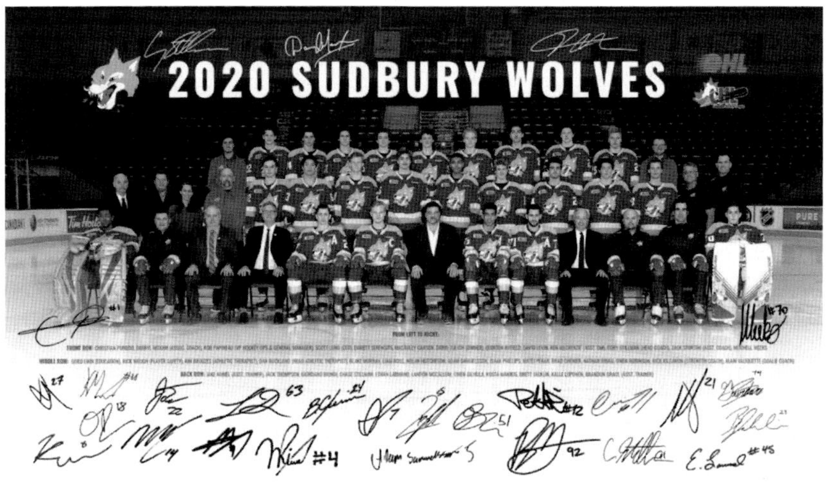

2019-2020 Sudbury Wolves. Provided courtesy of the Sudbury Wolves.

The Wolves selected Quentin Musty first overall in the 2021
OHL Draft after winning the league's first ever draft lottery.
Provided courtesy of the Sudbury Wolves.

The current logo of the Sudbury Wolves.
Provided courtesy of the Sudbury Wolves.

ever laid. Wideman was traded to London in early January in a package that included forward Chris Kelly. [24]

In spite of all this commotion, the Sudbury Wolves pieced together another fantastic regular season, and once again looked poised for a deep playoff run. For the second year in a row the Wolves went on a massive tear from mid-February to early March, winning nine consecutive games and tying another until they were beaten by the Toronto St. Michael's Majors on March 10. [25] The Wolves finished the regular season atop the Central Division with a record of 35-22-8-3, thereby earning the franchise's first division championship in twenty-five years. "I think it's quite an accomplishment ... The city and fans deserve it, too," Jason Jaspers told *The Sudbury Star* after the Wolves locked down the division title. [26] Captain MacKenzie led the team with 89 points and was also recognized with both the OHL and CHL Faceoff Awards due to his spectacular faceoff winning percentage of 67 percent. [27] As the postseason drew near, Sudbury was ranked among the top junior teams in Canada. [28]

Alexei Semenov rebounded beautifully from his preseason controversy, posting 21 goals and 63 points on the season. Many considered him a frontrunner for the Max Kaminsky Trophy, presented annually to the OHL's most outstanding defenceman, and even as a possible league MVP. "All I'm worried about his how I play ... hockey is a business for me now, and I'm a businessman," Semenov told *The Sudbury Star* when asked about the awards. The Russian blueliner was ultimately named the winner of the Max Kaminsky Trophy in May. [29]

In the playoff quarterfinals, Sudbury again crossed paths with the rival Barrie Colts. Hoping to exact revenge for the controversial Game 7 loss from the previous year, the Wolves came out firing against the defending OHL champions. Sudbury outplayed Barrie physically and on the scoresheet, winning the first three games of the series. Mike Smith, coming off a great season as the team's starting goaltender, posted his first career OHL playoff shutout in Game 3 as the "big, bad Wolves" trounced the Colts by a score of 6-0. Barrie fought back with a 4-1 win in Game 4 to keep the series alive. The Wolves completely controlled Game 5 at the Sudbury Arena, allowing the Colts only seventeen shots on net. Semenov's rocket from the point just over two minutes into the match proved to be the game-winner, as the Wolves won 2-0 on another shutout by Smith. "Revenge is a dish best served cold," wrote *The Star* after the Wolves ended the Colts' season. The players did not hide the added layer of satisfaction that came with beating Barrie, with MacKenzie stating that the Colts "got the last laugh last year … but it was real nice to get that win against them."[30]

Sudbury met the Toronto St. Michael's Majors in the second round of the postseason, a matchup that appeared to favour the Wolves. Sudbury had won five of six meetings with Toronto during the regular season, with MacKenzie alone racking up eight goals and seven assists over that span. The Wolves captured Game 1 at home by a score of 5-3, scoring all their goals on the man-advantage.[31] The next game of the Eastern Conference semi-final on April 8 was a lights-out performance for both teams—literally. During the second intermission, with the game tied 2-2, there was a power outage at St. Michael's Arena. Templeton, Toronto coach Dave Cameron, and OHL commissioner David Branch eventually agreed to postpone the game until the next day, the first time in league history that a playoff game had to be delayed in the middle of the match.[32] Play resumed the following evening at the start of the third period with the score still even. The Majors won 3-2 in overtime, bringing an end to a drawn-out game that the *Toronto Star* called "truly worthy of The Twilight Zone."[33]

The peculiar circumstances surrounding Game 2 were soon the least of the Wolves' worries. The team wrested back the series with a 5-1 win at the Sudbury Arena in Game 3. Jaspers posted his sixteenth point in eight games, while Kelly scored his league-leading tenth goal of the postseason. In Game 4, Fedorov netted four goals as the Wolves embarrassed the Majors by a score of 9-2; the series seemed all but over. The Majors refused to give up, however, and beat Sudbury 4-2 to force a sixth game. In that match Toronto reached deep and pulled off a hard-fought 3-1 victory on the back of a 40-save performance by goaltender Peter Budaj to tie the series. The tenacious Templeton remained calm in the face of adversity, stating that he was "sure we'll come up with a better effort next game."[34]

The Wolves and the Majors met at the Sudbury Arena on April 19 to decide which team would advance to the Eastern Conference finals. Templeton felt that Sudbury's vocal fans would be an invaluable asset as the Wolves tried to get rid of the pesky Majors once and for all. Semenov agreed: "This is our barn, filled with our fans, and they will help us out a lot. When you hear them going nuts it gives you power, like a shot of adrenaline." That energy was quickly drained after the Majors scored on their first two shots on goal by Matt Bannan and Michael Gough. Toronto made it 3-0 in the second frame before MacKenzie snuck in a shorthanded goal just before the intermission. That was all the Wolves could muster. The Majors, in front of "5,200 championship-starved fans" at the Sudbury Arena, put an end to Sudbury's season with a decisive 3-1 victory. Players and management were just as devastated. "I'm probably the one who's most upset of everybody," said veteran forward Kip Brennan, who had returned to Sudbury from the AHL in hopes of winning the Memorial Cup. "I'm confused as anybody as to why we didn't win. Full credit to St. Mike's, they never quit."[35]

For Wolves fans this latest anguish was salt in a decades-old wound. If the 2000-01 Sudbury Wolves were not destined for a Memorial Cup run, what hope did the franchise have? A letter to the editor published in *The Sudbury Star* a few weeks after Sudbury was eliminated reflected the sense of disappointment that seemed to plague the team and its followers:

'1932'–- that's what the banner says. And while the banner that hangs from the rafters of the Sudbury Arena–- commemorating the Wolves' last and only Memorial Cup–- is supposed to be looked upon with pride, it instead draws our attention to the frustration and failure that yearly befalls our hockey club. Now, it's happened again … And so we, the faithful fans, must wait again until next year, as Sudbury hockey fans have done since 1932. And we'll dutifully support our team, take our familiar seats, cough up $2 for a pitifully small bag of popcorn and, perhaps, during a particularly long stoppage in play, we'll stare up at that damn banner that says, 'Sudbury Wolves 1932 Memorial Cup Champions.'[36]

DIRTY THIRTY

The 2001-02 season was generally a forgettable one for the Sudbury Wolves, but a few players of local origin managed to make a notable impact. After snagging defenceman Ryan Hastings seventeenth overall in the 2001 OHL

Priority Selection, the Wolves used their second-round choice to take gritty winger and Sudbury resident Zach Stortini. "It's such a great town … I'm also looking forward to playing for Bert Templeton," the 16-year-old Stortini told *The Sudbury Star*.[37] The Wolves later added Sudburian forward Trevor Blanchard in a trade with Mississauga. Hometown rookie forward Bobby Chaumont led the Wolves in goals (24) and points (50). "It was an interesting situation because … they lost a lot of players the year I came in. I believe we were eight or nine rookies on the team," says Chaumont two decades later. "So, I got a chance right off the hop to play a lot in all situations."[38] Fellow rookie Stortini, meanwhile, racked up a whopping 187 penalty minutes that season. "I think it was something that was always part of my game, is that tough, physical aspect," Stortini, whose father Tim played for the Wolves in the 1970s, explains twenty years later. "And I always wanted the opportunity to play and earn that opportunity, so if there was a role that needed to be filled and a spot that would be created or opened up because of that, that was something I was always willing to do."[39]

Templeton was leading a young, inexperienced team, and its winless preseason was not especially encouraging. The regular season was scheduled to open on September 14 at the Sudbury Arena, but the game was postponed in the wake of the terrorist attacks against the United States on September 11, 2001.[40] On September 15, the Wolves dropped the first puck of the year against the Mississauga IceDogs, now coached by team owner Don Cherry. The Sudbury crowd erupted at the sight of Cherry, who was making his IceDogs coaching debut that evening. "It was unbelievable … A sell-out crowd, the first opener sold out here in 30 years, I understand. It must have been my suit," Cherry told *The Sudbury Star* after the game. The Wolves, led by their youngsters, defeated Cherry and the IceDogs by a score of 5-3. Hastings recorded a goal and two assists in his OHL debut.[41]

Unfortunately, the Wolves' youth was largely unable to sustain that success for the rest the season. The team won just four out of their first sixteen games and played particularly badly on the road all year long. This was attributable to a lack of offence, a situation that was worsened when John Winstanley, one of Sudbury's leading scorers, suddenly quit hockey and left the team for unspecified personal reasons in January. Management was also discouraged by the Wolves' performance. In December, after news broke that the North Bay Centennials would be relocating to Saginaw, Michigan, Wolves' governor and vice-president Blaine Smith bluntly told *The Sudbury Star* that "Somewhere along the line, the owners of the Sudbury Wolves will have to make a decision (like) the North Bay owners made … I would hate to see the Sudbury Wolves ever leave." This led one Wolves fan to denounce Smith's comments as "hogwash" and "one-sided, self-serving propaganda." Despite the team's struggles, attendance at the Sudbury Arena still remained among the best in the OHL.[42] The Wolves and Centennials played for the last time on March 9, 2002 at the North Bay Memorial Gardens, bringing an end to a twenty-year rivalry between the two Northern Ontario clubs. The Centennials won by a score of 4-1.[43]

On December 28, the franchise retired Randy Carlyle's No. 6 jersey in a pregame ceremony at the Sudbury Arena. "It's an honour and something that you'd never expect," Carlyle says twenty years later. "I was very, very surprised, and actually stunned by it. It's a huge honour to have your jersey retired in an arena that's very close to your hometown."[44] That night, Carlyle, who grew up in Azilda, now part of Greater Sudbury, received a three-minute standing ovation as his Wolves jersey banner was raised to the rafters. In a speech before the crowd of over 4,300 people, he remarked that "Junior hockey was an enjoyable experience for me, and it was all made possible by the management and coaches I played for with the Wolves." Carlyle compiled 151 career points with the Wolves before embarking on a nineteen-year NHL playing career that included winning the James Norris Memorial Trophy as the league's best defenceman in 1981 and a Stanley Cup in 2007 as the head coach of the Anaheim Ducks.[45]

The Wolves finished with a subpar record of 25-33-5-5, yet still qualified for the postseason. Sudbury met the Barrie Colts in the Eastern Conference quarterfinals. After Barrie bested Sudbury in the first two games of the series, Colts forward and assistant captain Tyler Hanchuk told *The Sudbury Star* that his team would sweep the series. This may have been what lit a fire under the Wolves in Game 3. Templeton pieced together several new lines, Smith had a fantastic 36-save performance, and forward Brody Todd scored "by far the biggest goal of my OHL career" in the early going of overtime to earn a 4-3 Wolves' win.[46] The Colts then backed Sudbury into a corner by capturing Game 4 and taking a 3-1 series lead. The Wolves fought hard in Game 5, rallying back from 2-0 and 3-2 deficits in the third period, but ultimately lost the game 4-3 and conceded the series to the Colts. "I'm not going to make any excuses," Wolves' captain Josh Legge said after his final major junior game. "They outworked us in the series and I am kind of disappointed about that."[47]

Another premature exit from the playoffs left the Wolves with a long summer to reflect on their future. It had been a less than glamorous way to conclude what happened to be Templeton's twenty-fifth season in the OHL. "I'd sure like to win a Memorial Cup here," he had told *The Star* a couple of weeks before the loss.[48] Little did Templeton know, his amazing career in major junior hockey was about to come to an unceremonious end. Wolves' fans appeared committed to the team despite another discouraging season. When an April Fool's joke was broadcasted over the radio in Sudbury stating that the franchise was moving to St. Ignace, Michigan, local Telemedia offices were flooded with phone calls in protest.[49]

WHAT COULD HAVE BEEN?

The Wolves entered the 2002-03 season with a modest outlook. Templeton and team officials believed their team would finish somewhere in the middle of the Eastern Conference standings, and with the right attitude and work ethic could surprise fans and observers alike. Fifteen players returned for another season, including Chaumont, Hastings, Blanchard, and Stortini, who was named team captain in September. Stortini had just turned 17-years-old, making him the youngest captain in the OHL at the time. "It was quite an honour and quite a privilege to be selected as captain by a legendary coach like Bert Templeton," recalls Stortini.[50] The Wolves still had one of the youngest teams in the league, and with Smith moving on to professional hockey, Joel Whitmarsh, a sophomore goaltender with a handful OHL games to his name, took over the starting job in goal.[51] With Templeton at the fore, supporters of the team believed the Wolves could remain competitive. As reporter Bruce Heidman of *The Star* wrote in the days leading up the 2002-03 season, Templeton had "brought the franchise a level of respect and continuity that had been missing at times over the club's 31-year history."[52]

The Wolves' season opener was an omen of what was to come. The Ottawa 67's walked into the Sudbury Arena on September 20 and pummeled the home team by a score of 7-1, thwarting what could have been Templeton's one-hundredth regular season win with the Wolves organization. "They just plain kicked our butts," said Sudbury's head coach.[53] Things went from bad to worse for the Wolves, with the 2002-03 season ending up as one of the most abysmal in team history. A brutal eleven-game winless streak starting in late October came to an end on November 22 when Joel Whitmarsh posted his first OHL shutout in a 3-0 Wolves win over the Majors.[54]

Overall, the season was a painful one for players, fans, and management. "It was a pretty dreadful season," remembers Chaumont.[55] The Wolves were plainly snake-bitten offensively. The team scored the second-fewest goals in the OHL, and Chaumont was the sole Wolf to crack the 20-goal barrier. The team's 2002 first rounder, forward Brett Connolly, recorded five points and zero goals in his rookie season; he was traded to the Greyhounds the following year. Fans responded to the Wolves' poor play; attendance dropped by an average of nearly 350 fans per game. On January 30, with twenty games remaining, Mark Burgess said that he owed it "to the fans, season ticket holders and our advertisers to make changes with management and coaching" if he did not see big improvements.[56]

In the end that was exactly what transpired. With a measly sixteen wins, the Wolves finished second last in the OHL standings. This marked the first time in Templeton's twenty-six-year career that he did not lead his team into the postseason. On March 21, it was announced that Templeton had been fired, a move which surprised both the coach and his players. For Burgess the logic behind the decision was simple: "We have just gone from 39 wins to 35 to 25 to 16 this year ... so changes had to be made." Templeton finished his stint in Sudbury with a coaching record of 115-124-22-11. At the time of his departure, he was one game short of being the longest-serving coach in Wolves' history, and sat second all-time for wins as well.[57] Templeton did not go quietly and sought payment for the fifth and final year of his deal along with punitive damages. In mid-September, *The Sudbury Star* reported that he and the Wolves had reached an out-of-court settlement. Around the same time, it came to light that Templeton was suffering from cancer, something which the coach had kept largely private since his diagnosis. Sadly, on December 5, 2003, he passed away at the age of 63.[58] "I learned a lot from him," Zack Stortini says of Bert Templeton all these years later. "I owe him a lot of thanks for the opportunity he gave me as a hockey player."[59]

The Templeton era had come to a tragic conclusion. The coach's tenure in Sudbury had begun with such great expectations, only to experience a host of bad breaks, close-calls, and what-ifs. A litany of future NHL players, including Derek MacKenzie, Alexei Semenov, and Mike Smith, had come and gone, yet the Wolves did not have much to show for it aside from a division championship. Fans were undoubtedly beleaguered by the closing of another Memorial Cup window, but had shown that they were committed to moving ahead alongside their team through thick and thin. The abrupt end to Templeton's colourful career and life seemed to typify what had been one of the more disappointing periods in the Wolves' history. Having shown so much potential, Sudbury Wolves fans, players, and management still cannot help but wonder—what could have been?

CHAPTER 9:

CINDERELLA STORY, 2003-2007

Bert Templeton's departure left a sizeable void in the Sudbury Wolves' organization. The franchise was in rebuilding mode but had no coach or general manager to lead the way. With an important offseason approaching, ownership needed to come up with a game plan fast. Blaine Smith served as interim general manager while leading the search for a replacement head coach. Mark Burgess made it clear that the Wolves were in no rush to hire a new bench boss, though he did allude to who his ideal candidate might be: "There's a certain person who is coaching in the AHL who is from Sudbury who, if he wants both roles, that would be fine."[1] In short order Burgess and the Wolves would get their man, and this individual would in due time bring Sudbury to the cusp of major junior hockey greatness.

SUDBURY'S FAVOURITE SON

The 2003-04 season was a turning point in Wolves history. The tides of change began for the organization as they so often do in the world of sports: the draft. In May 2003, the organization selected defenceman Marc Staal of the Thunder Bay Kings with the second overall pick in the 2003 OHL Draft. At six-foot-two and 185-pounds, the 16-year-old rearguard played a style of hockey that some compared to the likes of Chris Pronger and Rob Blake. "It's pretty exciting to get drafted that high ... I know Sudbury is a good hockey town and lots of good players have been through there," said Staal. The Wolves chose defenceman Adam McQuaid as well as winger Nick Foligno, son of Wolves' legend Mike Foligno, in the third and fifth rounds, respectively.[2]

Then, about one month later, Mike Foligno himself was hired as the new coach and general manager. An experienced AHL coach and a former NHL player, the return of Foligno to his hometown sent waves of enthusiasm throughout the city. One fan wrote to *The Sudbury Star* to proclaim that "Sunny days are here again ... for the long-suffering fans of the Sudbury Wolves." Burgess described the signing as "a great moment in the history of the Sudbury Wolves," while Foligno called it "a very exciting time for me and my family ... We're all coming back home." Bobby Chaumont describes Foligno as "definitely a player's coach," adding that "my relationship with Mike was great right off the hop ... Mike was a great coach to play for."[3] With the addition of Mike Foligno, the Wolves featured the most Sudburians in the organization since 1995: assistant general manager Oscar Clouthier, assistant coach Bryan Verreault, and players Stortini, Chaumont, Eric Larochelle, Jordan Prevost, and Mike Mills.[4]

The Sudbury Community Arena also became an increasingly prevalent topic around this time. The declining state of the complex, now over 50-years-old, had been a focus of discussion for years, especially in comparison to other OHL arenas throughout the province that were either recently remodeled or newly constructed. The City of Greater Sudbury had already contributed millions of dollars to upgrade the arena facilities in the recent past when in early 2003 the Wolves proposed a $2.4 million renovation to the Sudbury Arena. It would involve the construction of about a dozen corporate boxes along the arena's north side. Blaine Smith, at the time serving as interim general manager, stated that this would allow the franchise to diversify its revenue streams. Furthermore, he again alluded to the possibility of a relocation if the Wolves did not modernize, stating that "what happened to the North Bay Centennials ... is possible in any OHL city that falls behind the times." The idea was hailed by the local press as indicative of the Wolves' commitment to the community and as something that would greatly benefit the city, fans, and the team's business model. Although the plan had to be postponed because the club could not rally the required corporate sponsorships, it would certainly not be the last time that the city would be faced with decisions about the fate of the Sudbury Arena.[5]

Filled with a young, tough roster and fresh leadership, the rebuilding Wolves nevertheless strove to improve upon the previous season's dismal showing. Multiple media outlets, including *The Toronto Star* and *Canadian Press*, had projected the Wolves to miss the playoffs. An unphased Mike Foligno predicted that "It will be a good, competitive, physical product, one that will come together to win a lot of hockey games." This self-assuredness proved to be crucial during what was a grind of a season. Foligno, dubbed "Sudbury's favourite son," won his Wolves' coaching debut on September 19 when his team toppled the Erie Otters by a score of 4-0 in front of an energized home crowd. German goaltender Patrick Ehelechner, plucked by the Wolves in the 2003 CHL Import Draft, earned the shutout in his first OHL game. "I'm very proud of the team and thanked them for making me proud and winning it for me," said Foligno.[6]

The rest of the season was difficult for the Wolves, but they still managed to exceed expectations. Although Sudbury finished last in the Central Division with a record of 25-32-6-5, they squeezed into the OHL playoffs with the eighth and final seed in the Eastern Conference. Chaumont, who had attended the Detroit Red Wings' training camp over the summer, again led the team in goals (31), and tied for first in points (63) with teammate Rafal Martynowski, who had been acquired in October from the Kitchener Rangers. That year, Chaumont set a franchise record for most consecutive seasons as the team's leading scorer (three), and became the first Wolves' player in three seasons to be named to the OHL all-star team.[7] Captain and fan favourite Zack Stortini, now a prospect of the Edmonton Oilers after getting selected in the 2003 NHL Entry Draft, scored 20 goals while registering a characteristic 151 penalty minutes. The Wolves' defensive core was young, featuring rookies Staal, McQuaid, Kyle Lamb, and Jonathan D'Aversa, each of whom stepped up and embraced the challenge. Ehelechner was steady from start to finish, finishing with a goals-against average of 2.87, a .915 save percentage, and three shutouts.

The Wolves were matched with the conference-leading St. Michael's Majors in the first round of the playoffs in a classic case of David versus Goliath. Toronto was the only team in the Eastern Conference that Sudbury had not beaten that season, with the Wolves losing all six games.[8] The series did not start how the Wolves had hoped. The Majors blanked Sudbury 2-0 in Game 1 in Toronto. The Wolves responded in kind on March 21 at the Sudbury Arena with a 2-0 victory of their own, handing Toronto its first loss since February 22. Ehelechner posted the shutout, while Martynowski and Chaumont scored for Sudbury. However, the Wolves failed to harness this momentum, dropping the next two contests to Toronto by scores of 3-1 and 2-1. The stellar play of Majors' goaltender Justin Peters, along with some tough penalty calls, had put an already underdog Wolves team at a bigger disadvantage. After Sudbury's loss in Game 4, a frustrated coach Foligno remarked that "It's really difficult to figure out what kind of a game the referee is going to call. We know they may call it a little tight, but some of the calls were beyond belief."[9]

The threat of imminent elimination sprung the Wolves into action. In Game 5 the Wolves won their first match in Toronto that season with a huge 4-3 overtime victory. Stortini scored the game-winning goal, while rookie netminder Kevin Beech stopped every shot he faced after Ehelechner was forced to leave the game due to an injury. Ehelechner returned in Game 6 and posted another shutout as the home team downed the Majors 4-0 to tie the best-of-seven series. "We're riding really, really high right now, we have a ton of confidence and I don't think they do," overage defenceman Dene Poulin said after the win before over 4,600 roaring fans.[10]

Many Wolves supporters flocked south to Toronto to attend Game 7 on March 30. In fact, there were at least as many, if not more, Wolves fan in attendance as there were Majors fans at the St. Michael's College School Arena, leading to sporadic "Go Wolves Go" chants throughout the game. Within fifteen minutes the Wolves were losing 3-0, and despite goals by rookies Stefan Blaho and Benoît Pouliot, the Majors won by a score of 5-2. Toronto goalkeeper Peters scored his team's fifth goal on an empty net with about two minutes remaining in the game, which was believed to be only the second time a netminder scored a goal in the OHL. The Wolves had certainly put on a "gutsy" performance, wrote *The Toronto Star*. Mike Foligno applauded his team for nearly stealing the series and for disproving those who thought that "we wouldn't be winning any games at all." Remaining positive, the coach affirmed that "We're looking for bigger and better things next year."[11]

BIG BEN

The Wolves did, in fact, take a step forward in the 2004-05 season. With the entire NHL season lost to a lockout that year, the Wolves were the primary source of entertainment for hockey fanatics in Sudbury. Rafal Martynowski, Bobby Chaumont, and Zack Stortini once more provided scoring and a veteran presence up front, while the team's young defence core only grew stronger with time. Patrick Ehelechner remained Sudbury's go-to-guy between the pipes, but Kevin Beech made a case for himself with some solid play in the second half of the season.[12] A number of new faces in Sudbury's lineup had a positive effect as well. Nick Foligno made his Wolves' debut, accumulating 10 goals, 38 points, and over 100 penalty minutes in his rookie campaign. Fellow freshman Ryan McDonough, selected fifth overall by the Wolves in 2004, showed offensive potential by scoring 15 goals on the year. Even so, McDonough, like other top Wolves draft picks before him, did not last long in Sudbury. The following off-season, he requested a trade and was dealt to the Saginaw Spirit.[13]

The loss of this top prospect was overshadowed by the meteoric rise of Benoît Pouliot. Chosen 207th overall by the Wolves in the 2002 OHL Priority Selection, the six-foot-three, 180-pound left-winger earned a full-time roster spot with Sudbury in the 2004-05 season. Pouliot netted a hat trick in his second game of the season—a 6-1 win over the Erie Otters—and racked up

19 points in his first 14 games.[14] He proceeded to take the league by storm, scoring 29 goals and 67 points in 67 games and becoming the second player in Wolves history to win the Emms Family Award as the OHL's rookie of the year. "I was pretty surprised … I never thought I would get it, so it was a bonus. It was great," explained Pouliot upon receiving the news.[15] The native of St. Isidore, Ontario, must have been even more shocked when he was then selected as the CHL's Rookie of the Year, joining the ranks of players like Sidney Crosby, Vincent Lecavalier, and Joe Thornton before him.[16] Pouliot became the first Wolves' player to receive this award since its introduction in 1988. Having captured the attention of the entire hockey world, Pouliot was selected fourth overall by the Minnesota Wild in the 2005 NHL Draft ("The Sidney Crosby Sweepstakes"), while his teammate Marc Staal was chosen a few picks later by the New York Rangers.

On March 6, 2005 Bobby Chaumont also made headlines when he set an OHL record for most consecutive regular season games played. The Wolves travelled to Sarnia to take on the Sting, where Chaumont was met with a standing ovation from the rival crowd for skating in his 267th straight game, surpassing the OHL record previously held by Mike Oliveira. The Wolves and their fans honoured Chaumont with a ceremony at the team's next home game. By the end of the season Chaumont's streak totalled 272 games, which two decades later still remains the league record.[17] "Throughout my whole career I was always prided myself on playing no matter what," Chaumont explains. "So, it was a pretty cool feeling once I hit that." Chaumont went on to play professionally across North America and Europe before hanging up his skates for good in 2020 and settling back in his hometown where it all began.[18]

The regular season as a whole was a great success for the Wolves. Upon registering a winning record of 32-23-6-7, the team entered the postseason sitting fifth in a very tight Eastern Conference. Sudbury was not a team to be taken lightly. On December 17, 2004, for example, the Wolves defeated the London Knights by a score of 5-2 at the John Labatt Centre in London, bringing an end to the Knights' OHL record-setting streak of 31 consecutive games without a loss.[19] The Wolves even set a franchise record for fewest goals against (185) in a season. Mike Foligno received accolades for "building the Sudbury Wolves into a hard-working winner that emulates the blue-collar style of the City of Greater Sudbury." The Wolves completely sold out a record seven regular season games, while the average attendance at the Sudbury Arena that season (over 4,200) was the highest the team had ever seen. The increase of nearly 900 fans per game from the previous year was the largest jump in the league and put the Wolves fifth in the OHL in average attendance.[20] In the words of coach Foligno, the Wolves provided "an entertainment value ... to the city and to the people that live in the city. It's a sense of pride that the team performs, not only successfully, but performs very hard ... each and every night."[21]

The Wolves played the evenly matched Brampton Battalion in the opening round of the postseason. The Wolves had been the only team in the OHL to go winless in overtime that year, dropping thirteen games in the extra frame in the regular season; that all changed on March 24 in Game 1 at the Brampton Centre for Sports and Entertainment. Pouliot scored late in the third to tie it for Sudbury and force overtime. Less than halfway through the fourth period, Martynowski fed a pass to forward Kevin Baker, acquired from Owen Sound at the trade deadline in January, who buried his first career playoff goal and won the game for the Wolves by a score of 3-2. The Wolves went up 3-1 in the series but failed to clinch the round in Game 5 after the Battalion chased Ehelechner from the net in the first period and won the game.[22]

The Battalion travelled north to Sudbury to face the hungry Wolves in Game 6 of the Eastern Conference quarterfinals. The Wolves twice blew a two-goal lead before Nick Foligno scored his second of the night in the third period to put his team up by a score of 4-3. With over a minute left in the game, a desperate Brampton team pulled its goalie for the extra attacker. Forward Dan McDonald silenced the capacity crowd at the Sudbury Arena with his second goal of the game and pushed it into overtime. An additional twenty minutes of hockey solved nothing. Then, early in the second overtime period, Pouliot scored the series-winning goal in front of an ecstatic crowd of 5,085 fans. The Wolves had won their first playoff series since 2001. "It's been a long time coming you know," said Chaumont after the victory.[23]

The Ottawa 67's awaited the Wolves in the Eastern Conference semifinals. Sudbury held home-ice advantage in the series, leading Nick Foligno to declare that "Sudbury fans are unbelievable ... To have them through this series is unbelievable." There was a sombre atmosphere in Game 1 with the news of former Wolves defenceman Brad Morgan's sudden passing. The 25-year-old had been killed in a single-vehicle car accident in Toronto earlier that week; the Wolves organization held a moment of silence at the Sudbury Arena prior to the game in Morgan's memory. The 67's took Game 1 by a score of 3-2, with Ottawa goaltender Danny Battochio making 48-saves on the evening. Foligno made a change in net for Game 2, giving Beech his first career OHL playoff start. In that game the Wolves clawed back from a 2-0 deficit to the tie it up on goals by Jonathan D'Aversa and Stefan Blaho. Sudbury prevailed in double overtime for the second time in the postseason when Mike Mills chipped a rebound passed Battochio.[24] The Wolves headed east to the nation's capital with the series split.

Events took a negative turn for the Wolves in Game 3 at the Ottawa Civic Arena. The 67's won by a score of 6-2, but it was the conduct of Wolves forward Kyle Musselman that caught everyone's attention. In the third period, the 19-year-old Musselman punched 67's winger Mark Mancari in the head from behind. Ottawa coach and general manager Brian Kilrea told *The Ottawa Citizen* that the incident reminded him of Todd Bertuzzi's infamous punch on Steve Moore during the 2003-04 NHL season. Mike Foligno did not appreciate Kilrea's comments, calling them "really unnecessary and drew attention away from the real issue here." On April 15 the OHL handed down its judgement; Musselman received a lifetime ban from the league and the Wolves were fined $10,000. The Wolves' forward was shocked by the decision: "Did I mean to hurt him? No. Did it happen? Yes. The league dealt with it the way they saw fit and that's the way it goes."[25]

The Wolves did their best to ignore the fallout from the Musselman affair and focus on beating the 67's. Battochio and 67's forward Julian Talbot, both from Sudbury, were the first two stars in Game 4 as Ottawa trounced the Wolves by a score of 5-2 to take a 3-1 lead in the series. The Wolves bounced back with a 6-2 win in Game 5 before over 5,700 frenzied fans on multipoint nights by Stortini, Foligno, and Ryan Hastings.[26] Having cracked the almost superhuman Battochio for the first time, the Pack travelled back to Ottawa for Game 6 with renewed confidence. The 67's went up 4-1 in the second period, prompting Mike Foligno to pull Beech in favour of Ehelechner. It was too late, however, as Ottawa ended the Wolves' season with a 7-4 victory. Mancari netted a hat-trick and an assist, a storybook end for the target of Musselman's attack. Goaltending had been a decisive factor in the series, with Battochio averaging 43 saves per game. "He had one heck of a series," remembers Chaumont of Battochio's performance. Years later, Chaumont still looks back on his final season with the Wolves as probably his most enjoyable. "We had a great team. Unfortunately, we just fell short in the second round," he explains.[27]

It was also the end of major junior hockey for Zack Stortini, who remains the longest-serving captain in Wolves' history and the franchise's all-time leader in penalty minutes (746). Stortini went on to play over 250 NHL games for the Edmonton Oilers and Nashville Predators and also won two Calder Cups while playing in the AHL before retiring in 2019. Now serving as a member of the Wolves' coaching staff, Stortini still has fond memories of his days playing for the team, and states that "I owe a great deal and am very thankful for the opportunity the Wolves as a group have afforded me and my family."[28]

UNDERACHIEVERS

Mike Foligno and the Wolves entered the 2005-06 OHL season with a wealth of high-end talent. Eight Wolves players attended NHL training camps in the summer, including Marc Staal, who signed his first pro-hockey contract with the New York Rangers in September. Luckily for the Wolves, he would play two more years in Sudbury before entering the NHL. In September, Staal was named team captain, something that the 18-year-old defenceman took seriously: "To be named captain of any team is an honour, so to be named captain of the Sudbury Wolves feels good. It's something I take pride in." The Wolves were similarly blessed with the return of Benoît Pouliot in early October after he was one of the last cuts from the Minnesota Wild; he repeated his scoring ways by burying a hat trick in his first game back. Kevin Beech, recently drafted by the Tampa Bay Lightning, sat firmly as the team's number one goaltender. The trend of Sudbury's first-rounders failing to pan out continued with centre Brett Parnham, who was chosen thirteenth overall by the Wolves in May 2005 only to be traded to the Oshawa Generals at the following OHL trade deadline.[29]

Sudbury also acquired Nigerian-born rookie forward Akim Aliu from the Windsor Spitfires at the trade deadline. Aliu had demanded a trade from Windsor after a highly publicized clash with veteran teammate Steven Downie, who himself was traded to the Peterborough Petes. During a practice, just days after Aliu had refused to participate in degrading hazing activities, Downie purposefully sticked Aliu in the face, knocking out several of his teeth and prompting a fight between the two players. In 2020, in an article published by *The Player's Tribune*, Aliu recounted the confrontation in hope of shedding light on "the biggest problems facing the game I love – and how we can fix them." That same year, Aliu cofounded the Hockey Diversity Alliance, a group of current and former NHL players who strive to fight discrimination in hockey.[30]

It was a turbulent year for the Wolves, who went through glaring hot and cold streaks throughout. What the team lacked in consistency it made up for in physicality and fisticuffs; the Wolves led the OHL in total penalty minutes (1,820) in the 2005-06 regular season, having finished second overall (1,647) the previous year. Sophomore forward Devin Didiomete led the Pack with over 200 penalty minutes, while Hastings, Foligno, Pouliot, McQuaid, and Swedish import winger Anton Hedman all amassed over 100 minutes of their own. A noteworthy game for the Wolves occurred on September 30 against the Oshawa Generals, when a 15-year-old John Tavares played at the Sudbury Community Arena for the first time as an OHL player. Prior to the game, Tavares, whose mother is from Sudbury, told *The Sudbury Star* that the Wolves "were probably my favourite OHL team. I used to go and watch the games with my uncle." The young phenom and future NHL superstar scored a beautiful goal on his first shift that night, though the Wolves came out with a 6-2 win.[31]

The Wolves' top players led the team to a third-place finish in the Central Division. Nick Foligno sat atop the Wolves' scoresheet with 70 points on the season. Pouliot led the way with 35 goals, followed close by Kevin Baker who broke out with a 34-goal campaign of his own. In his inaugural season as captain, Staal upped his offensive game by posting 11 goals and 49 points. Both Staal and Pouliot made the Wolves proud by representing Team Canada at the 2006 World Junior Ice Hockey Championships in British Columbia. Canada defeated Russia in the final to win the gold medal on home soil and Staal was named the best defenceman of the tournament. Mike Foligno felt that his squad that year was "as good as any team in the league and we have as good a chance as anyone … What's really going to be important is that our players believe it and play like they believe it."[32]

As winter turned to spring, the OHL playoffs yet again provided the city of Sudbury with the opportunity to watch the Wolves compete for junior hockey supremacy. The Wolves played the Kingston Frontenacs in the opening round. The first game of the Eastern Conference quarter-finals at the Kingston Memorial Centre was a wild one. The first period ended with a ten-player scrum at centre ice that saw Akim Aliu square off with Kingston's six-foot-seven defenceman Justin Wallingford. Midway through the game the Wolves were ahead by a score of 3-1 on two goals by Pouliot, but it was the Frontenacs who replied with four unanswered goals and took Game 1. The series went to Game 6 at the Sudbury Arena, with the Wolves holding a 3-2 lead. Beech posted his second shutout of the series as the Wolves won 4-0 and advanced to the next round of the postseason. "They are a veteran club built for the playoffs. Their big players really performed well," Frontenacs' coach Jim Hulton told *The Kingston Whig*. Pouliot had a monster series, notching eight goals and three assists over six games.[33]

The Wolves next faced the powerhouse Peterborough Petes. Ranked among the top-ten teams in the CHL, the Petes featured top NHL prospect Jordan Staal, the younger brother of Wolves' captain Marc. The two brothers downplayed any suggestions of a sibling rivalry playing into the series, with both Marc and Jordan emphasizing they were focused on their respective teams advancing to the Eastern Conference finals. "But I'd definitely like to win," admitted Marc. "That would be a lot of fun." The Petes outmatched the Wolves from the get-go, capitalizing on the Wolves' discipline problems in the penalty-filled series. Peterborough scored three powerplay goals in Game 2 to win by a score of 6-1 and put the Wolves behind two games to none in the series.[34]

The Wolves found themselves at risk of getting swept following a third consecutive loss to the Petes. Fighting for their lives in Game 4 at the Sudbury Arena on April 11, the Wolves were without both an injured Pouliot and a suspended Hedman for the second consecutive game. The Pack fell behind 2-0 in the first fourteen minutes of the game. Goals by local resident Kyle Hope and rookie Gerome Giudice tied the game up before Steve Downie, "a player Sudbury fans love to hate," put the Petes ahead early in the third period. Minutes later, Downie took a double-minor penalty to put the Wolves on the powerplay. Nick Foligno stepped up with his first goal of the postseason with less than five minutes left in the match to send Game 4 into overtime. A bad five-minute checking-from-behind penalty against Mike Mills then put Peterborough on the powerplay. About three-and-a-half minutes into the penalty kill, Petes' forward Patrick Kaleta tipped a point shot that hit the post and then found its way past Beech to complete the sweep of the Wolves in four straight games. The franchise's second consecutive conference semi-final exit was a tough pill to swallow for the Wolves and their supporters, especially given how much promise this year's roster had shown. Wolves' forward and Sault Ste. Marie native Matt Dias summarized the feelings of his teammates, fans, and management when he stated "We did underachieve."[35]

CINDERELLA STORY

The Sudbury Wolves 2006-07 season marked the team's thirty-fifth season in the OHL. The year 2007 was also the seventy-fifth anniversary of the city's only Memorial Cup championship. But, before the year got underway, many fans were already jaded from the team's repeated playoff failure. Although the Wolves had improved their regular-season finish each year under Mike Foligno, a poll conducted by *The Sudbury Star* in September revealed that over 60 percent of Wolves fans believed that the team would either miss the playoffs or lose in the first round. This view was somewhat surprising given that that year's incarnation of the Pack was not lacking in skill. With Benoît Pouliot graduating to the professional ranks, Nick Foligno, picked by the Ottawa Senators in the first round of the 2006 NHL Entry Draft, was charged with leading the Wolves offence. Marc Staal returned as captain and as the figurehead on a blueline that still included Jonathan D'Aversa and Adam McQuaid. Sudbury chose winger Jared Staal, the youngest of the four Staal brothers, with its first-round selection in the 2006 OHL Draft.[36]

The Wolves struggled during the regular season and appeared to confirm the fears of their fanbase. In the season opener at the Sudbury Arena, the Wolves got smoked 10-4 by the Mississauga IceDogs. The Wolves secured their first win of the season one week later, a 6-0 victory against Toronto where, in a pregame ceremony at the Sudbury Arena, the franchise retired Ron Duguay's No. 10 jersey, honouring a local player that ranks second all-time in assists (230), third in goals (130), and third in points (360).[37] "I would like to express my sincere thanks to the Sudbury Wolves organization and to all the fans," said Duguay in a press release upon receiving the news that his number would be retired by his junior club.[38]

The team could not seem to get any rhythm going, prompting management to make some midseason moves to bolster the roster. In November, Sudbury sent a draft pick to the Belleville Bulls in exchange for 19-year-old left winger Andrew Self.[39] Months later, with the trade deadline drawing near, Mike Foligno made a handful of critical deals. He shipped Kevin Beech to the Otters to make room for Danish netminder Sebastian Dahm, who joined the Wolves from Sarnia in a separate trade. Foligno then swapped a third-round pick in 2007 for defenceman Zack McCullough from the Owen Sound Attack. In a blockbuster exchange on January 9, the Wolves grabbed dynamic scorer Justin Donati from the Majors in exchange for Jesse Messier, Justin Vaive, and a couple of 2008 draft picks.[40]

The Wolves did not end the season on a particularly strong note, but the team still displayed glimmers of something special. Despite losing seven of its final eight regular season games, the injection of new blood into the lineup was enough to get the Wolves into the playoffs as the sixth seed in the East Conference with a record of 29-30-3-6. Nick Foligno led the team with 31 goals and 88 points, while Donati brought much needed firepower by registering 35 points in 28 games with Sudbury. Four other Wolves scored at least 20 goals. On the backend, Marc Staal further solidified himself as one of the CHL's premier defenceman and won another gold medal with

Team Canada at the 2007 World Junior Ice Hockey Championships in Sweden. There were some struggles between the pipes as Dahm posted a 3.36 goals-against-average and .890 save-percentage in 24 games with his new team. Wolves' fans proved that Sudbury remained a bastion of OHL hockey, boasting one of the best home attendance figures in the league with about 4,200 fans per game and a strong season ticket base.[41]

The Wolves' first opponent in the 2007 OHL playoffs was the Mississauga IceDogs, the team that had scored the most goals in the entire CHL that year. The Wolves' chances of overcoming Mississauga seemed meagre, with 54.6 percent of *Sudbury Star* readers believing the local team would not escape the quarterfinals.[42] Several members of the 2006-07 Wolves shared their memories of the team's epic playoff run in a 2017 article written by Mike Commito. Nick Foligno, for example, reminisced that the team "was better than it probably was in the standings ... we just didn't come together until the playoffs really hit."[43] From the outset of the postseason, the Wolves completely elevated their play. Sudbury stole Game 1 in Mississauga by a score of 5-4, with Self scoring the game-winner late in the third period. The IceDogs defeated the Wolves in Game 2, but that proved to be the heavy favourite's only win of the series. The Wolves won the next three games in a row, dispatching Mississauga in five games. The top line of Foligno, Self, and Donati combined for 25 points in the series while Dahm stopped 91 of 97 shots he faced. Marc Staal drew widespread praise for his play in the first round, displaying defensive acumen, game-changing physicality, and enhanced offensive flair.[44]

Riding the wave of this upset, the Wolves met the rival Barrie Colts in the second round. The Colts finished first in the Eastern Conference and had won almost twenty more regular season games than the Wolves. The odds were not in Sudbury's favour. The Wolves stunned the Colts with a 4-3 overtime victory in Game 1. Donati, who scored the game-winning goal that night, later stated that "The first game in Barrie, we won in overtime, that was probably the moment where I thought maybe there is a chance we go far." In Game 2, McCullough scored in the second overtime period to secure another 4-3 win for Sudbury. The Wolves took advantage of the momentum and never looked back, sweeping the Colts in four straight games, including a third consecutive overtime win in Game 3 on a goal by DiDiomete. When the Wolves ended the series on April 11 in front of over 5,400 adoring fans with a 4-2 win, it marked the first time the franchise had swept an OHL four game series, and only the third time it ever advanced to the third round of the league playoffs. Broomsticks hit the ice of the Sudbury Arena to celebrate the slaying of Barrie, a team that had not lost three consecutive games all season long. Never in its history had the Colts been swept in a playoff series. "I think that sweep against Barrie really helped out our confidence and we kind of just built off of that," said Jonathan D'Aversa in an interview ten years later.[45]

As the Wolves prepared for the club's first Eastern Conference finals in twelve years, the players and coaching staff increasingly drew inspiration from a few unique sources. The most obvious was the atmosphere in the Sudbury Community Arena. "I'll never forget the arena … That was the most unbelievable thing to watch. Sudbury is such a great hockey town," once remembered Nick Foligno. "It was so physically loud," recalled Akim Aliu. "I remember standing beside Nick and Marc on the bench during 'O Canada' and I couldn't speak to them it was literally so loud in there." Adam McQuaid, a member of the 2011 Stanley Cup champion Boston Bruins, later acknowledged that "I've been fortunate to play in a lot of exciting atmospheres since then, but that was up there for sure."[46]

A lesser-known factor in the Wolves' sudden success came from Mike Foligno. Before the playoffs started, the Wolves coach introduced his team to a film and bestselling book by Rhonda Byrne entitled *The Secret*, which highlighted the power of positive thinking in achieving success.[47] "My Dad made us sit down and watch it … You roll your eyes at first but I don't think we realized how influential it was until we started getting on our roll in the playoffs," once explained Nick Foligno. According to D'Aversa, Mike Foligno "got everybody believing in *The Secret* and that kind of went like that throughout the playoffs. We kind of used that to fall back on if we had any ups and downs." Donati concurred, stating that "it was a great message to send to the team. Coach Foligno was a great motivator and he kept the guys on their toes. He was great at what he did and that was a big reason why we went as far as we did."[48]

By the time the Wolves entered the Eastern Conference finals, practically the entire city of Sudbury was stricken with hockey fever. Several local establishments opened their doors to allow fans to watch televised away games or sold out matches at home.[49] The Wolves faced the Belleville Bulls, a team that coincidentally featured Justin Donati's twin brother, Tyler. "We both really want to win," Tyler told *The National Post.* "We don't trash-talk or anything, but we both want it. We want to keep on playing and get to the Memorial Cup."[50] Sudbury lost Game 1 in Belleville, ending a seven-game playoff win streak and leaving the team trailing in a series for the first time that postseason. An unlikely hero emerged in Game 2 when rookie Jared Staal scored in overtime to give Sudbury the 3-2 win. After narrowly losing Game 3 at home in overtime, the Wolves took Game 4 by a score of 3-2 on another overtime goal by Justin Donati. Sudbury then registered a 4-1 win in Game 5, making Mike Foligno the winningest playoff coach in club history.[51]

The stage was set for an exhilarating Game 6 at the Sudbury Arena. Before the match, Baker encouraged Wolves fan to "just keep doing what they are doing. They make it hard for the visiting team to come in here." On April 27, the Wolves punched their ticket to the OHL championship in a nail-biting 4-3 triple overtime win. Matt Dias scored the decisive powerplay goal, the biggest of his young career. The 5,743 Wolves fans who packed the house that night "jumped from their seats and yelled with all their might" when Dias deposited the series-winning marker. After exchanging handshakes with the Bulls, Marc Staal, the "unparalleled leader" of the team, hoisted the Bobby Orr Trophy as the Wolves celebrated the organization's first-ever Eastern Conference championship.[52] Mike Foligno had been a player on the 1976 Wolves team that made their own run to the OHL finals, and now had a second shot at glory as a coach. The win was particularly special for Justin Donati: "Playing against my brother in the Eastern Conference championship and then beating him, I couldn't ask for more."[53]

The last test for the Wolves were the Western Conference champion Plymouth Whalers. The Michigan-based franchise had been the OHL's best defensive team during the regular season and sat third in goal-scoring, too. Sudbury fans were convinced that their team, the underdog, would prevail. On the eve of the OHL finals, *The Sudbury Star* commented that

"Regardless of what happens from here on out, the 2006-07 edition of the Sudbury Wolves will be a big part of the franchise lore, a collection that will be talked about for years to come."[54] The energy throughout Sudbury was truly unprecedented in modern memory. "It was incredible, the whole town, buses, churches had 'Go Wolves Go.' We couldn't pay for meals if we tried, it was unbelievable. It was the stuff kids dream about when they think of the OHL," remembered Aliu a decade later.[55]

It was indeed an historic moment for the Wolves and the community at large. Rick Bartolucci, Member of Provincial Parliament for Sudbury and a lifelong hockey fan, convinced members of the Ontario Legislature to wear "Go Wolves Go" buttons during the OHL championship series. Bartolucci praised the Wolves for "uniting the community through our collective pride for Sudbury and in our unanimous good wishes for the team." At a barbeque and pep rally hosted by the city the day before Game 1, Greater Sudbury Mayor John Rodriguez likewise stated that the Wolves had sparked the community like never before. "Your mayor is behind you, and you will carry all of the luck that I can possibly wish for you, because it's the luck of all the citizens of Sudbury," Rodriquez proclaimed before an audience of Wolves fans.[56] "It's been a long time coming for our club," said Nick Foligno on the eve of Game 1. Sudbury's leading playoff scorer with nine goals and 20 points entering the OHL finals, the young Foligno stated that "the history behind it is something special for everyone on the team to be able to be involved with."[57]

The first two games of the J. Ross Robertson Cup finals were played at the Compuware Arena in Michigan. Dias scored the opening goal of the championship series mere minutes into the game. The Wolves held on to the one-goal lead until the third period when the Whalers scored four consecutive goals.[58] Sudbury replied with a rousing 7-3 victory in Game 2. Dias stayed hot with a goal and three assists and Dahm stopped 41 shots on the night. Marc Staal garnered accolades of his own from team-mates, fans, and coaching staff for his leadership throughout the playoffs.[59] Coach Foligno traced the team's success back to a conversation he had with the team captain in January: "we asked him, 'Marc, where do you want to take this team?' And he said 'I think we can win.' From that point on, I think he took his game to the highest level I've ever seen. He's playing like an NHL hockey player."[60]

The city of Sudbury warmly welcomed the Wolves as they returned home for Game 3, the first OHL finals match hosted at the Sudbury Arena in over thirty years. On May 8, *The National Post* published an article capturing the wider significance of the Wolves' Cinderella story. Marc Staal was taken aback by the fans' response, stating that "The sense of pride Sudbury takes in the Wolves is amazing. And it's really opened my eyes." Local bars and restaurants noticed boosts in business as the team pushed deeper and deeper into the playoffs. Coupled with the rising price of nickel, claimed Mayor Rodriguez, the Wolves added "icing on the cake" to what was "a very optimistic time to be living in this city." Mike Foligno fully understood the magnitude of what was at stake: "The last time a Memorial Cup was won by the Sudbury Wolves, it was 1932 … I have a picture of the team in my office. And that team has been talked about for 75 years. I can guarantee you, that if we can take a trip to the Memorial Cup, they'll be talking about these players for the next 75 years."[61]

In the end it was not meant to be. Prior to Game 3, fans could pay a fee to smash an old Plymouth automobile with sledgehammers and cement blocks in a nearby parking lot outside of the Sudbury Arena.[62] The gimmick proved helpful as the Wolves won by a score of 5-4 in overtime thanks again to Donati, eliciting "a deafening roar" from the over 5,700 people at the Sudbury Arena.[63] The Wolves proceeded to lose the next two matches, including a backbreaking overtime defeat in Game 5, giving Plymouth the chance to win its first J. Ross Robertson Cup in Game 6 in Sudbury.[64] On Sunday, May 13, the Wolves and Whalers battled and pushed themselves into overtime for the third time in the series with the score locked 2-2. James Neal shattered the hearts of Wolves fans' everywhere when he scored the decisive goal three minutes into the extra frame, handing Plymouth a 3-2 victory and the league championship. The clock had struck midnight for the Sudbury Wolves.[65]

After a moment of silence as the shock of the sudden loss sunk in, Wolves fans showed one last gesture of support and gratitude for their team with a thunderous "Go Wolves Go" chant. Afterwards, everyone graciously watched the Whalers celebrate, among them Plymouth forward and Sudbury local Vern Cooper. A silver lining came when Marc Staal was awarded the Wayne Gretzky 99 Trophy as the OHL's most valuable player in the playoffs, having accumulated five goals and 20 points in 21 playoff games. Days earlier Staal had been named winner of the Max Kaminsky Trophy as the OHL's best defenceman for that season. Mike Foligno and the players, both proud and saddened that they came so close to winning it all, publicly thanked the people of Sudbury for everything they had offered along the way. "It was great seeing the support we got, just amazing … It blew us away. We were holding back emotions and stuff, but that made it easier to swallow when you know you still have that support from fans," McQuaid assured *The Sudbury Star.*[66]

It had been an astonishing time for Sudbury and the Wolves. The taste of a near-championship run had awakened an already rabid fanbase. Despite falling short of the J. Ross Robertson Cup, the underdog 2006-07 Wolves are still fondly remembered by many residents, and this speaks to just how meaningful this Cinderella story was for the people of Sudbury. "I'm upset it wasn't us but I'm excited for the day that I can be a fan in that stands and watch the team win a championship," said Nick Foligno in 2017. For Dahm, who posted a .934 save-percentage in the 2007 postseason, the Wolves' runner-up status was an achievement in and of itself. "Especially because it's such a hard-working city, a blue-collar city," he explained ten years after the historic run. "I think just the fact we worked so hard and achieved so much with what we came with that I think it was just such an incredible achievement for ourselves and the community."[67] It is this attitude that continues to fuel fans' loyalty to the Sudbury Wolves and keeps alive the shared dream of bringing a Memorial Cup back to the Nickel City.

CHAPTER 10:

AFTERMATH, 2007-2012

GROWING PAINS

Mike Foligno and the Sudbury Wolves shook off the disappointing ending to their amazing playoff surge as quickly as possible and got back to work. Most of the core components of the Bobby Orr Trophy-winning roster did not return to Sudbury for the 2007-08 season. In a rebuilding effort, the Wolves traded away some of their players over the summer, most notably Akim Aliu to the London Knights and Devin DiDiomete to the Sarnia Sting. Mike Foligno sought to strengthen the team's depleted blueline by drafting defenceman Dan Maggio in the first round of the 2007 OHL Priority Selection. The Wolves then snagged winger Marcus Foligno, Mike's younger son, in the second round. Upon becoming the third member of his family to join the Wolves franchise, Marcus said it was a "really great feeling" and that he was happy "to be staying home" in Sudbury. Marcus chose to wear No. 71 with the Wolves, the same number his brother Nick had chosen to wear with the Ottawa Senators and that their father wore with the Toronto Maple Leafs back in the day.[1] Before the season got started, Wolves alumni Randy Carlyle treated the City of Greater Sudbury to an up-close look at the Stanley Cup when he brought the trophy to a local arena as the head coach of the reigning champion Anaheim Ducks.

Long-awaited upgrades to the Sudbury Community Arena came to fruition that season. The Wolves organization had invested $1.5 million to renovate the interior of the building, and in exchange received a 15-year lease on the rink from the municipality. The changes included twelve corporate boxes, the conversion of nearly 1,000 seats into more upscale club seating, a lounge, modernized bathrooms and concessions, and new video terminals. By this time, both city and Wolves' officials were not overly concerned about the future of the nearly 60-year-old barn. When the deal had been announced in 2006, *The Sudbury Star* predicted that improvements would make it possible "to attract all-star games, international hockey events, concerts and even the Memorial Cup."[2] By the time the changes were unveiled in the fall of 2007, the reaction from fans was underwhelming. It was clear to many that this facelift did not put the Wolves' aging den on par with other OHL rinks.[3]

The 2007-08 season was practically the polar opposite of the previous one. The club opened the season with a seven-game road trip as the finishing touches on the Sudbury Arena were being completed. The Wolves' lost their first five games, finally winning on October 5 in London by a score of 3-2. Forward John Kurtz scored the game-winning goal that night, his first in a Wolves' uniform after joining the team in a preseason deal with the Windsor Spitfires. On October 19, the organization raised its first Eastern Conference championship banner to the ceiling of the Sudbury Arena in a pregame ceremony. The gathered crowd was treated to a video montage filled with highlights from the 2006-07 season before the banner was hoisted. The game itself was a "shockingly listless" one for the Wolves, who were shutout 3-0 by the Brampton Battalion and dropped to 2-9-0 on the year.[4]

The rest of the season was, for the most part, just as listless. The Wolves' inexperience shone through time and time again, much to the chagrin of veteran netminder Sebastian Dahm, who by early December had made an OHL-leading 871 saves. In mid-November, the Wolves defeated the Peterborough Petes by a score of 4-2 at the Sudbury Arena, with Marcus Foligno burying his first OHL goal; Sudbury proceeded to lose the next ten matches in a row. "We see ourselves as a team that will make the playoffs, and we'll continue to see ourselves that way until we see no light at the end of the tunnel," Mike Foligno confirmed after the tenth-consecutive loss. The very next game, the Wolves snapped the losing streak with a 4-3 win at home against the Sarnia Sting. Forward J.K. Gill, selected by the Wolves in the 2006 OHL Draft and believed to be the first Sikh to ever play in the OHL, had the first two-goal game of his major junior career that night.[5]

By the New Year, even Mike Foligno could no longer deny that this year's Pack was not destined for the playoffs. In January 2008, captain Kevin Baker, the team's leading scorer, was traded to the Oshawa Generals for centre Eric O'Dell and forward Dean Howard. Forward Gerome Guidice was named the Wolves' new captain. The day after the Baker deal, Dahm was flipped to the Niagara Falls IceDogs for goalie Andrew Loverock, defenceman Chris Van Laren, and two draft picks. "I had a great time in Sudbury, as I've always said … the fans are crazy hockey fans and I loved playing here," stated Dahm after the trade. Without arguably their most valuable player, the Wolves turned to Loverock and Sudbury native Alain Valiquette in goal.[6]

The Wolves finished the season with a record of 17-46-2-3, placing them at the very bottom of the OHL standings. Not since 2003 had the Wolves been out of the playoff picture, but the consensus seemed to be that Mike Foligno would get the team back to winning form in no time. A good pool of prospects in the system helped, too. The Wolves had secured the first overall selections in both the 2008 OHL Priority Selection and the CHL Import Draft, and players like O'Dell and Jared Staal, the latter of whom notched a team-high 21 goals, would be returning to Sudbury for at least another season. "I'm not surprised they didn't make the playoffs, but I hoped we could. I'm very optimistic for next year," one fan told *The Sudbury Star*.[7]

Local hockey enthusiasts found another source of satisfaction in late April when the Sudbury Nickel Capital Wolves, the local AAA midget team, defeated the heavily favoured Winnipeg Thrashers to win the 2008 Telus Cup national title. It was the first time a Sudbury team had won a national title at that level of play, and they did so against a Winnipeg team that had gone 58-1 against Canadian teams in the run-up to the finals. The Thrashers, led by future Vegas Golden Knights captain Mark Stone, were downed by the Nickel Caps by a score of 6-4 during the Sunday afternoon final that received national television coverage. "It is a team of which the community can be justifiably proud," wrote *The Sudbury Star*.[8]

THE MCFARLAND SWEEPSTAKES

As the 2008 OHL Priority Selection approached, the buzz around the league centred on John McFarland. In his draft year the 16-year-old forward from Richmond Hill had compiled 96 goals and 165 points in 76 games while playing for the Toronto Jr. Canadiens Minor Midget AAA team. The consensus top pick, everyone in the hockey community knew the Sudbury Wolves would be taking the six-foot-one, 190-pound superstar centreman well before the announcement was even made official. *The Sudbury Star* reported that "For the Wolves and their hungry fan base, there is something oh-so special about the 2008 OHL Priority Selection, creating a buzz like never before." Yet there were still some questions surrounding McFarland's temperament as the big day drew near. Described as having a "bad boy edge," McFarland sometimes channelled his intensity in a counterproductive way, leading to a few ejections from games and even some suspensions. Scouts seemed to believe he would grow out of it and that it could actually translate well into the OHL. McFarland acknowledged his tendency to lose his cool at times, but reasoned "there will be easier ways to take out my anger next year. In the OHL you can take a five-minute major for fighting and move on."[9]

On May 2, the day before the draft, the Wolves announced their intention to select McFarland first overall at one of Sudbury's largest ever sports media events. The young sniper personally came to town with his family to greet fans and enjoy the "John Tavares-like hype" surrounding him. In front of a full conference room at Sudbury's Travelodge Hotel, McFarland put on a Wolves' jersey with the No. 18 on the back, his preferred No. 6 having been retired by the franchise in honour of Randy Carlyle years earlier. "I hope one day we can retire No. 18," Mark Burgess told the crowd. The Wolves' previous record for early-bird season ticket sales was shattered in anticipation of McFarland's debut. "It's clearly a hockey town … I wanted to play in Sudbury," McFarland stated. In June, Sudbury chose Nikita Filatov with the first pick in the 2008 CHL Import Draft, but the Russian forward and Columbus Blue Jackets prospect never ended up donning a Wolves jersey.[10]

The addition of McFarland fortified a Wolves' lineup that was better, at least on paper, than its last-place finish from the previous season might suggest. Eric O'Dell was given a bigger role with the club after being drafted by the Anaheim Ducks in the 2008 NHL Entry Draft. Jared Staal, who himself was chosen by the Phoenix Coyotes only a few spots after O'Dell, also returned to the fold. Other familiar faces included captain Gerome Giudice, Marcus Foligno, and Matt Dias. Andrew Loverock and Alain Valiquette stayed in place as the Wolves' goaltending duo. "The Sudbury Wolves aren't going to get slapped around this season," defenceman Chris Van Laren declared before the 2008-09 season opener.[11]

The Wolves came out the gate hot only to have their expectations quickly tempered. In the season and home opener, the Wolves skated to a 7-4 win versus the Oshawa Generals that saw Sudbury native Kyle Tarini register two points and a fight. The Wolves next defeated the Barrie Colts and Sarnia Sting to start the year a perfect 3-0-0, but by the end of November owned a losing record. Early on John McFarland demonstrated that he was not, in the words of *The Star*, "a gift from the hockey gods willed onto the Earth to score 100-points and lead the Wolves to instant glory in his rookie season." The rookie forward recorded one assist in his first seven OHL games, only to follow up with six goals and 12 points in the next eight contests.[12]

The Wolves' unbalanced play was akin to Jekyll and Hyde, causing worry among the fanbase over whether the team would qualify for the 2009 postseason.[13] In early January, Akim Aliu, drafted by the Chicago Blackhawks in 2007, was reacquired by Mike Foligno from the London

Knights in exchange for draft picks. The six-foot-three, 216-pound forward scored ten goals and 26 points in 29 regular season games during his second stint in Sudbury.[14] John Kurtz broke out with 21 goals and 54 points of his own, and in February replaced Giudice as team captain after the latter was stripped of the role following an off-ice incident.[15] McFarland had a respectable rookie season, putting up 52 points in 58 games. Marcus Foligno did not register huge numbers in his sophomore year, but the power forward caught the eye of NHL scouts for his size, physicality, and work ethic. The Wolves clinched the eighth and final playoff spot in the Eastern Conference in the final game of the regular season by earning one point in a 5-4 overtime loss to the Mississauga St. Michael's Majors.[16]

The Wolves played the formidable Belleville Bulls in the playoff quarterfinals. The 2008 OHL championship runners-up, the Bulls were the top-seeded team in the Eastern Conference during the 2008-09 season. On March 18, Sudbury lost Game 1 of the series by a score of 3-1 at the Yardmen Arena in Belleville. The Wolves evened the series in Game 2 with a 2-1 victory; Loverock made 30 saves and McFarland scored his first ever OHL playoff goal in the effort. As the Pack prepared to take the series back to the Sudbury Arena, Aliu recalled the memory of the team's run to the OHL championship in 2007: "I wanted to play in the playoffs in front of these fans again. It's my favourite rink in the league. It's going to be unbelievable."[17]

The Bulls got the best of the Wolves and took a 3-1 series lead heading into Game 5 at the Sudbury Arena. With his team on the brink of elimination, Dias, playing in his final OHL season, had a career-night. He scored a natural hat trick in the first period to put the Wolves up 3-0, only to slip a fourth consecutive goal past Belleville goalie Mike Murphy. "It's pretty hard to score on Murphy, so I'm pretty happy about that," said Dias of his performance. Loverock finished with 43 saves and Sudbury kept their season going, beating their opponent 6-2 and sending it back to Belleville for Game 6. The Bulls saw red and stomped the Wolves by a score of 6-1 in that game, taking the series four games to two. The Wolves had put on an admirable showing against a talented hockey team, but it was nevertheless a disappointing conclusion to the year. "It's not the way we wanted to go out … We're not happy with our efforts," asserted McFarland.[18]

GROUNDHOG SEASON

The Wolves entered John McFarland's sophomore season with high hopes and a fusion of key veterans and young talent. The return of several players, including Marcus Foligno, drafted by the Buffalo Sabres that June, gave Sudbury reasonable hope for a competitive squad. Valiquette and Loverock again split duties in the crease. The team used its first three picks in the 2009 OHL Priority Selection to take defenceman Justin Sefton, regarded by many as the best player in the draft, blueliner Frank Corrado, and forward Kristoff Kontos, the son of former Wolves and NHL player Chris Kontos.[19] McFarland felt poised to take a leap forward as he prepared for the upcoming 2010 NHL Entry Draft. He also wanted to quiet any rumblings that he was dissatisfied with his lot in Sudbury. After helping with the annual rookie camp, McFarland told *The Sudbury Star* he wanted to "prove it to everyone who has doubts and shut up any rumours going around. Sudbury is where I want to be and where I'm going to be."[20] A poll conducted by *The Sudbury Star* in September indicated that nearly half the respondents believed the Wolves would make the playoffs, while ten percent thought they could win the Central Division.[21]

Another major change came when Mike Foligno announced he would be stepping down as head coach following the death of his wife, Janice, from cancer. "I don't think it's fair to the team to stay behind the bench when it doesn't have my complete focus," Foligno explained. He decided to remain as general manager, with Bryan Verreault, an assistant and associate coach under Foligno for six years, taking the lead behind the bench. The Wolves also added four-time Stanley Cup champion Jeff Beukeboom as an assistant coach.[22] The Foligno family continues to honour Janice's memory through the Janice Foligno Foundation, a charity that fundraises for cancer research and promotes awareness to aid early detection and prevention of the disease.

The Wolves organization ultimately made little progress in the 2009-10 season, leading one sports reporter to dub it "kind of like Groundhog Season for the Sudbury Wolves."[23] After going winless in the preseason, the Wolves dropped their season opener at the Sudbury Arena to the Erie Otters by a score of 4-3.[24] The team went on an early seven-game losing skid that came to an end on October 18 in Brampton as Valiquette stopped

32 shots for his first OHL shutout in a 3-0 Wolves win.[25] Following a 4-8-0-1 start, Foligno agreed to return as head coach at Burgess's request. Verreault was reportedly offered his old job as associate coach but turned it down and left the team. "I felt that our team needed to be more competitive … Mike is regarded as one of the best coaches in the OHL and we are very excited to have him back," Burgess maintained. Mike Foligno said he was glad to be back behind the bench: "It's great to be back out there on the ice with these young players … We are getting down to business right away."[26] The team won in Foligno's first game back over Sarnia by a score of 4-0, with Valiquette recording a second straight shutout.[27]

Foligno altered the lineup as the Wolves eyed a return to the playoffs. In early November, the organization picked up overage centre Steve Reese from Sarnia and defenceman Josh McFadden from Mississauga. Then, in January, the Wolves made a bold trade with the Guelph Storm for Atlanta Thrashers prospect Ben Chiarot, a six-foot-three, 222-pound defenceman in return for Chris Van Laren and a couple of draft picks.[28] Sudbury went on to finish with almost the same record (26-35-4-3) as the previous year, landing at the bottom of the Central Division and barely squeezing into the postseason as the eighth seed in the East. A few of its top players nonetheless enjoyed solid regular season performances. Eric O'Dell led the way in scoring with 68 points, while captain John Kurtz finished his OHL career with a strong 30-goal campaign. McFarland's second season in the OHL was hardly mind-blowing for a player of his stature, tallying 20 goals and 50 points in 64 games. The Florida Panthers decided to take a chance and selected him early in the second round at the 2010 NHL Entry Draft in June.

Come playoff time, Sudbury was no match for Barrie, the top-ranked junior team in Canada with players like Alex Pietrangelo, Alexander Burmistrov, and Zac Rinaldo. The Colts had won seven of eight meetings against the Wolves during the regular season, with Sudbury's only win coming from a 4-3 home victory back in late September. It appeared that things would be different in the postseason when McFarland scored just over one minute into Game 1 to give the Wolves a 1-0 lead. The wheels fell off almost immediately, however, after Barrie scored eight consecutive goals and won the match by a score of 11-4. "When they scored their first goal, I don't know what happened, but we fell a part [sic]," Jared Staal said.[29] In Game 3, with the Wolves down two games to none in the series, Colts forward Rinaldo earned a twelve-game suspension for a blindside hit against Marcus Foligno; the Wolves lost the match 6-2. The stacked Colts completed the sweep on March 24 at the Sudbury Community Arena with a 6-3 drubbing of the Wolves.[30]

IT STARTS NOW

The new decade marked a turning point in Sudbury Wolves history. Less than a month after being eliminated from the 2010 OHL playoffs, Mike Foligno formally resigned as head coach and general manager of the team. He departed as the longest-serving and winningest head coach in franchise history, with nearly 500 games over the course of seven seasons under his belt. Foligno initially decided to remain with the Wolves as the director of hockey development, noting that he "really enjoyed my time coaching the team … but now it's an opportunity for someone else."[31] By late June he had moved on entirely after accepting an assistant coaching position with the Anaheim Ducks alongside former teammate Randy Carlyle.[32]

The Wolves' front office obviously had some big shoes to fill. In May, the Wolves held a press conference to introduce Blaine Smith as the team's new general manager and Trent Cull as its new head coach. A former OHL defenceman who had worked as an assistant coach in both the OHL and AHL, this was the 36-year-old Cull's first head coaching gig. He relished the opportunity, professing that he "wanted to come somewhere where it is on me … I want to be the guy who is moving this organization in the right way." Former Wolves captain Derek MacKenzie had nothing but positive things to say about Cull, having played for him on the Syracuse Crunch of the AHL: "He is really hungry to be successful … hiring Trent is a step in the right direction." After having been led by three well-known coaches over the previous decade—Tom Watt, Bert Templeton, and Mike Foligno—Burgess decided to chart unfamiliar territory. The Wolves' owner was unconcerned by Cull's youth and relative lack of experience, citing the new coach's knowledge and perspective on the rapidly changing sport of hockey—which in North America was witnessing a shift away from an emphasis on size and physicality toward more of a focus on speed and skill—as central factors behind the hiring.[33]

Sudbury made significant on-ice changes, too. Picking fifth overall for the second straight year, the Wolves nabbed slick centre Mathew Campagna in the 2010 OHL Priority Selection. In the second round the Wolves chose two players with family connections to the organization, selecting Iroquois Falls forward Brody Silk, whose father Dennis had played for Sudbury in the 1970s, and winger Sam Schutt, nephew of the great Rod Schutt. All of these selections were part of a wider effort to shift the team's focus toward speed, skill, and goal-scoring, something that Cull believed was more crucial to winning than size and toughness alone. Smith made some offseason trades to align with this new philosophy, notably sending veteran defenceman and New York Rangers' prospect Dan Maggio to the Guelph Storm. Cull came up with the slogan "It starts now" as the theme of the Wolves' training camp that year.[34] Alain Valiquette took the lead in the Wolves' crease in what was his fifth and final OHL season.

The Wolves suffered through a rough opening to the 2010-11 season. The team lost its season opener on September 24 to the visiting Niagara Falls by a score of 6-2, and proceeded to win only one of the first eight contests to start the year. Early in the season the Wolves swung a trade with the Kitchener Rangers for American defenceman Charlie Dodero, and rumours soon began to circulate that John McFarland was going to be moved next. "There is nothing up at all ... Zero truth to it at all," Smith said in response to the suggestion.[35] Marcus Foligno, like his father before him, was named team captain in early November. In his first game with the 'C,' Foligno recorded a goal, an assist, and a fight, also known as a Gordie Howe hat trick, in a rowdy 6-4 Wolves victory against the Plymouth Whalers that featured five fights.[36]

On December 10, with the Wolves owning a disappointing 10-18-1-0 record, McFarland's time in Sudbury came to an end. The Wolves sent the former first overall selection, along with Ben Chiarot, to the Saginaw Spirit in exchange for centre Michael Sgarbossa, left winger Alex Racino, and blueliner Frank Schumacher. The clubs also swapped draft picks. Smith wished McFarland well with his new team and defended the young forward against criticism of his attitude. "In my dealings with him, he's been exceptional," the Wolves' general manager explained. Although McFarland's 112 points in 134 regular season OHL games with the Wolves was nothing to sneeze at, he had clearly fallen short of becoming the saviour of the franchise that fans had envisioned when he first arrived in Sudbury. McFarland went on to play only three NHL games for the Florida Panthers before retiring from professional hockey altogether in 2019.[37]

The Wolves play improved significantly not long after McFarland's departure. They had a strong second half and finished above .500 in the New Year.[38] Marcus Foligno had a breakout season that included a silver medal with Team Canada at the 2011 World Juniors. Michael Sgarbossa thrived with his new team and posted 62 points in 37 games. A number of young players took noticeable steps forwards, including rookie forward Josh Leivo, an eleventh-round pick by Sudbury in the 2009 OHL Draft. Valiquette played just under 60 regular season games, posting 27 wins and a 3.69 goals-against average. Smith did not make a single deal at the OHL trade deadline in January, despite multiple calls about Marcus Foligno. "There were a number of teams interested in Foligno, but we made it clear that our relationship with the Folignos spans more than four decades ... and Marcus made it clear he wanted to finish his career in Sudbury," Smith indicated.[39]

After finishing seventh in the Eastern Conference with a losing record, the Wolves once more found themselves unevenly matched in the 2011 Eastern Conference quarterfinals. With players like goaltender Peter Mrázek and Tyler Toffoli, who tied for the league-lead in regular season scoring, the Ottawa 67's did indeed appear to have the upper-hand over Sudbury. The outcome of Game 1 stunned the 67's as the Wolves pulled off a hectic 8-7 overtime win in Ottawa. Sgarbossa tied a franchise playoff record with a six-point performance, registering a goal and five assists. "It was just one of those nights, I guess," Sgarbossa said afterwards. Leivo and Andrei Kuchin, a Russian forward selected by the Wolves in the 2010 CHL Import Draft, each netted hat tricks, with Kuchin burying the game-winner in the extra frame. After the Wolves took Game 2 by a score of 5-3, the club's fans began praising Smith and Cull for piecing together a fast, skilled team that was clearly much different than "the big, bad Wolves in past years." The Wolves took a stranglehold on the series in Game 3 after rallying for a comeback 5-4 overtime victory at the Sudbury Arena.[40]

Finally, on March 31, 2011, the underdog Wolves completed the sweep of the 67's in Game 4 on the road. Josh McFadden, who had scored a hat trick in Game 3, potted the game-winning goal in the third period to give the Wolves the 3-2 win. The offensive defenceman called it "the most important goal in my hockey career." Trent Cull admitted the Wolves never thought they would sweep an Ottawa team that finished 31 points ahead in the standings, but added that he was "extremely proud of these young men … They have done a great job and they have worked hard."[41] The 67's and their fans, conversely, were left scratching their heads. "The 44-win season, the .684 winning percentage, the scoring champion and 57-goal scorer, and the drive to the East Division pennant are no longer what the 2010-11 edition of the Ottawa 67's will be remembered for," lamented *The Ottawa Citizen*. "We might have come into the playoffs a little cocky," confessed Tyler Toffoli. "We lost our worth ethic."[42]

The Wolves opponent in the Eastern Conference semifinals were the Mississauga St. Michael's Majors. The Majors had been awarded the Hamilton Spectator Trophy for holding the best record in the regular season and were also set to host the 2011 Memorial Cup. Nothing seemed insurmountable for the Wolves in the wake of their domination of the 67's. The organization held its first-ever playoff rally before Game 1, allowing fans to watch the Wolves practice and then take part in a meet and greet with the players.[43] The series began on April 8; this time, however, there was no upset. The Wolves lost four in a row to Mississauga, capped off by a tough 4-3 overtime loss in Game 4 at the Sudbury Arena. Nevertheless, as *The Sudbury Star* sports editor Bruce Heidman noted, "the 2010-11 edition of the Sudbury Wolves will be remembered by the faithful for years to come." Wolves' fans voiced their pride in a team that had surprised everyone. "You can now say that I am a fan … this little playoff round has turned me into a believer of this team," one Laurentian University student originally from southern Ontario told *The Star*.[44]

MICHAEL SCORE-BOSSA

The Sudbury Wolves celebrated some significant milestones during the 2011-12 season. First, it recognized its fortieth season of play in the OHL with an array of festivities, including the unveiling of throwback green and white jerseys. It also marked the Burgess family's twenty-fifth year of ownership, incidentally making them the longest-serving ownership group in the OHL. Mark Burgess admitted that he did not originally support his late father Ken's decision to buy the team, stating "It's not a secret that I was against it … But it was the best decision for bringing our family into the fortunes of the community." He added that the Wolves and his family were "still very hungry" for a championship.[45] In a pregame ceremony celebrating the ownership anniversary on November 25, Burgess thanked "the best junior hockey fans in Canada" and acknowledged the contributions of former and current players and staff.[46]

Berk Keaney officially retired from the microphone in 2011 at the age of 90-years-old after 59 years of service as the announcer for the Sudbury Wolves. "After all these years, it's almost time I retire … It feels great," he told *The Sudbury Star*. Upon his retirement Keaney received an outpouring of well-wishes and gratitude for his years of dedication. Marcus Foligno, for instance, wrote that "Mr. Keaney was one of the reasons I will always miss playing for the Sudbury Wolves. The way he announced goals and better yet, penalties, was my favourite. He made people appreciate 5 minutes for fighting!" Keaney, who passed way in 2012, was recognized for his contributions to team history in a farewell ceremony on December 2, 2011 at the Sudbury Community Arena. After the Wolves won the game, the players skated toward Keaney and raised their sticks in honour of his illustrious career. Today, Keaney's former public address spot, located high above section 19 at the east end of the Sudbury Arena, is officially known as the "Berk Keaney Announcer's Booth."[47]

The team largely stuck with a core of familiar faces for the 2011-12 season. Michael MacDonald, a gritty veteran left winger acquired from the London Knights in 2010, replaced Foligno as captain in November, though Josh McFadden was officially considered a co-captain.[48] Frank Corrado, Justin Sefton, and Josh Leivo all returned to Sudbury as newly drafted prospects of the Vancouver Canucks, San Jose Sharks, and Toronto Maple Leafs, respectively. Leivo was set to be reunited with electric linemates Sgarbossa and Kuchin. Exciting new players included rookie forwards Nathan Pancel and Nicholas Baptiste. Four different goaltenders played in the Wolves' crease during the year, but the team eventually settled with the tandem of Swedish import pick Johan Mattsson and Hearst native Joel Vienneau.[49] The day before the Wolves' season opener, Jeff Giffen of *The Sudbury Star* called it "one of the most anticipated season-opener [sic] in years."[50]

The Wolves rebounded from a dreadful start to have their most productive regular season in recent memory. They lost their first five games, including dropping an 8-2 contest to the London Knights and a road loss to the Sarnia Sting by a score of 7-2.[51] The team then began to turn things around after winning its first game of the year on October 7 by a score of 5-4 over the Niagara Falls IceDogs in Mattsson's OHL debut.[52] The team went on a six-game winning streak from late November to early December, twice beating the Soo Greyhounds along the way. At the trade deadline in January, Smith traded Kristoff Kontos and two other players in a string of deals that landed the Wolves forwards Derek Schoenmakers from the Majors and Michael Kantor from the Greyhounds, along with defenceman Mackenzie Braid from the Spitfires.[53] The Wolves dealt with injuries, suspensions, and a rigorous schedule for much of the year, yet managed to remain fairly competitive throughout. The club finished the 2011-12 season with a winning record (36-26-4-2) for the first time since 2005-06, and 78 points in the standings, the team's best total since the 2000-01 season.[54]

One player in particular left his stamp on Wolves' history that year. Michael Sgarbossa entered the Wolves' final regular season game on March 18 tied with Ottawa's Tyler Toffoli for the OHL points lead. Playing in Kingston on a Sunday afternoon, the 19-year-old native of Campbellville, Ontario, scored a hat trick and added an assist in a 5-1 Wolves win to perch himself atop of the league's scoring podium. With 47 goals and 102 points, Sgarbossa became only the second Wolves player to lead the OHL in scoring after Mike Foligno had done so in 1978-79. An undrafted free agent, Sgarbossa had signed with the San Jose Sharks in 2010 before his rights were traded to the Colorado Avalanche in February 2012. The sniper credited his teammates with helping him secure the scoring title, and wasted no time looking toward the upcoming postseason: "It's right back to business, preparing for Brampton."[55]

Sitting fifth in the Eastern Conference, the Wolves faced the Brampton Battalion in what was anticipated to be a closely matched quarterfinal series. Nevertheless, lingering injuries and bad penalties cost the Wolves dearly against the tight-checking and veteran Battalion squad. The Wolves lost the first two games in Brampton. In Game 3 in Sudbury, the Battalion won by a score of 6-1 to take a three-game series lead. With their season on the line, the Wolves turned to Vienneau in goal in Game 4, giving him his first start of the playoffs after Mattsson was yanked in Game 3. Goals by Leivo, Sgarbossa, and Schoenmakers kept the Wolves in a match that went into double overtime. The Wolves do-or-die mentality was not enough, however, as Brampton's Cameron Wind scored to give his team a 4-3 win and a series sweep. Trent Cull told his players to take this as "a good learning tool" about the importance of work ethic and across-the-board effort.[56]

CHAPTER 11:

PEAKS AND VALLEYS, 2012-2016

WORLDWIDE WOLVES

The summer of 2012 was unusually eventful for the Wolves. The team had another busy draft day in April, bolstering its blueline with fourteenth overall pick Conor Cummins from the Whitby Wildcats. The team also used one of its third-round picks to take forward Connor Burgess, the son of team owner Mark, of the Sudbury Nickel Capital Wolves.[1] About a month later, Sudbury chose Dominik Kubalík and Dominik Kahun in the CHL Import Draft, two offensively minded European forwards. Team management hoped to fill the gaps up front caused by the departures of multiple key veterans, most notably Michael Sgarbossa.[2]

In late August, shortly after extending Trent Cull's contract until the 2013-14 season, the Wolves travelled to Omsk, Russia to play in the 2012

Junior Club World Cup as representatives of the CHL. A ten-team tournament, Sudbury defeated junior clubs from Finland, Belarus, and Denmark before meeting the Waterloo Black Hawks of the United States Hockey League in the finals. The Wolves won the goal medal game by a score of 2-0, with Joel Vienneau earning the shutout victory. Michael Kantor was named the tournament's top forward, and Josh Leivo finished as the top scorer with eleven points in six games. "It was unbelievable … It's great for the start of the season, a good bonding moment for our team," said Leivo afterwards.[3]

Only five years after undergoing a series of renovations, the status of the 60-year-old downtown Sudbury Community Arena was once again called into question. Following a power outage that delayed an exhibition game between Sudbury and the Soo, Blaine Smith expressed concern over the barn's deficiencies, including aging electrical wiring and a leaky roof. The idea that the Wolves and the city of Sudbury needed a new rink was gaining groundswell support. City councillor Jacques Barbeau agreed with Smith, asserting that "it needs to happen … In order to get better hockey, if we want to hold the Memorial Cup here … we have to get there."[4] Executing this vision, of course, was easier said than done.

It took some time for the Wolves to translate their success on the international stage back to Canadian soil. Despite winning their first two games of the season, the Wolves got off to an all-too-familiar sluggish start. In mid-November, sitting with a record of 8-11-0-2 and riding a four-game winless streak, Sudbury captain Frank Corrado affirmed that "It's not up to one guy or one line to get out of this slump, it's everybody."[5] The leader's words did not immediately spark his club, but by the New Year things were starting to look upward. On December 30 the Wolves downed the Greyhounds at the Sudbury Arena by a score of 4-1 to start off a six-game winning streak. Mathew Campagna pieced together an 18-game points streak from November 24 to January 13, registering eight goals and 24 assists. The third-year forward likewise set a Wolves' franchise record for most consecutive games with an assist, recording at least one helper for fifteen matches in a row.[6]

In management's eyes, it was still time for a change. Days before the trade deadline in January, the Wolves dealt Corrado, Leivo, and Vienneau to the Kitchener Rangers in exchange for goalie Franky Palazzese, defenceman Cory Genovese, and rookie forward Matt Schmalz. The very next day the Wolves traded Justin Sefton to the London Knights for 19-year-old blueliner Kevin Raine. It was a bold series of moves, especially given that Sudbury had been among the OHL's hottest teams at the time of the deals. "It has been some time since we have moved some of our graduating players for a chance to add some skilled, experienced young players to our lineup," Blaine Smith reasoned. In his Wolves' debut, Palazzese, statistically the league's best goaltender before arriving in the Nickel City, posted a 27-save shutout versus the Mississauga Steelheads in a 2-0 Wolves win at the Sudbury Arena.[7]

The Pack remained relevant for the rest of the season, finishing third in the Central Division. Campagna had a career year with a team-leading 68 points and his line-mate Nathan Pancel led all Wolves with 26 goals. Kantor was named captain after the Corrado trade. Palazzese played well as Sudbury's new starting goaltender.[8] Trent Cull received praise from players and analysts alike for his coaching in general and the Wolves' revved-up play in the second half of the season in particular. Nicholas Baptiste credited Cull for the turnaround, stating that the coach "had played the biggest role … He's the leader of this ship." Some thought that Cull might even be considered for the Matt Leyden Trophy as the OHL's coach of the year.[9]

Sudbury met Brampton in the OHL quarterfinals for the second consecutive season. The outcome in 2013 was completely different for the more experienced, reshaped Wolves team. After dropping Game 1 in Brampton, the Wolves won the next three games, all on winning goals by Kubalík and supported by Palazzese's stellar goaltending. On March 29, the Wolves and the Battalion clashed at the Powerade Centre for Game 5 with Sudbury leading the series three games to one. A back-and-forth contest, the game was scoreless entering overtime. Just over six minutes in, rookie defenceman Evan de Haan buried his first OHL playoff goal past Battalion goaltender Jake Smith to win the game by a score of 1-0 and end the series in favour of the Pack.[10] This happened to be the final game the Battalion played in Brampton, as the franchise relocated to North Bay for the start of the 2013-14 season and commenced the new era of the Highway 17 rivalry with Sudbury.

The Wolves were challenged by the Eastern Conference-leading Belleville Bulls in the semifinals. Sudbury lost all four games to Belleville. Over 3,500 fans at the Sudbury Community Arena on April 11 gave the home team a standing ovation after the untimely elimination in Game 4 that saw the Wolves lose by a score of 5-0. "Honestly, I couldn't have asked for a better group of guys to be captain of … I have never been on a team that's so close and I'll miss them. I'll always remember this year," said Michael Kantor.[11]

THE DROUGHT CONTINUES

It was another busy summer for the Wolves organization in 2013. Trent Cull abruptly resigned from the Wolves in July to take his former job as an assistant coach with the Syracuse Crunch of the AHL. Cull denied media suggestions that his relationship with management had become strained, explaining that he simply was jumping at a promising opportunity. "I have had the pleasure of coaching some great young men in my time here and I will miss working with those great kids," Cull said in a statement released by the Wolves organization. He was replaced by Paul Fixter, who had been hired weeks earlier as an associate coach after five seasons with the Kitchener Rangers. Fixter had two Stanley Cup rings as a member of the Colorado Avalanche's coaching staff.[12] In August, the Wolves returned to Russia to defend the Junior Club World Cup championship, but the team did not even qualify for the semifinals this time around.[13]

The Pack were expected to have a strong team in the 2013-14 season with a nucleus of veteran players. The Wolves' blueline was led by captain Kevin Raine and fourth-year defenceman Jeff Corbett, rounded out by youngsters such as Kyle Capobianco, the seventh overall selection in the 2013 OHL Priority Selection.[14] The top line of Mathew Campagna, Nicholas Baptiste, and Nathan Pancel was tasked with driving the Wolves' offence. In early September, the club acquired defenceman Jimmy McDowell and left-winger Connor Crisp, a Montreal Canadiens' prospect, from the Erie Otters in exchange for Cory Genovese and a couple of draft picks. Baptiste, drafted by the Buffalo Sabres in the third round of the 2013 NHL Entry Draft, stated that the team wanted "Nothing short of winning an OHL championship."[15]

Led by one of the best forward lines in the OHL, the Wolves had a generally solid campaign. The year could not have gotten off to a worse start, however, as the Wolves were pounded by the Soo Greyhounds 10-3 at the Essar Centre in the season opener.[16] Injuries continued to hamper the team early on, but starting on November 27 the Wolves caught fire. They won nine straight games in December and twelve in a row on home ice.[17] At times it did not seem outrageous to call the Sudbury Wolves potential contenders for the J. Ross Robertson Cup. Blaine Smith felt confident enough in this squad to trade Dominik Kubalík to the Kitchener Rangers for 19-year-old centre and Dallas Stars' prospect Radek Faksa, as well as to pick up defenceman and Carolina Hurricanes' draft pick Trevor Carrick from the Mississauga Steelheads. "This is the first time I've been in a situation to really load up a team like this … and hopefully win a championship," the Wolves' general manager maintained.[18]

On January 31, the Wolves franchise retired Dale Hunter's No. 15 jersey in a pregame ceremony against the London Knights, a team that Hunter now coached and co-owned. After playing for Sudbury in the late 1970s and early 1980s, Hunter went on to play 1,407 NHL games, becoming the only player in league history to register more than 3,000 penalty minutes and over 1,000 points in his career. He also led the London Knights to the Memorial Cup in 2005, a feat that he would repeat again in 2016. In retiring his jersey, the Wolves were immortalizing a player who collected 76 goals and 119 assists, along with 377 penalty minutes, in only 120 games with Sudbury from 1978 to 1980. "You fans, you're the key," Hunter told the audience at the Sudbury Arena. "You're some of the best fans in the league." The Knights defeated the Wolves on Hunter's big night by a score of 3-2.[19]

A poor finish to the regular season made it hard to feel optimistic. Sitting first in the Central Division in early February, the Wolves tumbled down the standings and won only three of their final twelve games. The Wolves did win their final match of the regular season over the Oshawa Generals by a score of 2-1, backstopped by rookie backup goaltender Troy Timpano.[20] At the season's conclusion, Baptiste and Pancel each had 40-plus goals, while Campagna sat among the OHL's top playmakers with 59 assists. Palazzese had a fantastic year in net, posting a .916 save percentage and five shutouts through 60 games.

As the fifth seed in the Eastern Conference (33-24-3-8), the Wolves failed to secure home-ice advantage in the opening round of the postseason versus defenceman Aaron Ekblad and the Barrie Colts. The Wolves and the Colts were set to kick-off the seventh ever playoff meeting between the two evenly matched clubs. The teams were tied at three series wins a piece, and both teams had finished with 77 points in the standings that year. Sudbury had won three of five contests against Barrie during the regular season. Fixter planned to counteract the Colts' speed, skill, and grittiness with discipline, sound defence, and physicality. "We have to play better than we have, and we're capable of that," the Wolves head coach stated.[21]

The first two games of the series seemed to demonstrate that the Wolves and Colts were in fact closely matched. In Game 2, with the Colts having won the series' opener by a one-goal margin, the Wolves held 1-0 and 2-1 leads before falling behind 3-2 in the third period. Campagna then tied the game with only ten seconds left in regulation. Barely a minute into overtime, Barrie's Zach Hall scored his second of the evening to put the Wolves down two games to none.[22] On March 25, at the Sudbury Arena, the Wolves dropped Game 3 by a score of 6-4; the team now needed to win four straight games to advance to the next round of the playoffs. Sudbury kept the series alive in Game 5 on a 31-save performance by Palazzese and a game-winning goal by North Bay native Danny Desrochers. The Colts squashed any hope of a Wolves' comeback, however, with a 7-0 thumping of their northern opponents in Game 5.

Bruce Heidman of *The Sudbury Star* called the 2013-14 season "a new low" for the Sudbury Wolves. The team's ugly second half of the season had cost the franchise a division title. The club had traded five second-round picks and a promising rookie defenceman, Stefan Leblanc, to land rental players Carrick and Faksa, only to put on a meek showing versus the Colts. With multiple veterans departing the major junior ranks and a depleted stock of draft picks, the Wolves' immediate future seemed bleak. Reflecting on forty-three years of team history, Heidman remarked that the "real losers in all this is the team's championship-starved fan base … By any measuring stick, the track record is awful, worst in the league."[23]

MAKING HISTORY – FOR THE WRONG REASONS

The Wolves were gearing up for a full-fledged rebuild and everybody knew it. The team traded Mathew Campagna to the Plymouth Whalers in August for three draft picks and were projected by *The Hockey News* to finish last in the OHL for the 2014-15 season.[24] In spite of the return of a host of players, the Wolves clearly lacked the firepower and depth needed to compete every night with other teams in the league. Troy Timpano and Sam Tanguay, a 19-year-old rookie goaltender, were an unproven duo in net. In the first round of the 2015 OHL Priority Selection, the Wolves nabbed forward Michael Pezzetta of the Mississauga Senators. "It was pretty cool to get drafted that day and then find out I was going to Sudbury," said Pezzetta in a 2020 interview with the Wolves organization. "I remember the first time I got there … It was a great atmosphere. Right away, you kind of notice that the fans were pretty invested in the team."[25] The Wolves also added Czech forward Pavel Jenyš and Russian winger Ivan Kashtanov through the 2014 CHL Import Draft.[26] The Wolves went with two captains, alternating the 'C' between veterans Nicholas Baptiste and Brody Silk.[27]

It is unlikely that anyone could have predicted precisely how painful the 2014-15 season was going to be for Sudbury. The Wolves won their season opener at home versus the Niagara Falls IceDogs on September 26 by a score of 3-1. Rookie Pezzetta recorded his first OHL goal in his major junior debut.[28] "I always wanted to score in my first OHL game … I kind of just stepped in from the blueline and just shot one—couldn't really see the net—and then I saw that it went in and I was pretty excited," he once recalled years later.[29] It was all downhill from there for the Wolves, however. The team lost the next thirteen games in a row, among them an 8-1 defeat at the Sudbury Arena to Connor McDavid and the Erie Otters.[30] During that span, following a blowout loss to the Soo, a frustrated Paul Fixter directed an expletive at a reporter during a postgame interview. A video of the interaction was posted online and went viral. "I lost my cool," Fixter later admitted. "You know, for that I apologized publicly."[31] The Wolves strung together a separate eighteen-game winless streak from December to February, setting a franchise record for consecutive losses.[32] The Wolves lost their final game of the season on March 22 against the

67's, in which they were blown out by a score of 6-0 in Ottawa. The team had officially established an historic organizational low by winning only 12 games, sporting a record of 12-54-1-1. It was truly the worst season in the history of the Sudbury Wolves.[33]

As one would expect, management made serious adjustments to the team throughout the season and loaded up for the future. First, in early November, Evan de Haan was sent to the Ottawa 67's in exchange for defenceman Jonathan Duchesne and a draft pick. A few weeks later, Nicholas Baptiste was traded to Erie for Cole Mayo, Travis Wood, and four draft picks. In January, with the Wolves owning a 7-25-1-1 record, Fixter was fired and replaced by associate coach David Matsos. At the trade deadline, the club flipped Nathan Pancel, the team's top scorer, to the Peterborough Petes for two draft picks. That same day the Wolves nabbed 16-year-old rookie defenceman Reagan O'Grady from the Kingston Frontenacs.[34]

One of the more noteworthy storylines of the year occurred just eight games into the season when forward Connor Burgess suddenly retired from the OHL. A winner of the Ivan Tennant Memorial Trophy as the OHL's top academic high school student, Burgess decided to leave the Wolves so he could pursue his postsecondary studies on a full-time basis. Due to some of his on-ice struggles and the fact that his family owned the franchise, at times during his tenure with the team there had been fans and observers that questioned whether he had truly earned his roster spot. "I don't let it bother me … I just have to play my game. I know what I'm capable of," Connor told *The Sudbury Star* in 2013. In an interview with the *Northern Life* about one year after Connor had left, Mark Burgess said that his son "enjoyed his time here in Sudbury, and playing hockey, but now it's the next stage of his life."[35]

There were some redeeming aspects to this otherwise dark season. Pavel Jenyš, a Minnesota Wild prospect, led the team with 45 points. Kyle Capobianco posted ten goals and 40 points in his sophomore season, prompting the Arizona Coyotes to nab him in the third round of the 2015 NHL Entry Draft. Matt Schmalz had a breakout season and scored 24 of the Wolves' league-worst 149 goals; he was taken by the Los Angeles Kings in that same draft. The Wolves allowed the most-goals against in the OHL that year (323), but goalkeeper Troy Timpano showed flashes of brilliance behind his team's scattered play. Above all, the Wolves' last place finish meant the club had secured the first overall selection in the 2015 OHL Priority Selection. It was time to put a horrible year behind them.

BABY STEPS

The Wolves sought to ensure that the 2014-15 season remained a distant memory. On draft day in April 2015, the Wolves chose David Levin, an Israeli winger with a unique hockey background. Levin left Israel for Canada at the age of twelve to pursue a professional hockey career, leaving behind his parents and brother to live with his aunt and uncle in Richmond Hill. Up to that point he had mostly played roller hockey and only skated on ice a handful of times. With no consensus number one pick in this year's draft class, the Wolves decided to go with the five-foot-ten, 162-pound Levin after he put up 80 points in 55 games with the 'AAA' minor midget Don Mills Flyers. "It's the best feeling ever … Wearing this jersey and wearing this hat, can't get better," said the thrilled 15-year-old.[36] On June 30, Sudbury picked third overall in the CHL Import Draft and chose Russian left winger Dmitry Sokolov.[37] The team added a veteran presence to the blueline in mid-August by acquiring 20-year-old defenceman Patrick Murphy from the Erie Otters in exchange for a late-round pick in the 2018 OHL Priority Selection.[38]

The organization also shuffled its front office in preparation for the 2015-16 season. In August, the Wolves announced that Barclay Branch, an executive with the Belleville Bulls and the son of OHL commissioner David Branch, had been hired as the team's next general manager. Blaine Smith continued as team president. Upon his hiring, Branch called the Wolves "a cornerstone franchise of junior hockey" and expressed excitement over the team's pool of young talent. "I, along with the rest of the staff, want to put together a team the fans in Sudbury are proud of," Branch told *The Sudbury Star*.[39] As David Matsos prepared for his first full season as the Wolves' bench boss, he stressed that "Consistency, structure and worth ethic" needed to "become part of our team's DNA."[40]

The Wolves had a marginally less terrible year with Levin in the fold. Forward Danny Desrochers was announced as team captain the day before the 2015-16 regular season opener; the Wolves lost that game to the IceDogs at home by a score of 8-1.[41] The team continued to falter and almost tied the franchise record losing streak after dropping seventeen straight games until they finally stopped the bleeding on December 13 with a 4-2 road victory against the Guelph Storm. The Wolves simultaneously set a record for their longest consecutive home losing streak with fourteen uninterrupted defeats at the Sudbury Community Arena from late October to early January.[42]

With a 16-46-5-1 record, Sudbury finished ahead of only the lowly Storm that season. Branch made multiple trades to try to save another sinking ship. In October, he acquired netminder Zack Bowman from the Flint Firebirds.[43] Both Troy Timpano and Bowman played in at least 30 games for the Wolves as the team once again allowed the most goals in the OHL (328). To be sure, sloppy defence was not the only source of the team's woes. The Wolves also scored the second-fewest goals in the league, prompting management and coaching staff to make moves to spark the stagnant offence. In November, Branch dealt Pavel Jenyš to the IceDogs for Danish forward Mikkel Aagaard and defenceman Zach Wilkie. With an extra blueliner in the mix, the Wolves shifted the veteran defenceman Murphy to the wing. "We're going to give it a go … Goal production has been thin," Matsos advised.[44]

A handful of players drove the Wolves' meagre offence. Levin had a decent rookie campaign with nine goals and 30 points through 47 games while battling nagging-injuries all year long. Sokolov and Alan Łyszczarczyk, an American-born Polish centre signed by the Wolves as a free agent in 2015, led the team with 50-plus point seasons each. Sokolov became the fifth player in team history to score 30 goals as a rookie and the first to do so since Norm Milley in 1996-97. The Minnesota Wild selected the Russian sniper in the seventh round of the 2016 NHL Entry Draft that June, while teammate Michael Pezzetta was chosen by the Montreal Canadiens a round earlier.[45] Captain Desrochers netted a career-high 15 goals and ended his major junior career by playing his 264th match with the Wolves, placing him fifth all-time in games played with the organization.[46]

The Wolves topped off the regular season with nine straight losses before preparing for a lengthy offseason. Branch believed the team was on the right track after another gruelling campaign that witnessed some of the worst attendance numbers at the Sudbury Community Arena in years. "Long term, we would like to be a team that is competitive every year, and we don't want to get into a situation where we are dipping too far down in the standings and have an element of consistency year to year, and that is the end goal," he stated at the conclusion of his first season as the general manager of the Wolves.[47] Branch, along with the fans, must have felt relieved that it was over.

CHAPTER 12:

NEW ERA, 2016-2022

THE WOLVES LIVE FOREVER

After two horrible seasons in a row, it seemed inevitable that the junior hockey cycle would run its course and the Sudbury Wolves would find themselves trending upward in the OHL standings. With the second overall pick in the 2016 OHL Priority Selection, Barclay Branch's first as general manager, the Wolves chose Owen Lalonde, a right-shot defenceman who averaged over a point per game with the Windsor Junior Spitfires.[1] No one doubted Lalonde's pedigree, but Branch and the management team stirred up a minor controversy within local hockey circles for its later draft choices. While seven different players from the Sudbury Wolves AAA minor midget program were ultimately chosen by OHL teams that year, including future Minnesota Wild prospect Damien Giroux by the Saginaw Spirit, the

Wolves passed on all of them. With some of the greatest players in franchise history coming from Sudbury, many felt the Wolves should have pounced on the opportunity to add at least one highly coveted local to their system. Branch defended the Wolves' draft day in the face of criticism, reasoning that the "goal was to take the best player available … I understand there will be discontent, but it was not for lack of trying." The Wolves did select Sudbury native Christian Gaudreau, although he had been playing for the Mississauga Senators in his draft year.[2]

A watershed moment in franchise history occurred in the summer of 2016. On July 29, following months of speculation, it was revealed that the Burgess family, after thirty years of ownership, had officially sold the Sudbury Wolves to local businessman and real estate developer Dario Zulich.[3] After coming to an agreement, Zulich recalls an exchange he had with Mark Burgess that still resonates with him. "He said … 'You'd be, as far as I'm concerned, the best custodian of the Sudbury Wolves.' And that just made me feel so good, him endorsing me as this 'custodian,'" explains Zulich. "I'll always remember that because there's been a lot of owners before me, and there's going to be owners after me, so this is just a temporary gig, but the Wolves are going to live forever and they're going to stay here in Sudbury forever."[4]

The OHL board of governors formally approved the sale in mid-August, ending the Burgess family's tenure as the longest-serving owners in the OHL and marking the beginning of Dario Zulich's stewardship of the Sudbury Wolves. Mark Burgess, the principal owner and public face of the organization since the mid-1990s, thanked "everyone for their support over the past 30 years."[5] Zulich remembers being interviewed by the other OHL owners as part of the process to purchase the team. "Afterwards, one guy came up to me and said 'Congratulations, you just bought the number one brand in the second-best hockey league in the world,'" he explains. "And it's true. Everywhere I go, people … recognize the Wolves logo, they recognize Sudbury. Coast to coast."[6] Bruce Heidman of *The Sudbury Star* proclaimed that "A new era is about to dawn for the Sudbury Wolves."[7]

Dario Zulich's purchase of the local OHL franchise further intensified discussions centering around the fate of the Sudbury Community Arena, a structure which by now virtually everyone in town agreed needed to be replaced. Well before he even purchased the Wolves, Zulich had proposed to Sudbury city council his vision for an events centre located on the eastern end of the Kingsway across from Levesque Street. Originally dubbed the "True North Strong Centre," the project was officially approved by local officials in 2017. The Wolves' owner visualized an event centre that included a 6,000-seat arena, a casino, a hotel, and other entertainment venues at a cost ranging between $60-$100 million.[8] As of June 2022, construction of the complex, now known as the Kingsway Entertainment District (KED), has not yet commenced. The KED has been the subject of a number of legal challenges, and therefore has been unable to move forward until those matters are resolved. For the time being, the Sudbury Arena remains the Wolves' den.[9]

The new ownership was quick to make its mark on the team. Zulich acquired a train horn from the Canadian Pacific Railway as the team's new goal buzzer in order to, in his own words, "raise the roof on this building every time the Sudbury Wolves score."[10] On a broader level, Zulich sought to implement a new culture and management philosophy in the organization. The Wolves adopted a formal mission statement, which outlined the club's objective to turn its players from "16-year-old boys into 20-year-old gentlemen of character" by the time they left junior hockey. "At the end of the day, one out of a hundred of them are going to make the NHL," Zulich says frankly, "but the ninety-nine of them, they are going to be influenced by what we teach them in those formative years." At the same time, ownership also displayed an appreciation for history and tradition, assuring fans that the trademark wolf-on-a-wire was staying with the team, even when a new arena gets built.[11]

The 2016-17 season was a refreshing one for the Wolves and their fans. In goal the team went with Zack Bowman and rookie Jake McGrath, drafted by Sudbury in 2015, after Troy Timpano was traded to the Erie Otters over the summer. Kyle Capobianco, named team captain on September 30, returned to the fold with several other veterans, while David Levin and sophomore centre Macauley Carson hoped to have big years.[12] New additions to the team included twin brothers Drake and Darian Pilon, a pair of scrappy forwards from Sault Ste. Marie signed by the Wolves as free agents in the offseason. Behind the bench, the Wolves hired assistant coach Darryl

Moxam, who played for the Wolves in the mid-1990s. Sudbury opened the season at home against the Oshawa Generals, sounding the train horn four times and winning the game by a score of 4-3.[13]

The Wolves returned to the playoffs in Zulich's first season as owner. The team benefitted from a weak Central Division, finishing second despite owning a losing record. Dmitry Sokolov scored at a torrid pace all season and finished with 48 goals. He sat second among OHL goal-scorers that year, behind only Alex DeBrincat of the Erie Otters. Carson exploded for 30 goals of his own, a huge leap from the five he scored in his rookie season. Levin continued to develop and posted 53 points in 66 games. The Wolves locked up their first postseason appearance since 2014 when they defeated the North Bay Battalion 5-2 at the Sudbury Arena on St. Patrick's Day.[14]

The sixth-seeded Wolves took on the Oshawa Generals in the 2017 OHL playoffs. The two clubs had not met in the postseason since 1994 when Sudbury eliminated Oshawa in the quarterfinals in five games. Thirteen Wolves players made their OHL playoff debuts in Game 1 on March 24, 2017 at the Tribute Communities Centre in Oshawa. The Wolves won the game by a score of 5-2, with McGrath making 33 saves and Drake Pilon contributing a goal and a fight.[15] The Generals responded and evened the series heading into Game 3 in Sudbury on March 28; Sokolov scored for the third straight game and the Wolves won 3-2 to take a 2-1 series lead. Oshawa won the next three matches, however, eliminating the Wolves in Game 6 by a score of 3-1 at the Sudbury Arena. No one could deny that this maturing Pack had shown a lot of progress and effort over the season despite the early exit. "Let's be honest, those guys are the future of this team … they worked and that's all you can ask of them," Matsos said of his team.[16] For developing professionals like Michael Pezzetta it had been an invaluable experience. "When we started getting into the playoffs … I couldn't believe I was missing out on that for the first two years, so definitely learned a lot," he acknowledged in hindsight a few years later.[17]

BACK TO THE BASEMENT

The Wolves' front office and coaching staff underwent a shakeup in the weeks following the end of the season. In April Barclay Branch resigned his position with the team after being named general manager of the Flint Firebirds. He was replaced by vice-president and Sudbury native Rob Papineau, who had previously worked as a scout for the Carolina Hurricanes.[18] About a month later, the Wolves and head coach David Matsos mutually agreed to part ways. Two days after that, the organization held a press conference to announce that Cory Stillman had been hired as the team's next bench boss. Stillman had played over 1,000 games in the NHL and won consecutive Stanley Cups in 2004 and 2006 (owing to the entire 2004-05 season being locked out) with the Tampa Bay Lightning and Carolina Hurricanes, respectively. He had been working in player development for the last six seasons with the Hurricanes, where he first met Papineau. "We're going to be a hard team to play against," maintained Stillman. "It will be judged game to game, period to period, shift to shift and throughout practice."[19] The Wolves unveiled modernized jerseys for the 2017-18 season, giving a sleeker look to the famous blood-toothed wolf.[20]

Papineau took to his new role and pounced at the chance to remold the Wolves' roster. In late August, he sent defenceman Owen Lalonde to the Guelph Storm in return for defenceman Nolan Makkonen and six draft picks. The former second overall selection had played only one season in Sudbury, registering two goals and 10 assists in his rookie campaign. Papineau explained it was a forward-looking move, one that would enrich the Wolves' prospect pool in the coming years. The next day, Papineau moved Alan Łyszczarczyk and Zack Bowman to Owen Sound, and in September added 19-year-old blueliner Cole Candella, a Vancouver Canucks' prospect, in a trade with the Hamilton Bulldogs.[21]

It looked as if coach Stillman had a team of comparable skill to the previous season's squad, but things went south in a flash. Much to Sudbury's pleasant surprise, Dmitry Sokolov was sent back for another year of major junior hockey by the Minnesota Wild, as was new Wolves' captain Michael Pezzetta by the Montreal Canadiens.[22] The club still lost its first five games of the year. Rookie centre Blake Murray, selected seventh overall by Sudbury in the 2017 OHL Priority Selection, scored his first three OHL goals in a 6-5 loss to North Bay on September 27.[23] By January 2018, with the Wolves showing no marked improvement, the writing was on the wall. Papineau was a full participant in one of the most active trade deadline periods in recent OHL history, unloading five veteran players, most notably Sokolov to the Barrie Colts and Pezzetta to the Sarnia Sting, and gaining players like defender Peter Stratis from the Ottawa 67's. Overage defenceman Kyle Rhodes replaced Pezzetta as captain for the remainder of the season. After the dust had settled, Stillman informed his players that "this is the team moving forward, this is who we are, it's a great opportunity for guys to come and play and we expect to win every night."[24]

The Wolves finished with the worst record (17-42-0-9) in the OHL during the 2017-18 season. Blake Murray was one of the league's most productive rookies, leading the Wolves with 21 goals and 44 points. David Levin was limited to fewer than 50 games due to injury in his NHL draft year, contributing to him going undrafted in June.[25] The Pilon brothers, No. 28 Drake and No. 29 Darian, showed tenacity and some scoring ability in their sophomore seasons, becoming fan favourites in a city that valued sandpaper-style hockey. As the end of the season approached, Stillman gave a few starts in goal to rookie David Bowen, the son of Joe Bowen. The young goalie got his first OHL win in his second start with the Wolves in a 4-2 victory versus North Bay on March 8.[26] In the Wolves' final home game of the season, Sokolov scored his fiftieth goal of the year against his former club as the visiting Colts won by a score of 6-4. The Wolves honoured Sokolov with a tribute video and round of applause in a pre-game ceremony, something which Sokolov confessed "hurt my heart … I was almost crying."[27]

Fans and management had reason to believe something wonderful would rise from the ashes of this crumbled season. The Wolves had earned the first overall pick in the imminent OHL Priority Selection for the second time since 2015. The team also owned a top-three pick in the CHL Import Draft, and was set to pick first in the OHL Under-18 (U18) Midget Priority Selection, introduced by the league in 2017 to allow late-bloomers another chance to get chosen by an OHL club.[28] The reality that the Wolves were a last-place team had a "stinging" effect on Zulich, but the franchise owner stayed optimistic. "It takes a mile to turn a ship around, we just bought this team 18 months ago, but we've put together a program and it's starting to turn. We can feel it turning," he indicated as a tough year came to an end.[29]

PULLING A UPL-TURN

The Sudbury Wolves had inadvertently chosen the perfect season to finish at the bottom of the OHL. The 2018 OHL Priority Selection was headlined by Quinton Byfield, a six-foot-four centre from Newmarket, Ontario who played minor midget hockey for the York-Simcoe Express. It was a no-brainer for the Wolves to take the 15-year-old first overall after he posted 92 points in 34 games with the Express. "He's a great hockey player … This was the easiest pick I think we could have made ever," stated Rob Papineau. Byfield was eager to come to Sudbury, predicting the Wolves "will be a great fit for me … It's going to be a great experience." The rookie chose to wear No. 55 with Sudbury, a "lucky" number he started donning in his youth because he idolized NHL defenceman Sergei Gonchar.[30] At the CHL Import Draft in June, Sudbury chose 19-year-old goaltender Ukko-Pekka Luukkonen with the third overall pick. The six-foot-four, 195-pound native of Espoo, Finland had already signed a contract with the Buffalo Sabres after getting drafted by the club in the 2017 NHL draft, and the Wolves hoped to lure the young netminder to the OHL to enhance his development. The Wolves were ecstatic when Luukkonen formally committed to the team in August, with Papineau calling him a "first-rate goaltender."[31]

The early part of the 2018-19 season showcased that Quinton Byfield and Ukko-Pekka Luukkonen (often abbreviated as "UPL") had come to Sudbury just as advertised. The Wolves won their season opener versus the Guelph Storm by a score of 4-2, and Byfield recorded his first OHL goal and assist in that game. UPL made his debut on September 28 versus the Oshawa Generals, backstopping Sudbury to a 5-2 win.[32] It was the start of an MVP season for UPL, a player the Wolves depended on heavily night-in and night-out. When he left in mid-December to represent Team Finland at the 2019 World Juniors in Vancouver, the Wolves lost seven consecutive games. Luukkonen, meanwhile, was named the top goaltender of the tournament and led Finland to a gold medal finish before returning to Sudbury.[33]

The Wolves won again on November 2 against the Erie Otters by a score of 6-1, the same night that the franchise retired Rod Schutt's No. 8 jersey. Schutt told *The Sudbury Star* that he "was surprised and honoured … there is a real sense of community and pride that I feel."[34] The honour was certainly a long-time coming for a player who still holds the Wolves' single-season goal-scoring record with 72 markers in the 1975-76 season. "What a shot he had, an unbelievable shot. And that was a fun night," says Dario Zulich of Schutt and the ceremony that immortalized him in Wolves' history. "By doing that, a man and his name and his number will be remembered for the rest of time, and he deserves that."[35]

Although UPL and Byfield were the centrepieces of Sudbury's resurgence, a range of players contributed to the team's finest season since 1994-95. Cory Stillman did not name a team captain for 2018-19, instead rotating alternate captains amongst several players throughout the year. The Wolves went on an eight-game winning tear prior to Luukkoken's departure for the World Juniors, and in February went on another nine-game undefeated spurt.[36] Byfield led the Wolves in scoring with 61 points, Blake Murray scored a team-high 30 goals, and veteran forward Shane Bulitka recorded a career-best 54 points. David Levin's injury troubles continued, but he played at a near point-per-game pace when in the lineup. The defensive corps were highlighted by Cole Candella, sophomore Liam Ross, and rookie Jack Thompson. Just before the trade deadline, Papineau added Slovakian forward Adam Ružićka, a Calgary Flames prospect, from the Sarnia Sting and 19-year-old American defenceman Anthony DeMeo from the Soo Greyhounds.[37] The Wolves tied a franchise record for the second-most regular season wins with 43 victories in the 2018-19 campaign, and were especially dominant at home with a 27-6-1-0 record. Fans returned to the Elgin Street barn in waves to watch the local club vie for a shot at a championship title.[38]

Sudbury faced the Mississauga Steelheads in the playoff quarterfinals. With 91 points in the standings, the Wolves sat fourth in the Eastern Conference and held home-ice advantage. The Wolves won Game 1 on March 22 at the Sudbury Arena by a score of 5-2. Luukkonen made 29 saves and sophomore forward Nolan Hutcheson buried three goals. Byfield scored his first OHL playoff goal in Game 2 as the Wolves won 3-2 in overtime on a game-winner by Levin. The team kept rolling when they travelled south to Mississauga for Game 3, winning that match to take a 3-0 vice-grip on the series. On March 27, the Wolves completed the sweep at the Paramount Fine Foods Centre with a 4-1 victory over the Steelheads. It was Sudbury's first playoff series win since 2013 versus the Brampton Battalion, and their first four-game sweep since 2011 over the Ottawa 67's. Luukkonen stopped 32 of 33 shots he faced in Game 4; Stillman called the goaltender "the backbone of our team."[39]

The Wolves were matched with the Eastern Conference-leading Ottawa 67's in the second round of the postseason. The Pack were outgunned from the drop of the first puck, losing Game 1 in Ottawa by a score of 8-5 and from then on never getting their footing in the series. The Wolves fell behind three games to none heading into Game 4 on April 11 at the Sudbury Arena. An otherworldly goaltending display by UPL and goals by Ružićka and Hutcheson kept the Wolves tied 2-2 with the 67's all the way into triple overtime. A controversial slashing penalty against Wolves forward Owen Gilhula proved fatal. Ottawa connected on the powerplay and tucked the series-winning goal passed Luukkonen, who had stood on his head all night and finished with 60 saves. Sudbury had been swept in four straight games, but the season as a whole was nevertheless an immense success. "They went out hard … There's a lot of positive to take out of the season and the playoffs, but you're never ready for it to end," Stillman said of his team, the most improved in the entire OHL.[40]

While the Wolves failed to bring home the J. Ross Robertson Cup, members of their all-star cast received recognition with hardware of their own. In April Luukkonen was named OHL goaltender of the year following a vote by the league's general managers. The first member of the Wolves to win the award, UPL had posted a 38-11-2-2 record with a 2.50 goals-against average, a league-leading .920 save-percentage, and six shutouts in 2018-19. His goals-against average, save-percentage, and shutout totals for the year set new franchise records. Two weeks later, UPL was selected as the winner of the Red Tilson Trophy as the league's most outstanding player, becoming the first European to earn the honour and the second Wolves' player since Mike Foligno in 1978-79. "I am so honoured," the 20-year-old Finnish netminder said. "I want to thank the Sudbury Wolves organization for giving me a chance to play."[41]

At the same time, Quinton Byfield was named both OHL Rookie of the Year and CHL Rookie of the Year. He became the second player in franchise history to be recognized as the CHL's top rookie after Benoît Pouliot in the 2004-05 season. "I was incredibly humbled … I couldn't be more thankful for the opportunity that I received this year with the Sudbury Wolves," the 16-year-old phenom told *The Sudbury Star* after receiving the awards. Cory Stillman was also the runner-up in voting for OHL Coach of the Year, but the award went to André Tourigny of the Ottawa 67's. For the Wolves, the 2018-19 season was a fitting example of how much can change in the course of only one year.[42]

THE GREATEST SEASON THAT NEVER WAS

The fact that a number of players would be returning to the lineup for the 2019-20 season did not hold the Sudbury Wolves back from trying to improve their team. The club selected centre Landon McCallum with the fifteenth overall pick in the 2019 OHL Priority Selection in April. In the draft's second round, Sudbury chose forward Chase Stillman, son of Cory Stillman. Born in St. Louis, Missouri, and a dual Canada-U.S. citizen, the younger Stillman had played for the Sudbury Wolves minor midgets during his draft year while his father coached the local OHL club. "It's super exciting … There's a lot to look forward to right now," Chase commented at the time.[43]

A few staffing changes came as well. In August, the Wolves announced that former captain Zack Stortini would be joining the team as an assistant coach. "I never knew what was going to happen after hockey," admits Stortini regarding his transition into coaching upon the end of his fourteen-year playing career. He credits Mike Vellucci, his coach while playing for the Charlotte Checkers of the AHL, for having a major influence on his decision to pursue coaching. After talking with Stillman and Papineau about the possibility of joining the Wolves as an assistant coach, Stortini knew it was the right fit. "Any time that you're able to come to Sudbury and be a coach for one of the best teams here in the OHL, and obviously with a storied history, it's a tremendous opportunity," he says.[44] Along with associate coach Darryl Moxam and goalie coach Alain Valiquette, the Wolves organization now had three of its former players behind the bench for the 2019-20 season.[45] In September, vice-president of hockey operations Blaine Smith parted ways with the team after 31 years of service upon the expiration of his contract.[46]

The Wolves carried their groove from the previous year into the 2019-20 season. Cory Stillman at last filled the team's captaincy void by naming forwards Macauley Carson and Shane Bulitka as co-captains in September. The Wolves started the year with a three-game road trip, returning to Sudbury for their home opener on September 27 with a 1-2-0 record. Playing the rival North Bay Battalion, the Wolves danced to an 11-3 win at the Sudbury Community Arena. Wolves' goaltender Christian Purboo, acquired from the Battalion in early September, made 27 saves against his former team.[47] Purboo shared time in the crease that season with Mitchell Weeks, a native of Barrie, Ontario, whom the Wolves had made the first overall selection in the 2018 OHL U18 draft. Quinton Byfield, a projected top-three pick for the upcoming 2020 NHL Entry Draft, and Blake Murray, the Carolina Hurricanes' sixth-round pick in 2019, once more anchored the Wolves' offence. David Levin for the most part stayed healthy and had a career-best 73 points in his final OHL season. Draft-eligible defenders Jack Thompson and Isaak Phillips patrolled the blueline.[48] Byfield was a member of the Team Canada squad that captured a gold medal at the 2020 World Junior Championship in the Czech Republic, during which time the Wolves lost seven of eight games without their superstar centreman. Upon Byfield's return to Sudbury in early January, the Wolves owned a 19-18-1-0 record.[49]

Team captain Macauley Carson etched his name in a major category of the Sudbury Wolves' record book in his final year of junior hockey. On March 5, in a road game versus the Barrie Colts, Carson played in his 302nd career game with the Wolves, breaking Jamie Matthews' record for career games played with the franchise. Drafted by Sudbury in the second round of 2015 OHL Priority Selection, the 20-year-old forward had been a mainstay in the team's lineup since his rookie season. "The franchise has been here since '72 and that record has been standing for 26 years," Carson said as his record-breaking milestone approached. "It's nice to have one record before my time here is done, and it's a pretty special one for me, too." The Wolves won the landmark game by a score of 8-3 in front of a number of Carson's friends and family in Barrie, a stone's throw from his hometown of Midhurst. He finished his OHL career with 85 goals and 182 points in his 304 games in a Wolves' uniform.[50]

In March 2020, the world watched as COVID-19 morphed into an international pandemic. As governments across the globe enacted restrictions in an effort to halt the spread of the disease, the sporting industry, at all levels, was particularly hard-hit. On March 18, the OHL cancelled the remainder of the regular season, and the following week the CHL cancelled the postseason and Memorial Cup championship. "I think it's the right decision during these times," said Papineau of the decision.[51] It was an unexpected end to a fantastic season for Sudbury Wolves. In preparation for the postseason, the team had acquired 19-year-old winger Matej Pekar from the Barrie Colts at the trade deadline and sent Bulitka to North Bay for a package that included veteran forward Brad Chenier, a resident of Hanmer in Greater Sudbury. The Wolves won their last game of the season on March 8, defeating the Kingston Frontenacs by a score of 8-0, and were second in the Eastern Conference with 70 points in the standings at the time of the season's cancellation. This automatically allowed the Wolves to clinch their first division title since 2001, having been the best team in the Central Division when the pandemic hit.[52]

It was a small consolation prize for what could have been a great postseason for Sudbury and a difficult way for players like Carson and Levin to end their OHL careers. "We had a strong team, for sure, and we could have gone far … It was one of our best seasons in a while and we got the division title, so I think we could have made a strong push," Byfield said after his draft year was cut short. "That's what you play all season for, so having it cancelled just sucks for all of us." The Wolves centre had managed to put up 32 goals and 82 points in only 45 regular season games in the 2019-20 season, placing him among the most coveted young hockey prospects in the world as the postponed 2020 NHL Entry Draft drew near.[53]

THE LOST SEASON

In August 2020, the OHL announced a tentative start for the 2020-21 season, but the ever-evolving COVID-19 situation threw a wrench in those plans. The league aimed to begin a 64-game regular season from December 2020 to April 2021, followed by a 16-team playoff format and a Memorial Cup tournament held in either Sault Ste. Marie or Oshawa in June. Dario Zulich affirmed that the Wolves organization's top priority had always been the health and safety of players, staff and fans throughout the COVID-19 pandemic, but added that "We cannot wait to welcome everyone back to the Sudbury Community Arena this summer."[54] Unfortunately, after pushing back its return-to-play initiative several times in response to Ontario's province-wide COVID-19 restrictions, in April 2021 the OHL officially announced the cancellation of the entire 2020-21 season. "Today we had to face the hardest news and we are all very heartbroken that we could not provide you with a 2020-21 Sudbury Wolves hockey season," said Zulich in a public statement. "As we continue to battle the COVID-19 virus, we need to respect the decision that was made in the best interest and well-being of everyone ... We cannot wait to have you back to cheer on your Wolf Pack."[55]

Other league business took place as usual under the circumstances. The 2020 OHL Priority Selection was hosted in April, where the Wolves used the eleventh overall selection to take centre David Goyette, a native of Hawkesbury, Ontario.[56] In mid-December, Cory Stillman announced he would be stepping down as head coach of the Wolves and would be accepting a position as an assistant coach with the Arizona Coyotes of the NHL. "I really enjoyed coaching in Sudbury," he said upon announcing his departure. "It's a great spot to play and they love the Wolves." Stillman guided the Pack to a record of 94-89-16 during his tenure behind the bench. The Wolves organization was once again on the hunt for a new coach.[57]

Several members of the Sudbury Wolves kept busy while the status of the 2020-21 season remained in limbo. At the 2020 NHL Entry Draft in October, conducted in a remote format via videoconferencing, the Los Angeles Kings selected Quinton Byfield with the second overall selection. Byfield became the highest drafted NHL player in Wolves history, surpassing Mike Foligno's record of third overall to the Detroit Red Wings in 1979, and also became the highest drafted black player in NHL history. The young centre said afterwards that "hearing my name was a big relief off my shoulders and I can't wait to go to L.A. now." Byfield signed a professional contract with the Kings shortly after the draft and was later assigned to the AHL to start the 2020-21 season. Other Wolves chosen at the NHL draft were defencemen Jack Thompson to the Tampa Bay Lighting and Isaak Phillips to the Chicago Blackhawks.[58] About two months after he was chosen by Los Angeles, Byfield played at the 2021 World Juniors—held in Edmonton with no spectators for any of the games—where Canada took home a silver medal after losing 2-0 to the United States in the deciding match.[59]

The Sudbury Wolves were blessed with a stroke of good fortune in May 2021. Following the cancellation of the 2020-21 season, the OHL decided to hold a lottery to determine its first-round draft order for the 2021 OHL Priority Selection in June. It was the first time the league had ever held a draft lottery, with the results being determined by a computerized random number generator. Every team had an equal chance of drawing the first overall pick, and on May 5 it was revealed that the Wolves had earned that right. "It was shocking," Mike Taylor, the team's head scout, told *The Sudbury Star*. "I just didn't think we'd have that kind of luck. It was unreal."[60]

On June 3, the day before the OHL draft was set to take place, the Wolves organization announced in a press conference that it would be selecting Quentin Musty first overall. Born and raised just outside of Buffalo, New York, the young power forward had recorded 23 goals and 33 assists with the North Jersey Avalanche of the Atlantic Youth Hockey League. "He's a tremendous young man," said Rob Papineau of the 15-year-old American prospect. "He competes and does everything on the ice well." Musty officially committed to the Wolves just hours after he was made the first pick in the 2021 draft. "I am thrilled to sign with the Wolves today," he said in a press release on June 4. "I can't wait to get to the city and meet all my teammates and coaches."[61]

The Wolves capped off an eventful summer by hiring Craig Duncanson as its new head coach. On July 14, the organization announced that the former Wolves captain and Greater Sudbury native would be taking over behind the bench, supported by two other Wolves alumni and local products, Zack Stortini and Darryl Moxam, as assistant coaches. "I have been proud to be a member of the Sudbury Wolves alumni for a long time," said Duncanson at a press conference. "I can't express enough how elated I am to be actively back in the Wolves family. There are Wolves fans all over the world and we will strive to make each and every one of them proud!" Duncanson had previously served as the head coach of the Laurentian University men's hockey team since 2013, but, in early 2021, it was revealed that Laurentian had liabilities totalling over $320 million and had filed for creditor protection. In April, as part of the institution's restructuring under the Companies' Creditors Arrangement Act, both the men and women's ice hockey programs, among other varsity sports teams, were completely cut. Over 60 academic programs and more than 100 faculty and staff were also terminated, a devastating blow to not only the people directly impacted and their families, but the Sudbury community at large.[62]

READY TO RUN

The 2021-22 OHL season was characterized by excitement and a few surprises for the Sudbury Wolves. In the fall of 2021, the OHL returned to play after over a year-long hiatus caused by the COVID-19 pandemic. The Wolves roster had some notable names, including Tampa Bay Lightning prospect Jack Thompson, who was named captain in October, and Chase Stillman, who had been drafted by the New Jersey Devils in the first round of the 2021 NHL Draft. On October 8, the team opened the season at home against the Peterborough Petes—playing in front of spectators at the Sudbury Community Arena for the first time since March 2020—and won by a score of 6-3. By late November, the Wolves had won six of its seven home games, but had mustered only one win in twelve games on the road, prompting a perplexed head coach Craig Duncanson to comment that "It's so blatantly polarized, but it's hard to put a finger on why."[63]

This lack of consistency soon became a secondary concern once it was revealed that twelve Wolves players had tested positive for COVID-19. In early December it was reported that the club would suspend all team activities and postpone its upcoming games. In the weeks that followed the virus impacted other OHL teams as well, leading to the rescheduling of many games across the league. Sudbury's Jack Thompson was dealt an additional blow when Hockey Canada confirmed that he would now not be able to attend its selection camp for the upcoming 2022 World Junior Ice Hockey Championships due to COVID-19 protocols. Only a few weeks later, after several games were played, the tournament was cancelled entirely and tentatively rescheduled for August 2022. Back in the OHL, the Wolves finally returned to action on December 29 after a month-long break, losing 5-4 in overtime to the Soo Greyhounds.[64]

By the New Year the Sudbury Wolves organization had turned its attention to the future despite further complications caused by COVID-19. Although the Ontario government imposed new restrictions which called for no spectators at sports and entertainment venues for three weeks commencing January 5, 2022, the OHL reaffirmed its commitment to continue on with the season. Days later, the Wolves made a series of high-profile trade deadline deals. The team sent Thompson to the rival Greyhounds, Stillman to the Peterborough Petes, and local product Gio Biondi to the Hamilton Bulldogs. When it was all said and done, the Wolves collectively acquired Sudbury native Alex Pharand, forward Marc Boudreau, and defenceman Jacob Holmes, along with multiple draft picks. Veteran blueliner Liam Ross was later named the new team captain.[65]

While these moves suggested that the franchise was in rebuilding mode, the new-look Wolves still continued to fight for a playoff spot. On January 14, Sudbury travelled to Kingston to take on the Frontenacs in an empty Leon's Centre. Although there were no fans in the arena, the nationally televised contest certainly drew an audience, with much of the focus on Kingston's Shane Wright, the projected first overall pick in the 2022 NHL Draft. It was the Wolves who stole the spotlight, however, winning the game by a score of 8-4 on a hat trick by David Goyette, a two-goal performance by Quentin Musty, and a 43-save night by Mitchell Weeks. Despite flashes of promise and potential, injuries and inconsistent play proved problematic down the stretch, and before the season's end the team's postseason hopes had slipped from their grasp. The Wolves were statistically eliminated from playoff contention on April 9 following a 5-1 loss to the Greyhounds in Sault Ste. Marie. The team then closed out the regular season on home ice on

Good Friday with a 3-1 loss to the North Bay Battalion, leaving the Wolves' final record at 23-38-3-4. Sudbury also led the OHL in penalty minutes in 2021-22 with exactly 900 on the year.[66]

The Wolves concluded the season with plenty of reasons to remain optimistic that a return to the playoffs was not far off. Goyette not only led the team with 33 goals and 73 points, but he also led all OHL rookies in scoring. Musty had a respectable rookie year of his own with 31 points in 50 games played. Several other expected returnees, such as Evan Konyen and Kocha Delic, round out a promising core for the Wolves. Another top draft pick in the 2022 OHL Draft—one highlighted by the 15-year-old forward Michael Misa who was granted exceptional player status and thus became eligible for the draft one year early—will only strengthen this young roster as the club prepares for its fiftieth anniversary.

CONCLUSION:

MORE THAN A HOCKEY TEAM

The complications caused by COVID-19 do not change the fact that the year 2022 is full of milestones for the Sudbury Wolves. The month of April already marked the ninetieth anniversary of the Wolves' first and only Memorial Cup championship. Most of all, September 2022 will mark exactly fifty years since the modern Sudbury Wolves franchise dropped the puck for its first game, a moment which launched a storied history that this book has aimed to capture and commemorate.

Despite a lack of championship banners, this junior hockey team from Northern Ontario has clearly had a huge impact on the city of Sudbury over the last half-century. "The Sudbury Wolves are more than a hockey team," says Zack Stortini. "It's incredible that you see fans of the game years later and they're still talking about different games and you have that connection with people because of the game of hockey and because of the Sudbury

Wolves' organization. And I think it's made the Sudbury community a lot stronger."[1] Dario Zulich shares a similar perspective, reiterating his role as the so-called custodian of a team that will live on long after he eventually passes the ownership torch to somebody else. "When people are on the street and you see them, they don't say 'Oh, Dario won,' they say 'We won.' And they use 'we' because it's not my team, it's our team," emphasizes Zulich. "And again, I'm just the custodian, as Mark [Burgess] clearly and eloquently put it. So, this is not my team, it's our team. And so, when we win, we are on a high, and it brings us all together."[2]

A big part of the team's future rests with how it pays tribute to its past. "The history of the Sudbury Wolves, there is no place for it yet," says Joe Bowen. "Now, I understand that when the new arena is built that there may be a hall of fame or something of that nature, but I think it's badly overdue."[3] Celebrating the club's history is an essential component of galvanizing long-time supporters while also inspiring the next generation, the latter of which will be essential to keeping the Wolves a central part of the community. "It takes people that are committed and it takes people that are passionate about the Sudbury Wolves," asserts Randy Carlyle. "And it should remain that way because it is a great franchise, it's produced a lot of A-quality players and people, and it's the greatest game on earth."[4]

What lays ahead for the Sudbury Wolves? The team and its fanbase hope the floodgates will finally open and end the city's nearly century-long Memorial Cup drought. It would be a fitting reward for what have been several eventful and sometimes gruelling decades for the club, and one that the people of Sudbury greatly deserve. Regardless, what is certain is that the last fifty years of Wolves history has witnessed an array of legendary figures and timeless memories that continue to serve as a bond for much of the city. There is only more to come as the Sudbury Wolves organization skates toward its centennial anniversary and beyond.

ACKNOWLEDGMENTS

There are several people and organizations that I would like to thank for helping make *Leading the Pack* a reality.

I would first like to thank Heather Campbell and her team at Latitude 46 Publishing. I appreciate the support they offered during the process of writing, publishing, and promoting this book.

I owe a huge thank you to the Sudbury Wolves organization for the support and resources it provided. Dario Zulich graciously offered his time for an interview and his enthusiasm about the project was very encouraging. Miranda Swain-Boivin and her staff were also incredibly helpful in coordinating interviews, providing photographs, and promoting the book itself.

Thank you as well to the staff at both the City of Greater Sudbury Archives and the Greater Sudbury Public Library (especially at the Main Library located downtown). Everyone I dealt with while conducting my research was always professional and helpful.

I want to thank everyone who agreed to sit down with me for an interview about their experiences with the Sudbury Wolves. The full list of interviewees can be found in the bibliography, but I still would like to acknowledge each of them here (listed in alphabetical order by last name): Joe Bowen, Mervin "Bud" Burke, Ken Campbell, Randy Carlyle, Bobby Chaumont, Joe Drago, Craig Duncanson, Gord Ewin, Tim Stortini, Zack Stortini, and Dario Zulich. Each of you offered a unique and invaluable perspective about the history of the Sudbury Wolves which I know fans will be interested in reading about for years to come.

A couple of friends read early drafts and I appreciated their input. It seems fitting that Mark Kuhlberg was the first one to read my initial draft considering that I was first given the opportunity to explore my interest in this subject in one of his undergraduate classes at Laurentian University in the mid-2010s. Who would have thought a relatively brief essay about the 1932 Memorial Cup champion Sudbury Cub Wolves would eventually lead to an entire book about the history of the Sudbury Wolves? Mark's feedback was as insightful then as it is now, and I am fortunate that he took the time out of his busy schedule to read my work even though I have not been a student of his for a number of years now. Likewise, Mike Commito not only wrote a great foreword for this book, but he also offered helpful comments. A stamp of approval from the Team Historian for the Sudbury Wolves is a pretty nice endorsement to have.

Lastly, I am thankful for my parents for not only supporting my decision to embark on the process of writing my first book, but for everything they do. Despite her admitted lack of understanding of just about anything to do with hockey, my mom, Lori, is amongst the biggest fans of *Leading the Pack*. My dad, Brian, read over the manuscript several times and his glowing (although perhaps biased) review was reassuring as I prepared to release my writing into the public eye. Him and I have attended countless Wolves games together (including my very first one nearly thirty years ago!) and I look forward to watching many more.

BIBLIOGRAPHY

INTERVIEWS

Bowen, Joe. Interview by Miller, Scott. 21 September 2020.

Burke, Mervin "Bud." Interview by Miller, Scott. 7 October 2020.

Campbell, Ken. Interview by Miller, Scott. 15 June 2020.

Carlyle, Randy. Interview by Miller, Scott. 26 September 2020.

Chaumont, Bobby. Interview by Miller, Scott. 15 November 2021.

Drago, Joe. Interview by Miller, Scott. 16 January 2021.

Duncanson, Craig. Interview by Miller, Scott. 23 September 2020.

Ewin, Gord. Interview by Miller, Scott. 2 November 2020.

Rothschild, Sam. *Memories & Music.* Interview by Peck, Gary. Sudbury Public Library. June 1982.

Marson, Mike. *CBC Morning North.* Interview by Schwabe, Mark. https://www.cbc.ca/player/play/2682789886 (accessed 15 June 2020).

Pezzetta, Michael. Interview by Scott, Branden. https://www.youtube.com/watch?v=S2cIXujgQh4 (accessed 11 August 2020).

Stortini, Tim. Interview by Miller, Scott. 24 September 2020.

Stortini, Zack. Interview by Miller, Scott. 24 September 2020.

Zulich, Dario. Interview by Miller, Scott. 25 September 2020.

PRIMARY SOURCES

NEWSPAPERS

- *Calgary Herald*
- *Edmonton Journal*
- *Globe*
- *Globe and Mail*
- *INCO Triangle*
- *Montreal Gazette*
- *National Post*
- *Northern Life*
- *Ottawa Citizen*
- *Kingston Whig*
- *Windsor Star*
- *Toronto Star*
- *Vancouver Sun*
- *Sudbury Star*
- *Sudbury Journal*

SECONDARY SOURCES

Bray, Matt and Ernie Epp, eds. *A Vast and Magnificent Land: An Illustrated History of Northern Ontario*. Toronto: Ontario Ministry of Northern Affairs, 1985.

Commito, Mike. *Hockey 365: Daily Stories from the Ice*. Toronto: Dundurn Press Limited, 2018.

Cruise, David and Griffiths, Alison. *Net Worth: Exploding the Myths of Pro Hockey*. Toronto: Penguin Books Canada, 1991.

Hunter, Douglas. *Yzerman: Making of a Champion*. Random House of Canada Limited, 2004.

Kuhlberg, Mark and Scott Miller. "'Protection to the Sulphur-Smoke Tort-feasors': The Tragedy of Pollution in Sudbury, Ontario, the World's Nickel Capital, 1884-1927." *Canadian Historical Review* 99, no. 2 (June 2018): 225-257.

Logothetis, Paul. *Toe Blake: Winning Is Everything*. Toronto: ECW Press, 2020.

Miller, Scott. "Devil Copper: War and the Canadian Nickel Industry, 1883-1970." *Canadian Military Journal* 20, no. 1 (Winter 2019): 31-39.

Nelles, H.V. *A Little History of Canada*. Oxford University Press, 2004.

Pagnucco, Frank. *Home-Grown Heroes: A Sports History of Sudbury*. Miller Publishing, 1982.

Ross, Nicola. *Healing the Landscape: Celebrating Sudbury's Reclamation Story*. City of Greater Sudbury, 2008.

Saarinen, Oiva W. *From Meteorite Impact to Constellation City: A Historical Geography of Greater Sudbury*. Waterloo: Wilfrid Laurier University Press, 2013.

Sarlo, Dr. Frank S. *Hound Town: One of the Best Hockey Towns Anywhere*. Victoria: Friesen Press, 2016.

Shea, Kevin and Jason Wilson. *The Toronto Maple Leaf Hockey Club: Official Centennial Publication, 1917-2017*. McClelland & Stewart, 2016.

Wallace, C.M. and Ashley Thomson, eds. *Sudbury: Rail Town to Regional Capital*. Toronto: Dundurn Press Limited, 1993.

ONLINE SOURCES

"1989-90 Sudbury Wolves interviews," https://www.youtube.com/watch?v=mcOgZsxua9w (accessed 6 November 2020).

"1990 London Knights at Sudbury Wolves – Part 1," https://www.youtube.com/watch?v=Vc4R1PuGN4c (accessed October 10 2020).

"Against the Odds: Remembering Mike Marson's Career with the Caps," https://www.nhl.com/capitals/news/against-the-odds-remembering-mike-marsons-career-with-the-caps/c-305201080 (accessed 23 August 2020).

"Breaking Barriers," *The Agenda with Steve Paikin*, https://www.youtube.com/watch?v=qURwlyzcCA4 (accessed 23 August 2020).

Campbell, Ken. "OHL owner's son retires after scoring zero goals in 95 games," *The Hockey News*, 16 October 2014. https://thehockeynews.com/news/article/ohl-owners-son-retires-after-scoring-zero-goals-in-95-games (accessed 18 May 2020).

Commito, Mike. "Jamie Rivers Reflects on 40-WinSeason in 1994-95," https://sudburywolves.com/

articlejamie-rivers-reflects-on-40-win-season-in-1994-95 (accessed 14 December 2020).

Commito, Mike. "Macauley Carson Set to Make Wolves History," https://sudburywolves.com/article/macauley-carson-set-to-make-wolves-history (accessed 25 January 2021).

Commito, Mike. "Pat Verbeek: Wolves Fire, Flash and Finesse – From Record Books to Lightning Leadership," https://sudburywolves.com/article/pat-verbeek-wolves-fire-flash-and-finesse-from-record-books-to-lightning-leadership (accessed 14 October 2020).

Commito, Mike. "Perseverance and determination: Sean Venedam's incredible comeback,"

https://sudburywolves.com/article/perseverance-and-determination-sean-venedams-incredible-story-back-onto-the-ice (accessed 25 October 2019).

Commito, Mike. "Sudbury's Iron Man: Bobby Chaumont,"

https://sudburywolves.com/article/sudburys-iron-man-bobby-chaumont (accessed 25 August 2019).

Commito, Mike. "Ten Years Later: Remembering the Wolves' Historic Run." https://sudburywolves.com/article/10year_anniversary_magic_run (accessed 24 June 2020).

Commito, Mike. "The Stuffed Wolf: A Howling Good Time." https://sudburywolves.com/article/the-stuffed-wolf-a-howling-good-time (accessed 24 June 2020).

Commito, Mike. "The Sudbury Wolves' First NHL Draft Pick: Morris Titanic." https://sudburywolves.com/article/the-sudbury-wolves-first-nhl-draft-pick-morris-titanic (accessed 21 August 2020).

"End of an Era," https://sudburywolves.com/end-of-an-era (accessed 29 August 2020).

Hardy, Stephen and Holman, Andrew. "Hockey Towns: The Making of Special Places in America and Canada." https://smu.ca/webfiles/4Hardy-Holman.pdf (accessed 7 August 2020).

"History of Memorial Cup," https://chlmemorialcup.ca/ (accessed 17 August 2020).

Leeson, Ben. "Sudbury Accent: Remembering the 1975-76 Wolves," https://www.thesudburystar.com/2016/04/16/sudbury-accent-remembering-the-1975-76-wolves/wcm/27c39ff3-6447-110a-93f4-006c787cdd94 (accessed 26 September 2020).

"ONE-ON-ONE with Sudbury Wolves Owner Mark Burgess," https://www.youtube.com/watch?v=XbbV96eQj2k (accessed 18 May 2020).

"Schmalz Cup Trophy," http://pjhl.pointstreaksites.com/view/pjhl/about-us/history-1/schmalz-cup-trophy (accessed 26 August 2020).

"The Hockey Factory," https://sudburywolves.com/the-hockey-factory (accessed 18 August 2020).

"Wolves open 35th season with style," https://www.sudbury.com/sports/wolves-open-35th-season-with-style-213804 (accessed 20 January 2021).

APPENDICES

All of the following information/data has been gathered from the Official Site of the Sudbury Wolves (www. sudburywolves.com) and other relevant sources. The author has attempted to make these lists as comprehensive as possible, but accepts responsibility for any errors/omissions.

RETIRED NUMBERS

- *Randy Carlyle: #6*
- *Rod Schutt: #8*
- *Ron Duguay: #10*
- *Dale Hunter: #15*
- *Mike Foligno: #17*

ONTARIO HOCKEY LEAGUE (OHL) TROPHIES AND AWARDS

Bobby Orr Trophy (Eastern Conference Playoff Champions)

- *2006-07: Sudbury Wolves*

Dan Snyder Memorial Trophy (Humanitarian of the Year)

- *1998-99: Ryan McKie*

Dave Pinkney Trophy (Lowest Team Goals-Against-Average)

- *1975-76: Jim Bedard*

Eddie Powers Memorial Trophy (Scoring Champion)

- *1978-79: Mike Foligno*
- *2011-12: Michael Sgarbossa*

Emms Trophy (Central Division Regular Season Champion)

- *2000-01: Sudbury Wolves*
- *2019-20: Sudbury Wolves*

Emms Family Award (Rookie of the Year)

- *1981-82: Pat Verbeek*
- *2004-05: Benoît Pouliot*
- *2018-19: Quinton Byfield*

OHL Executive of the Year

- *1989-90: Sam McMaster*

F.W. "Dinty" Moore Trophy (Lowest Rookie Goals-Against-Average)

- *1994-95: David MacDonald*

Hamilton Spectator Award (Best Regular Season Record)

- *1975-76: Sudbury Wolves*

Ivan Tennant Memorial Award (Top Academic High School Player)

- *2012-13: Connor Burgess*

Jack Ferguson Award (OHL First Overall Draft Pick)

- *1984: Dave Moylan*
- *1987: John Uniac*
- *2008: John McFarland*
- *2015: David Levin*
- *2018: Quinton Byfield*
- *2021: Quentin Musty*

Jim Mahon Memorial Trophy (Top Scoring Right Winger)

- *1978-79: Mike Foligno*
- *1998-99: Norm Milley*

Leyden Trophy (East Division Regular Season Champion)

- *1975-76: Sudbury Wolves*

Matt Leyden Trophy (OHL Coach of the Year)

- *1975-76: Jerry Toppazzini*

Max Kaminsky Trophy (Most Outstanding Defenceman)

- *1985-86: Jeff Brown*
- *1993-94: Jamie Rivers*
- *2000-01: Alexei Semenov*
- *2006-07: Marc Staal*

Mickey Renaud Trophy (Best Captain/Leadership)

- *2009-10: John Kurtz*

Red Tilson Trophy (Most Outstanding Player)

- *1978-79: Mike Foligno*
- *2018-19: Ukko-Pekka Luukkonen*

Wayne Gretzky 99 Award (Most Valuable Player in Playoffs)

- *2006-07: Marc Staal*

Canadian Hockey League (CHL) Awards

CHL Rookie of the Year

- *2004-05: Benoît Pouliot*
- *2018-19: Quinton Byfield*

FRANCHISE RECORD HOLDERS

Individual Records - One Season Mark (Limited List)

Goals: Rodney Schutt – 72 (1975-1976)

Assists: Ron Duguay – 92 (1975-76)

Total Points: Mike Foligno – 150 (1978-79)

Most Goals by a Defencemen: John Baby – 32 (1976-77); Jamie Rivers – 32 (1993-94)

Most Assists by a Defencemen: Jamie Rivers – 89 (1993-94)

Most Points by a Defencemen: Jamie Rivers – 121 (1993-94)

Career Leaders – Regular Season (Limited List)

Games Played: Macauley Carson – 304 (2015-20)

Goals: Norm Milley – 167 (1996-2000)

Assists: Jamie Matthews – 249 (1989-94)

Points: Jamie Matthews – 369 (1989-94)

Penalty Minutes: Zack Stortini – 746 (2001-05)

Career Goaltending Leaders – Regular Season (Limited List)

Games Played: Mike Sands – 146 (1980-83)

Shutouts: Mike Smith – 6 (2000-02); Patrick Ehelechner – 6 (2003-05); Franky Palazzese – 6 (2012-14); Ukko-Pekka Luukkonen – 6 (2018-19)

Best Goals-Against-Average: Ukko-Pekka Luukkonen – 2.50 (2018-19)

Career Coaching Leaders – Regular Season (Limited List)

Wins: Mike Foligno – 163 (2003-09)

NATIONAL HOCKEY LEAGUE (NHL) DRAFT PICKS/ALUMNI

- Adduono, Jeremy
- Aliu, Akim
- Allison, Mike
- Armstrong, Derek
- Baby, John
- Barnes, Ryan
- Baptiste, Nicholas
- Beaupre, Don
- Bedard, Jim
- Beech, Kevin
- Belland, Brad
- Bennett, Adam
- Best, Bill
- Bonsignore, Jason
- Bodkin, Rick
- Brennan, Kip
- Brown, Jeff
- Byfield, Quinton
- Capobianco, Kyle
- Carlyle, Randy
- Carrick, Trevor
- Chaumont, Bobby
- Chitaroni, Terry
- Colley, Tom
- Convery, Brandon
- Corrado, Frank
- Crowley, Paul
- Dale, Andrew
- Dafoe, Kyle
- De Fazio, Dean
- DiDioMete, Devin
- DiPietro, Paul
- Duguay, Ron
- Duncanson, Craig
- Faksa, Radek
- Farrish, Dave
- Fedorov, Fedor
- Fisher, Mike
- Fitzpatrick, Rory
- Foligno, Marcus
- Foligno, Mike
- Foligno, Nick
- Fox, Jim
- Frawley, Dan
- Gagne, Luc
- Gagnon, Sean
- Gazdic, Mike
- Goverde, David
- Gratton, Josh
- Green, Geoff
- Grennough, Glenn
- Gruhl, Scott
- Hansen, Max
- Hansen, Richie
- Hillier, Randy
- Hinks, Rod
- Holt, Randy
- Hunter, Dale
- Hunter, Dave
- Hudson, Mike
- Hrynewich, Tim
- Jancevski, Dan
- Jarvis, Wes
- Jaspers, Jason
- Jenyš, Pavel
- Kahun, Dominik
- Kelly, Chris
- Kerr, Chris
- Kontos, Chris
- Koudys, Jim
- Kovacs, Bill
- Kubalik, Dominik
- Laforge, Marc
- Lalonde, Todd
- Leivo, Josh
- Lenarduzzi, Mike
- MacDonald, David
- MacDonald, Kevin
- MacKenzie, Derek
- Maggio, Dan
- Matthews, Jamie
- Mattsson, Johan
- Mara, Paul
- Marini, Hector
- Marson, Mike
- Martin, Mike
- McCarthy, Dan
- McCourt, Dale
- McFarland, John
- McGrattan, Brian
- McKee, Jay
- McKendry, Alex
- McLean, Don
- McLeod, Glenn
- McQuaid, Adam
- McRae, Chris
- McRae, Ken
- McTavish, Gord
- Mercier, Paul
- Middendorf, Max
- Mikhnov, Andrei
- Milley, Norm
- Moher, Mike
- Moore, Barrie
- Moreau, Ethan
- Moylan, Dave
- Murray, Blake
- Murray, Glen
- Nadjiwan, Jamie
- Nedved, Zdenek
- O'Dell, Eric
- O'Donnell, Sean
- Peca, Michael
- Perkins, Frank
- Pezzetta, Michael
- Philips, Isaak
- Pierce, Randy
- Poirier, Joel
- Pouliot, Benoît
- Pyatt, Taylor
- Raycroft, Andrew
- Rivers, Jamie
- Rivers, Shawn
- Rychel, Warren
- Ryder, Dan
- Sands, Mike
- Savage, Mike
- Schutt, Rod
- Schmalz, Matt
- Sefton, Justin
- Semenov, Alexei
- Sgarbossa, Michael
- Shanahan, Ryan
- Simon, Jason
- Smith, Brad
- Smith, Mike
- Sokolov, Dmitry
- Staal, Jared
- Staal, Marc
- Staios, Steve
- Stortini, Zack
- Suderman, Matt
- Swan, Shane
- Sylvestri, Don
- Tanner, John
- Titanic, Morris
- Thompson, Jack
- Vail, Eric
- Valiquette, Steve
- Volpe, Bob
- Verbeek, Pat
- Watson, Dave
- Wideman, Dennis
- Wilson, Mike
- Wilson, Rob
- Young, Barry
- Young, Jason
- Young, Tom

ENDNOTES

INTRODUCTION:
SUDBURY AND THE WOLVES, A SYNONYMOUS HISTORY

1   C.M. Wallace, "The 1930s" in *Sudbury: Rail Town to Regional Capital*, ed. C.M. Wallace and Ashley Thomson (Toronto: Dundurn Press Limited, 1993), 160-161.

2   Stephen Hardy and Andrew Holman, "Hockey Towns: The Making of Special Places in America and Canada," https://smu.ca/webfiles/4Hardy-Holman.pdf (accessed 7 August 2020).

3   Dr. Frank S. Sarlo, introduction to *Hound Town: One of the Best Hockey Towns Anywhere* (Victoria: Friesen Press, 2016), xi-xiii.

4   C.M. Wallace, "The 1980s" in *Sudbury: Rail Town to Regional Capital*, ed. C.M. Wallace and Ashley Thomson (Toronto: Dundurn Press Limited, 1993), 275.

5   Craig Duncanson, interview by Scott Miller, 23 September 2020.

6   "The Hockey Factory," https://sudburywolves.com/the-hockey-factory (accessed 18 August 2020); Mike Commito, "The Sudbury Wolves' First NHL Draft Pick: Morris Titanic," https://sudburywolves.com/article/the-sudbury-wolves-first-nhl-draft-pick-morris-titanic (accessed 21 August 2020).

7   "Stortini signs with Oilers," *The Sudbury Star*, 16 September 2004.

8   Joe Bowen, interview by Scott Miller, 21 September 2020.

9   "Wolves bring us together," *The Sudbury Star*, 30 March 2006.

10   Joe Drago, interview by Scott Miller, 16 January 2021.

11   "Wolves key thread in community's fabric," *The Sudbury Star*, 25 March 2004.

12   Dario Zulich, interview by Scott Miller, 25 September 2020.

13   "History of Memorial Cup," https://chlmemorialcup.ca/ (accessed 17 August 2020).

14   Dario Zulich, interview by Scott Miller, 25 September 2020.

15   Joe Bowen, interview by Scott Miller, 21 September 2020.

16   "Wolves' impressive playoff run 'icing on the cake' in Sudbury," *The National Post*, 8 May 2007.

17   "Greyhounds fan backs Wolves bid for OHL championship," *The Sudbury Star*, 3 May 2007.

18   Randy Carlyle, interview by Scott Miller, 26 September 2020.

19   "Wolves did Sudbury proud in playoffs," *The Sudbury Star*, 16 April 2004.

CHAPTER 1: WOLVES OF THE NORTH, 1892-1972

1   "Crushing Blow to Collingwood: Sudbury Overwhelm O.H.A. Intermediate Champions in Sudden-death Game," *The Globe*, 12 March 1920.

2   "Sports happenings in 1920," *The Sudbury Star*, 11 June 2000; "Historically Speaking: Sudbury was a hockey town as far back as 1892," *The Northern Life*, 24 November 1976.

3   Ashley Thomson, "The 1890s" in *Sudbury: Rail Town to Regional Capital*, ed. C.M. Wallace and Ashley Thomson (Toronto: Dundurn Press Limited, 1993), 29, 47; "Historically Speaking: Sudbury was a

hockey town as far back as 1892," *The Northern Life*, 24 November 1976.

4   Frank Pagnucco, *Home-Grown Heroes: A Sports History of Sudbury* (Miller Publishing, 1982), 68-69.

5   "Hockey: An Ontario Hockey Association," *The Globe*, 28 November 1890.

6   "Gordon Cup comes to Sudbury," *The Sudbury Journal*, 1 April 1915.

7   Pagnucco, 69-73.

8   Mark Kuhlberg and Scott Miller, "'Protection to the Sulphur-Smoke Tort-feasors': The Tragedy of Pollution in Sudbury, Ontario, the World's Nickel Capital, 1884-1927," *Canadian Historical Review* 99, no. 2 (June 2018): 225-257.

9   Pagnucco, 75-76.

10   "Historically Speaking: Sudbury was a hockey town as far back as 1892," *The Northern Life*, 24 November 1976.

11   "Sudbury, Wolves of North, Defeat Allan Cup Holders 6-2," *The Globe*, 18 March 1920.

12   Pagnucco, 78.

13   "Rothschild's History of the Sudbury Wolves," *The Northern Life*, 18 December 1974.

14   Sarlo, xv.

15   Joe Greaves, "Sports and Recreation," in *A Vast and Magnificent Land: An Illustrated History of Northern Ontario*, ed. Matt Bray and Ernie Epp (Toronto: Ontario Ministry of Northern Affairs, 1984), 191.

16   "Granites Decisively Beaten in Sudbury Round By 11 to 3," *The Globe*, 22 March 1920.

17   "Fast and Heavy U. Of T. Wear Sudbury Down, Holding Wolves 2 to 2 in Allan Cup Semi-Finals," *The Globe*, 23 March 1920.

18   Pagnucco, 79; "It's Unjust," *The Globe*, 24 March 1920.

19   "Wolf Mascot Reaches Town," *The Sudbury Star*, 26 October 1921.

20   "Wolf Mascot is Given Name," *The Sudbury Star*, 16 November 1921.

21   Pagnucco, 79-80.

22   "Green's Departure Tragedy in Sudbury," *The Globe*, 23 November 1923; "Sudbury Drops Out of Senior Hockey," *The Globe*, 8 December 1923.

23   Kevin Shea and Jason Wilson, *The Toronto Maple Leaf Hockey Club:*

Official Centennial Publication, 1917-2017 (McClelland & Stewart, 2016), 27; Pagnucco, 80.

24 Sam Rothschild, interview by Gary Peck, *Memories & Music*, Sudbury Public Library, June 1982.

25 Paul Logothetis, *Toe Blake: Winning Is Everything* (Toronto: ECW Press, 2020), 26-31; Pagnucco, 80; "Historically Speaking: Sudbury was a hockey town as far back as 1892," *The Northern Life*, 24 November 1976.

26 H.V. Nelles, *A Little History of Canada* (Oxford University Press, 2004), 175.

27 C.M. Wallace, "The 1930s" in *Sudbury: Rail Town to Regional Capital* (Toronto: Dundurn Press Limited, 1993), 138-139, 143, 160-162.

28 Oiva W. Saarinen, *From Meteorite Impact to Constellation City: A Historical Geography of Greater Sudbury* (Waterloo: Wilfrid Laurier University Press, 2013), 201.

29 "New mayor of Sudbury living sports legend," *The Globe and Mail*, 8 December 1965; "Hockey first love for Sudbury mayor," *The Globe and Mail*, 6 October 1966.

30 Saarinen, 202.

31 Logothetis, 26-31; Pagnucco, 81.

32 "The History of the Sudbury Wolves," *The Northern Life*, 18 December 1974.

33 "Sudbury District Acclaims its Worthy Champions," *The Sudbury Star*, 6 April 1932; Pagnucco, 81; "1932 – Sudbury Cub Wolves," https://chlmemorialcup.ca/1932-sudbury-cub-wolves/ (accessed 20 December 2021).

34 "NOHA Group Opener at Sudbury Set Back for a Week as Sault Lacks Ice," *The Sudbury Star*, 9 January 1932; "Sudbury Cub Wolves Win NOHA Opener With Sault Hounds by Default," *The Sudbury Star*, 20 January 1932; "Sudbury Wolves Lace Sault Greyhounds by 11-2 Score for a Starter," *The Sudbury Star*, 27 January 1932; "Sudbury Juniors Defeat Sault by 2-1 Score in Kitty-Bar-the-Door Affair," *The Sudbury Star*, 3 February 1932.

35 "Chapleau Defaults After 14-0 Lambasting and Cubs Enter NOHA Finals," *The Sudbury Star*, 24 February 1932.

36 "Cub Wolves Lose Final to Monteith But Capture NOHA Junior Title," *The Sudbury Star*, 5 March 1932.

37 Ibid.

38 Shea and Wilson, 48.

39 "Cub Wolves Make Hockey History by Shutting Out Champions of OHA 3-0," *The Sudbury Star*, 16 March 1932.

40 "Cub Wolves Win Round from Marlboros by 5-4 in Thrilling Overtime Encounter," *The Sudbury Star*, 19 March 1932.

41 "Sudbury Cub Wolves Outplay Shamrocks at Home 3-2 to Capture Round 5-2," *The Sudbury Star*, 23 March 1932.

42 "Cub Wolves Are Champions of all Eastern Canada – In Finals with Winnipeg," *The Sudbury Star*, 30 March 1932.

43 Ibid.; Pagnucco, 81-82.

44 Pagnucco, 83.

45 "Sudbury Cub Wolves Win Memorial Cup and Dominion Junior Championship," *The Sudbury Star*, 6 April 1932; Pagnucco, 82-84.

46 "Applause Pours from All North on Wolves' Win," *The Sudbury Star*, 6 April 1932; "Civic Welcome Awaits Victorious Cubs," *The Sudbury Star*, 6 April 1932; "All Northern Ontario Greets You!" *The Sudbury Star*, 6 April 1932; Pagnucco, 83-84.

47 Pagnucco, 84-85; "Cub Wolves Scamper Through Porkies to Win Junior Title," *The Sudbury Star*, 13 March 1935.

48 "First Contest Thrown Out, O.H.A. Tells Sudbury Club Must Drop One of Imports," *The Sudbury Star*, 23 March 1935; "Maxie's Boys Outlast Majors," *The Sudbury Star*, 27 March 1935; "Silverman Had Toughest Task Handling Cubs," *The Sudbury Star*, 27 March 1935; Pagnucco, 85.

49 "Don Grosso and Hiller Shine as Woofers Outclass Verdun," *The Sudbury Star*, 27 March 1935; "Grosso's Four Tallies Feature Scoring Splurge at Montreal," *The Sudbury Star*, 30 March 1935; Pagnucco, 86.

50 "Sudbury Springs Surprise, Ottawas Are Outclassed in Speed and Team Play," *The Sudbury Star*, 30 March 1935; "Richardson Cup Comes to Sudbury," *The Sudbury Star*, 3 April 1935; "Master Touch of Silverman Spells Glory," *The Sudbury Star*, 3 April 1935; Pagnucco, 86.

51 "Monarchs Win 7-6 to Gaine One Game Lead Over Woofers," *The Sudbury Star*, 10 April 1935; "Complaint Sent by Tom Faught to C.A.H.A Head," *The Sudbury Star*, 10 April 1935; "Monarchs Adopt Dirty Tactics," *The Sudbury Star*, 13 April 1935; Pagnucco, 86-87.

52 "Big Welcome and Parade as Wolves Return," *The Sudbury Star*, 17 April 1935; Pagnucco, 87-88.

53 "Sudbury Team Returns Home," *The Globe and Mail*, 21 March 1938.

54 "Silverman Sizzles: Denounces World Tourney; Canadians Not Attacked," *The Globe and Mail*, 17 February 1949; "Wolves Win Pair: Overwhelm Danes, 47-0: Canucks Open Puck Series, Scoring Pair of Shutouts," *The Globe and Mail*, 14 February 1949; Pagnucco, 94-97; Graeme S. Mount, "The 1940s" in *Sudbury: Rail Town to Regional Capital*, ed. C.M. Wallace and Ashley Thomson (Toronto: Dundurn Press Limited, 1993), 185; Mike Commito, *Hockey 365: Daily Stories from the Ice* (Toronto: Dundurn Press Limited, 2018), 58.

55 Scott Miller, "Devil Copper: War and the Canadian Nickel Industry, 1883-1970," *Canadian Military Journal* 20, no. 1 (Winter 2019): 33-37.

56 O.W. Saarinen, "The 1950s" in *Sudbury: Rail Town to Regional Capital*, ed. C.M. Wallace and Ashley Thomson (Toronto: Dundurn Press Limited, 1993), 197, 209; "Wolves, N.Y. Sign Working Agreement," *The Globe and Mail*, 31 August 1957; Pagnucco, 97.

57 "Wolves Setting An Attendance Mark in NOHA," *INCO Triangle* 13, no. 10 (January 1954), 10.

58 Saarinen, 201.

59 Mike Commito, "The Stuffed Wolf: A Howling Good Time," https://sudburywolves.com/article/the-stuffed-wolf-a-howling-good-time (accessed 24 June 2020).

60 "Sudbury Wolves Win Ontario Senior Crown, defeating Mercs, 4-1," *The Globe and Mail*, 9 April 1954; Pagnucco, 97-99.

61 "Max Silverman: Hockey first love for Sudbury Mayor," *The Sudbury Star*, 6 October 1966; Pagnucco, 100.

62 "Berk Keaney Sr.; You have your diehard sports fans and then you have...," *The Sudbury Star*, 3 December 2011.

63 "Penticton Snares Senior Puck Title With 3-2 Victory," *The Globe and Mail*, 17 May 1954.

64 Pagnucco, 99-101.

65 "Leafs Send Six Players to Sudbury," *The Globe and Mail*, 19 September 1960.

66 "Royals Capture Game and Title," *The Globe and Mail*, 21 April 1960;

"Fronts Snare EPHL Title for Kingston," *The Globe and Mail*, 18 April 1963.

67 "St. Mike's Keon Paces Sudbury to 5-2 Victory," *The Globe and* Mail, 16 April 1960; Pagnucco, 101.

68 "Pact Will End Raids on NOHA Junior Clubs," *The Globe and Mail*, 13 June 1963; "Hall-bound Gasparini founded Wolves," https://www.thesudburystar.com/2013/05/10/hall-bound-gasparini-founded-wolves/wcm/bcbb73f7-b34c-aadf-1dc8-d493db48c1bd (accessed 13 October 2020).

69 "Wolves Run Wild Over North Bay Trappers, 14-1," *The Sudbury Star*, 6 November 1971.

70 "Wolves Need Big Victory Tonight in Soo," *The Sudbury Star*, 7 April 1970; "Wolves Win NOHA Jr. 'A' Championship Over Soo," *The Sudbury Star*, 20 March 1971; "Wolves Lose 8-5; Hounds Go Against Guelph," *The Sudbury Star*, 27 March 1972.

71 "Blanchard Equals Scoring Record as Wolves Whip Hounds in Finale," *The Sudbury Star*, 3 February 1971.

72 "Bud wants to sell out," *The Sudbury Star*, 3 January 1978.

73 Mervin "Bud" Burke, interview by Scott Miller, 7 October 2020.

74 Randy Carlyle, interview by Scott Miller, 26 September 2020.

75 "Soo, Sudbury players on move: Shuttle flights play role in NOHA final," *The Sudbury Star*, 4 April 1970.

76 "Wolves not ready for OHA," *The Sudbury Star*, 8 February 1971.

77 "Wolves Franchise Bid for OHA Club Received by NOHA," *The Sudbury Star*, 5 March 1971; "Rumours Were Flying, But Franchise Bid Still Up in the Air," *The Sudbury Star*, 5 April 1971.

78 "Now comes another NOHA vote," *The Sudbury Star*, 15 April 1971; "OHA entry can cause problems," *The Sudbury Star*, 15 April 1971; "NOHA could fold by decision," *The Sudbury Star*, 15 April 1971; "OHA Council Votes Down Expansion, Franchise Transfer Only Door Open," *The Sudbury Star*, 21 April 1971.

79 "Rumours Were Flying, But Franchise Bid Still Up in the Air," *The Sudbury Star*, 5 April 1971; "OHA Council Votes Down Expansion, Franchise Transfer Only Door Open," *The Sudbury Star*, 21 April 1971.

80 "OHA accepts Jr. A entry from Sudbury," *The Globe and Mail*, 2 May

1972; "11 Flyers to Sudbury," *The Globe and Mail*, 6 May 1972; "Wolves' first fan still with the team," *The Sudbury Star*, 28 September 2011.

82   "Owners reconsider, grant Soo franchise in OHA junior loop," *The Globe and Mail*, 12 May 1972; Sarlo, 1-4.

CHAPTER 2: TRIAL BY ICE, 1972-1976

1   Dieter K. Buse, "The 1970s" in *Sudbury: Rail Town to Regional Capital*, ed. C.M. Wallace and Ashley Thomson (Toronto: Dundurn Press Limited, 1993), 243-246.

2   "Wolves want Greg Neeld badly," *The Sudbury Star*, 20 June 1972.

3   "OHA to settle 'rights war'," *The Sudbury Star*, 12 October 1972.

4   Mike Marson, interview by Markus Schwabe, *CBC Morning North*, https://www.cbc.ca/player/play/2682789886 (accessed 23 August 2020).

5   "Mackenzie happy with Wolves' tryout," *The Sudbury Star*, 7 September 1972.

6   Mike Marson, interview by Markus Schwabe.

7   Mervin "Bud" Burke, interview by Scott Miller, 7 October 2020.

8   "Wolves will open Friday night at Arena against Ottawa 67's," *The Sudbury Star*, 28 September 1972.

9   "Wolves home ice drought ends in scoring sprees," *The Sudbury Star*, 16 October 1972; "Wolves defeated 7-3; eight players ejected," *The Sudbury Star*, 10 November 1972.

10   "Wolves open OHA major Junior 'A,' Oldtimers from 1932 Cubs on hand," *The Sudbury Star*, 29 September 1972.

11   "Ottawa gives Wolves lesson in OHA hockey," *The Sudbury Star*, 30 September 1972.

12   "Wolves outplay Hamilton Red Wings, veteran players lead team to win," *The Sudbury Star*, 4 October 1972; "Win lightens players' load," *The Sudbury Star*, 7 October 1972.

13   "Wolves part with two draft picks to get defenceman Greg Neeld," *The Sudbury Star*, 17 October 1972; "Chorus of boos ends the honeymoon with fans," *The Sudbury Star*, 21 October 1972; "Goalies turn plumber and fix problem between Wolves' pipes," *The Sudbury Star*, 3 November 1972.

14   "Greyhounds crouched, ready to streak past Wolves tonight," *The*

Sudbury Star, 14 November 1972; "Hounds' howl 'beat Wolves,'" *The Sudbury Star*, 15 November 1972.

15   "Reminder of short gone old days in the now defunct NOHA loop," *The Sudbury Star*, 12 December 1972; "Wolves trainer out in cold, players refused to practise," *The Sudbury Star*, 16 December 1972; "Burke raps media," *The Northern Life*, 24 November 1976.

16   Mervin "Bud" Burke, interview by Scott Miller, 7 October 2020.

17   "Kitchener vacates OHA Jr. 'A' cellar, beats Wolves 9-6," *The Sudbury Star*, 11 November 1972; "Petes pushed by Wolves to earn late 3-3 draw," *The Sudbury Star*, 12 December 1972.

18   "Wolves usher new coach into OHA Jr. 'A' ranks on 5-5 tie," *The Sudbury Star*, 8 January 1973; "Chrysler goes to St. Kitts for three players," *The Sudbury Star*, 11 January 1973; "Wolves name 19-man roster for OHA, one local player, McCourt, gets nod," *The Sudbury Star*, 11 January 1973; "It was some homecoming Generals had planned," *The Sudbury Star*, 12 January 1973.

19   Tim Stortini, interview by Scott Miller, 24 September 2020.

20   "Cubs close checking upsets parent Wolves," *The Sudbury Star*, 23 January 1973.

21   "Rangers domination of Sudbury entry bright spot on the year," *The Sudbury Star*, 10 February 1973; "New Sudbury Wolves' coach gets rough initiation into OHA," *The Sudbury Star*, 12 February 1973; "Vail tallies two as Wolves beat Rangers," *The Sudbury Star*, 24 February 1973.

22   Commito, "The Sudbury Wolves' First NHL Draft Pick: Morris Titanic."

23   "Wolves couldn't handle hit, score strategy," *The Sudbury Star*, 29 March 1973; "Wolves coming out licking chops," *The Sudbury Star*, 31 March 1973; "Wolves step closer to end of season in OHA Junior 'A' play," *The Sudbury Star*, 2 April 1973; "'They took penalties, we got goals' a good assessment of Wolves' last game," *The Sudbury Star*, 4 April 1973.

24   Commito, "The Sudbury Wolves' First NHL Draft Pick: Morris Titanic."

25   "The Sports Scene with Cummy Burton," *The Northern Life*, 12 September 1973.

26 "The Sports Scene with Cummy Burton," *The Northern Life*, 6 June 1973.

27 "Neeld a General," *The Globe and Mail*, 1 September 1973.

28 Joe Bowen, interview by Scott Miller, 21 September 2020.

29 "Gord McTavish leads Wolves to 6-4 victory over Greyhounds," *The Sudbury Star*, 28 September 1973.

30 "The Wolves Hot and Hungry," *The Northern Life*, 24 October 1973.

31 Tim Stortini, interview by Scott Miller, 25 September 2020.

32 "The Sports Scene with Cummy Burton," *The Northern Life*, 27 December 1973.

33 Buse, 244.

34 "The Sports Scene with Cummy Burton," *The Northern Life*, 19 December 1973.

35 Tim Stortini, interview by Scott Miller, 25 September 2020.

36 Ken Campbell, interview by Scott Miller, 15 June 2020.

37 "Wolves defeat Russians with close checking," *The Sudbury Star*, 27 December 1973.

38 Ken Campbell, interview by Scott Miller, 15 June 2020.

39 "Wolves defeat Russians with close checking," *The Sudbury Star*, 27 December 1973.

40 Mike Marson, interview by Markus Schwabe, *CBC Morning North*, https://www.cbc.ca/player/play/2682789886 (accessed 23 August 2020).

41 "Stubborn Wolves lose to Rangers in series," *The Sudbury Star*, 1 April 1974.

42 "Breaking Barriers," *The Agenda with Steve Paikin*, https://www.youtube.com/watch?v=qURwlyzcCA4 (accessed 23 August 2020).

43 "Against the Odds: Remembering Mike Marson's Career with the Caps," https://www.nhl.com/capitals/news/against-the-odds-remembering-mike-marsons-career-with-the-caps/c-305201080 (accessed 23 August 2020).

44 "Sports Roundup," *The Globe and Mail*, 6 April 1974.

45 "Tugging at long locks a no-no," *The Globe and Mail*, 6 November 1975.

46 "The Sports Scene with Cummy Burton," *The Northern Life*, 5 June 1974.

47 Joe Drago, interview by Scott Miller, 16 January 2021.

48   "Schmalz Cup Trophy," http://pjhl.pointstreaksites.com/view/pjhl/about-us/history-1/schmalz-cup-trophy (accessed 26 August 2020).

49   "The 'Pack' is back!" *The Northern Life*, 11 September 1974.

50   "'B' league all-stars offensive-minded, talent-rich Wolves' tamers," *The Sudbury Star*, 31 January 1973; Randy Carlyle, interview by Scott Miller, 26 September 2020.

51   "Coach Duncan plans new strategy for Wolves, speedsters hard to catch in rough going," *The Northern Life*, 5 June 1974.

52   "Duncan aims Sudbury Wolves for top of the Major rung on the Junior 'A' ladder," *The Northern Life*, 18 September 1974.

53   "Berk Keaney finally sets the record straight!" *The Northern Life*, 4 December 1974.

54   "Marlies over-come second period plunge," *The Northern Life*, 20 November 1974; "He'll be gone next year," *The Northern Life*, 19 March 1975.

55   "Wolves' Rod Schutt selected to team as OHA released 1974-75 dream squad," *The Sudbury Star*, 8 April 1975.

56   "Wolves on prowl!" *The Northern Life*, 26 March 1975; "Play-off fever hits town," *The Northern Life*, 26 March 1975.

57   "Play-off fever hits town," *The Northern Life*, 26 March 1975.

58   "Wolves maul 67s 6-1 in first contest," *The Sudbury Star*, 26 March 1975.

59   "Make-or-break contest for Wolves vs. Ottawa," *The Sudbury Star*, 4 April 1975.

60   "Ottawa goaltender stops Wolves in attempt to wrap up playoff," *The Sudbury Star*, 5 April 1975.

61   "Wolves fight back to enter semi-finals," *The Northern Life*, 9 April 1975.

62   "'We're ready' says Duncan as Wolves visit Marlies," *The Sudbury Star*, 9 April 1975.

63   Joe Bowen, interview by Scott Miller, 21 September 2020.

64   Randy Carlyle, interview by Scott Miller, 25 September 2020.

65   "Coach Duncan yanks Bedard, benches Farrish as Marlies romp to easy 8-1 victory," *The Sudbury Star*, 10 April 1975; "Wolves facing must game against Marlies with team attitude important ingredient," *The Sudbury*

Star, 11 April 1975; "Egg on ice 'no yoke' for Marlies; Wolves' spurt wins game," *The Sudbury Star*, 12 April 1975.

66 "Wolves show off true grit in 4-4 draw with Marlies," *The Sudbury Star*, 14 April 1975; "Wolves take command of series with 5-3 victory over Marlboros," *The Sudbury Star*, 15 April 1975.

67 "Goal judge 'avoids rush,' angers Duncan … and Marlies win," *The Sudbury Star*, 16 April 1975.

68 Ibid.

69 "Magical effect gone as Wolves triumph," *The Sudbury Star*, 17 April 1975; "Hamilton … or bust tonight as Wolves play deciding game at home," *The Sudbury Star*, 19 April 1975.

70 "Wolves eliminated by Marlboros in overtime of eighth game," *The Sudbury Star*, 21 April 1975.

71 Joe Bowen, interview by Scott Miller, 21 September 2020.

72 Ibid.; "One bad pass and it was all over," *The Northern Life*, 23 April 1975.

73 "Tugging at long locks a no-no," *The Globe and Mail*, 6 November 1975.

74 Randy Carlyle, interview by Scott Miller, 26 September 2020.

75 Joe Bowen, interview by Scott Miller, 21 September 2020.

76 Ben Leeson, "Sudbury Accent: Remembering the 1975-76 Wolves," https://www.thesudburystar.com/2016/04/16/sudbury-accent-remembering-the-1975-76-wolves/wcm/27c39ff3-6447-110a-93f4-006c787c-dd94 (accessed 26 September 2020).

77 Ken Campbell, interview Scott Miller, 15 June 2020.

78 Joe Bowen, interview by Scott Miller, 21 September 2020.

79 Randy Carlyle, interview by Scott Miller, 26 September 2020.

80 Ben Leeson, "Sudbury Accent: Remembering the 1975-76 Wolves."

81 Randy Carlyle, interview by Scott Miller, 26 September 2020.

82 "Fight-filled third period," *The Sudbury Star*, 29 March 1976.

83 "Greyhounds score impressive 4-2 win," *The Sudbury Star*, 31 March 1976.

84 "Young Fox leads 8-0 win by Wolves," *The Sudbury Star*, 1 April 2020; "Wolves eliminate Greyhounds," *The Sudbury Star*, 5 April 1976.

85 "Wolves bounced 7-4 in first game," *The Sudbury Star*, 8 April 1976;

"Wolves put emphasis on Lee for 7-3 playoff win," *The Sudbury Star*, 10 April 1976; "Duguay sparks Wolves to victory," *The Sudbury Star*, 12 April 1976.

86 "Roast beef dinner sparks Wolves to convincing victory over 67s," *The Sudbury Star*, 14 April 1976; "Class of OHA, Wolves and Fincups to meet in final showdown," *The Sudbury Star*, 15 April 1976.

87 "Game 1: Wolves host Fincups," *The Sudbury Star*, 19 April 1976.

88 Joe Bowen, interview by Scott Miller, 21 September 2020.

89 Randy Carlyle, interview by Scott Miller, 27 September 2020.

90 "First loss since Nov. 13," *The Globe and Mail*, 17 December 1975.

91 "Wolves defence absent in game as Fincups romp to 8-3 victory," *The Sudbury Star*, 20 April 1976.

92 "Wolves get important 7-5 win but penalties prolong outcome," *The Sudbury Star*, 24 April 1976; "Fincups take 4-2 win," *The Sudbury Star*, 27 April 1976; "Former 'Hound scores winning goal," *The Sudbury Star*, 29 April 1976.

93 Ken Campbell, interview by Scott Miller, 15 June 2020.

94 Ibid.

95 Ben Leeson, "Sudbury Accent: Remembering the 1975-76 Wolves."

96 Joe Bowen, interview by Scott Miller, 21 September 2020.

97 Randy Carlyle, interview by Scott Miller, 26 September 2020.

98 Ibid.

99 "Hockey on Topper's mind as Wolves set for camp," *The Sudbury Star*, 1 September 1976.

100 Ben Leeson, "Sudbury Accent: Remembering the 1975-76 Wolves."

101 "Wolves can hold heads high despite losing playoff set," *The Northern Life*, 29 April 1976.

CHAPTER 3: REBUILD AND REBOUND, 1976-1980

1 Buse, 246.

2 "Canadians will provide Wolves with stiff puck test," *The Sudbury Star*, 23 September 1976.

3 Ibid.

4   "Wolves sign 18 players on roster," *The Sudbury Star*, 18 September 1976.

5   "Wolves ink goalies; 'showdown' planned," *The Sudbury Star*, 24 September 1976.

6   "Wolves blow season opener," *The Sudbury Star*, 25 September 1976; "Wolves look to avenge loss against 67's at Arena tonight," *The Sudbury Star*, 8 October 1976.

7   "Wolves now in second," *The Sudbury Star*, 12 October 1976; "Shaw aids Wolves in win, not happy to see new goalie," *The Sudbury Star*, 8 November 1976.

8   "Upcoming trade likely for veteran," *The Sudbury Star*, 12 November 1976; "Duguay breaking club rules," *The Sudbury Star*, 16 November 1976.

9   "Wolves win easily over lowly Generals," *The Sudbury Star*, 20 November 1976.

10   "Papers have space," *The Sudbury Star*, 26 November 1976; "Wolves re-impose ban on The Star," *The Sudbury Star*, 2 December 1976; "The Star Won't Get Anything Out of Us!" *The Sudbury Star*, 3 December 1976.

11   "Porketta bingo is Sudbury's delicious passion," *The Toronto Star*, 16 December 2011.

12   "Wolves pick ex-NHLer Price as new coach," *The Sudbury Star*, 28 January 1977.

13   "Emms Division against Leyden Division," *The Sudbury Star*, 2 February 1977; "McCourt shines in all-star contest," *The Sudbury Star*, 3 February 1977.

14   "For May, 1978: City gets Memorial Cup playoffs," *The Sudbury Star*, 3 February 1977.

15   "The word from Ron is 'I'll be alright,' *The Northern Life*, 9 March 1977.

16   "Wolves Dump Canadians: Marini deadly around net," *The Sudbury Star*, 26 February 1977.

17   "Canadians win opener," *The Sudbury Star*, 19 March 1977; "Wolves' success in Kingston ended with loss," *The Sudbury Star*, 21 March 1977; "Canadians hold six point lead," *The Sudbury Star*, 23 March 1977; "Wolves get playoff tie," *The Sudbury Star*, 26 March 1977; "Pierce's tally pulls out win," *The Sudbury Star*, 28 March 1977; "Canadians eliminate

Wolves," *The Sudbury Star*, 30 March 1977.

18   "Long season ahead," *The Sudbury Star*, 13 September 1977.

19   "Greyhounds trounce inept Wolves squad," *The Sudbury Star*, 7 September 1977.

20   Dario Zulich, interview by Scott Miller, 25 September 2020.

21   "Trim Greyhounds by 7-5 score," *The Sudbury Star*, 28 September 1977.

22   "Familiar voice on the line," *The Sudbury Star*, 15 November 1977.

23   "Wolves disappointing fans," *The Sudbury Star*, 14 November 1977; "Wolves sign Bep Guidolin," *The Sudbury Star*, 16 November 1977.

24   "Fired Guidolin suing Wolves," *The Sudbury Star*, 21 February 1978; "New skipper finds success, Wolves grab upset triumph," *The Sudbury Star*, 21 February 1978.

25   "The decision must come," *The Sudbury Star*, 5 January 1978; "Jarvis paces way in Spitfires' win," *The Sudbury Star*, 3 February 1978; "Walker sparks win," *The Sudbury Star*, 13 February 1978.

26   Buse, 245.

27   "Wolves' mascot found in Toronto," *The Northern Life*, 18 January 1978.

28   "Sobey's Hometown Hockey: Sudbury's 'Wolf on a Wire,' https://www.sportsnet.ca/nhl/video/sudburys-wolf-wire-one-best-least-understood-traditions/ (accessed 25 January 2022).

29   "Greyhounds confirm inevitable fact: Wolves destined to place last," *The Sudbury Star*, 8 March 1978.

30   "Bud wants to sell out," *The Sudbury Star*, 3 January 1977.

31   "Wolves' first fan still with the team," *The Sudbury Star*, 28 September 2011.

32   "Sudbury Wolves on selling block," *The Sudbury Star*, 28 January 1978.

33   "Tickets going quick for cup event here," *The Sudbury Star*, 29 November 1977; "Opener Saturday," *The Sudbury Star*, 5 May 1978.

34   "1932 Cub Wolves were the toast of the town once again," *The Sudbury Star*, 17 May 1978.

35   "Face Soo Greyhound tonight: Laing optimistic over new season," *The Sudbury Star*, 13 September 1978; "Wolves seek improved year with youthful skating club," *The Sudbury Star*, 21 September 1978.

36   "Foligno key figure in Wolves' season," *The Sudbury Star*, 8 September

1978.

37   "Wolves dance to a winning tune," *The Sudbury Star*, 23 September 1978; "Natives are restless," *The Sudbury Star*, 28 November 1978; "Wolves face crucial test," *The Sudbury Star*, 1 December 1978.

38   "Wolves blanked by 67's 6-0; not since '74," *The Sudbury Star*, 15 January 1979.

39   "Remembering 1978-79," *The Sudbury Star*, 9 January 2010.

40   "Wolves 'could go all the way,' says coach," *The Northern Life*, 29 August 1979.

41   "MacQueen leads Sudbury attack against London," *The Sudbury Star*, 12 March 1979.

42   "Beaupre gains first shutout: Wolves blank Rangers with ease," *The Sudbury Star*, 14 November 1978; "Beaupre outstanding for Wolves spearheading win over Generals," *The Sudbury Star*, 24 March 1979.

43   "Curling, hockey pioneers to be inducted June 13," *The Sudbury Star*, 15 May 2001.

44   "Wolves follow Hollywood script," *The Sudbury Star*, 8 March 1979; "Foligno adds four points in 8-2 rout," *The Sudbury Star*, 10 March 1979; "MacQueen leads Sudbury attack against London," *The Sudbury Star*, 12 March 1979.

45   Gord Ewin, interview by Scott Miller, 2 November 2020.

46   "Gruhl paces Wolves in playoff win," *The Sudbury Star*, 17 March 1979; "'Brawling' tactics help Wolves take series lead," *The Sudbury Star*, 26 March 1979; "Laing – 'Oshawa pussycats on road'," *The Sudbury Star*, 27 March 1979.

47   "Wolves advance to Leyden Division final round," *The Sudbury Star*, 28 March 1979.

48   "Laing optimistic as Wolves prepare to pound Peterboro," *The Sudbury Star*, 5 April 1979; "Wolves edged once again as Petes assume command," *The Sudbury Star*, 7 April 1979; "Wolves take crucial win as Lekun provides spark," *The Sudbury Star*, 9 April 1979; "Wolves vanish from scene as Petes continue search," *The Sudbury Star*, 14 April 1979.

49   Joe Drago, interview by Scott Miller, 16 January 2021.

50   "Sports Roundup Hockey," *The Globe and Mail*, 18 June 1979.

51 "Wolves 'could go all way,' says coach," *The Northern Life*, 29 August 1979.

52 Mervin "Bud" Burke, interview by Scott Miller, 7 October 2020.

53 "Bowen replaces Hewat on Leaf NHL broadcasts," *The Globe and Mail*, 27 September 1982.

54 Gord Ewin, interview by Scott Miller, 2 November 2020.

55 "Wolves shift onus to defence this season," *The Northern Life*, 26 September 1979.

56 "Wolves hurting but confident of victory," *The Sudbury Star*, 16 November 1979; "Woofers having problems," *The Sudbury Star*, 26 November 1979; "Petes bite Wolves in clean game," *The Sudbury Star*, 14 December 1979.

57 "Wolves on road in weekend play," *The Sudbury Star*, 31 January 1980.

58 "Goal judge's decision helps Wolves end season with a win," *The Sudbury Star*, 14 March 1980.

59 "Wolves whip Kingston in opener," *The Sudbury Star*, 17 March 1980; "Wolves in series command after win over Canadians," *The Sudbury Star*, 19 March 1980; "Wolves move on with third win," *The Sudbury Star*, 21 March 1980.

60 "Sudbury takes series opener on 4 by Allison," *The Globe and Mail*, 28 March 1980.

61 "Allison holds birthday fete as Wolves trip Peterborough," *The Sudbury Star*, 28 March 1980.

62 "'Captain Colorado' rides again: Overtime victory goes to Wolves 6-5," *The Sudbury Star*, 31 March 1980.

63 "Petes tie playoff series on Cirella's clutch goal," *The Sudbury Star*, 2 April 1980.

64 "Wolves end 1979-80 season with loss to Petes," *The Sudbury Star*, 5 April 1980.

65 "The Seventies are Now History," *The INCO Triangle*, January 1980.

66 Sarlo, 1-17.

CHAPTER 4: GREEN, WHITE, AND RED, 1980-1985

1 C.M. Wallace, "The 1980s" in *Sudbury: Rail Town to Regional Capital*, ed. C.M. Wallace and Ashley Thomson (Toronto: Dundurn Press Limited, 1993), 275-77; "Sudbury economy to get facelift," *The Globe and Mail*, 27 November 1982.

2 "1990 London Knights at Sudbury Wolves – Part 1," https://www.youtube.com/watch?v=Vc4R1PuGN4c (accessed October 10 2020).

3 Craig Duncanson, interview by Scott Miller, 23 September 2020.

4 "OMJHL will receive new name in 1981," *The Globe and Mail*, 25 November 1980; "Roundup Hockey," *The Globe and Mail*, 9 May 1987; "Generals take aim at Memorial Cup," *The Globe and Mail*, 9 May 1987.

5 "New Leaf Allison was the heart of the Wolves," *The Toronto Star*, 20 August 1986.

6 "Laing returns along with 80 Wolves hopefuls," *The Northern Life*, 27 August 1980.

7 "'Hounds stun Wolves," *The Sudbury Star*, 26 September 1980; "Wolves react to pressure by whipping London squad," *The Sudbury Star*, 30 September 1980.

8 "Wolves' coach suspended," *The Globe and Mail*, 29 November 1980; "Wolves cruise past Spits with third period thrust," *The Sudbury Star*, 29 November 1980.

9 "Wolves feast on Emms again, devour Marlies," *The Globe and Mail*, 16 February 1981.

10 "Boy injured: Sudbury mascot hit by penalized player," *The Globe and Mail*, 5 January 1981; "Roundup," *The Globe and Mail*, 9 January 1981.

11 "'Hounds grab top spot," *The Sudbury Star*, 14 March 1981; "Wolves end dismal season," *The Sudbury Star*, 16 March 1981.

12 "Wolves' first fan still with the team," *The Sudbury Star*, 28 September 2011.

13 Joe Drago, interview by Scott Miller, 16 January 2021.

14 Gord Ewin, interview by Scott Miller, 2 November 2020.

15 "OHL shuffles divisions; schedule unbalanced," *The Globe and Mail*, 30 May 1981; "Bulls aim to build competitive squad," *The Globe and Mail*, 1 June 1981.

16   Douglas Hunter, *Yzerman: Making of a Champion* (Random House of
      Canada Limited, 2004), 19-37.

17   "Marlies, Wolves swap centres," *The Globe and Mail*, 21 October 1981;
      "Drago raps defenceman following Wolves' loss," *The Sudbury Star*, 31
      October 1981.

18   "Strapped for cash, fans: Sudbury Wolves in tailspin," *The Globe and
      Mail*, 7 January 1982.

19   "Another OHL team may follow Guelph," *The Globe and Mail*, 6
      February 1982.

20   "Wolves end slump with 6-5 triumph," *The Globe and Mail*, 11 February
      1982; "Wolves defeat Flyers 9-7," *The Sudbury Star*, 15 February 1982.

21   "Greyhounds shade lowly Wolves 6-5," *The Sudbury Star*, 13 March
      1982.

22   Mike Commito, "Pat Verbeek: Wolves Fire, Flash and Finesse – From
      Record Books to Lightning Leadership," https://sudburywolves.com/
      article/pat-verbeek-wolves-fire-flash-and-finesse-from-record-books-to-
      lightning-leadership (accessed 14 October 2020).

23   "Greyhounds shade lowly Wolves 6-5," *The Sudbury Star*, 13 March
      1982.

24   "Guidolin out in Brantford shakeup," *The Globe and Mail*, 22 October
      1981; "Top midget pick on the move," *The Globe and Mail*, 31 May
      1982.

25   "Wolves meet Cornwall," *The Sudbury Star*, 15 October 1982; "Wolves
      lose again with poor display," *The Sudbury Star*, 11 December 1982;
      "Agreement paves way for Memorial Cup play," *The Globe and Mail*, 15
      December 1982; "Roundup Hockey," *The Globe and Mail*, 16 December
      1982.

26   "Roundup Hockey," *The Globe and Mail*, 14 May 1983; "Tough chore
      awaits coaches as OHL opens," *The Globe and Mail*, 21 September 1983.

27   "Wolves eliminated from playoff hunt," *The Sudbury Star*, 7 March 1983.

28   C.M. Wallace, "The 1980s," 276; "Layoff extended for 4,000: Falco
      closed 'til January as nickel market shrinks," *The Sudbury Star*, 11
      September 1983.

29   "Junior hockey sags in Northern Ontario," *The Globe and Mail*, 10
      February 1983.

30   "Q: 'Would it upset you if the Sudbury Wolves moved out of this city?"
     The Sudbury Star, 7 February 1983.

31   "Last hurrah for Wolves?" *The Sudbury Star*, 26 February 1983.

32   Gord Ewin, interview by Scott Miller, 2 November 2020.

33   Joe Drago, interview by Scott Miller, 16 January 2021.

34   Craig Duncanson, interview by Scott Miller, 23 September 2020.

35   "Gain no ground: Poor display by Wolves," *The Sudbury Star*, 12
     November 1983; "Harris given axe by junior Wolves," *The Sudbury Star*,
     10 January 1984; "Wolves fire Harris as coach," *The Globe and Mail*, 10
     January 1984; "Spruce to coach OHL Wolves," *The Globe and Mail*, 11
     January 1984.

36   "Spruce's debut spoiled: Kitchener raps Wolves," *The Sudbury Star*, 12
     January 1984.

37   "New height set in Wolves loss," *The Sudbury Star*, 14 January 1984.

38   Craig Duncanson, interview by Scott Miller, 23 September 2020.

39   "What's ahead for the Sudbury Wolves," *The Northern Life*, 17 March
     1984.

40   "Draft threatens junior league," *The Globe and Mail*, 21 January 1984.

41   "Wolves eye defenceman," *The Globe and Mail*, 26 May 1984.

42   Craig Duncanson, interview by Scott Miller, 23 September 2020.

43   "Wolves show early signs of respectability," *The Sudbury Star*, 15 October
     1984.

44   "Wolves trade McRae," *The Sudbury Star*, 27 October 1984; "Two more
     setbacks for Wolves," *The Sudbury Star*, 29 October 1984; "Kenny's
     debut spoiled: Errors prove costly as Wolves defeated," *The Sudbury Star*,
     19 November 1984; "Brian Verbeek," *The Kingston Whig-Standard*, 3
     December 1985.

45   "Fault clock face saver: Hapless Wolves wounded by powerplay of Cents,"
     The Sudbury Star, 10 December 1984.

46   "Wolves end winless ways," *The Sudbury Star*, 26 January 1985; "Wolves
     eliminated from playoff picture again," *The Sudbury Star*, 2 March 1985.

47   Sarlo, 25-35.

48   Craig Duncanson, interview by Scott Miller, 23 September 2020.

CHAPTER 5: ROAD TO REDEMPTION, 1985-1989

1   Wallace, "The 1980s," 277-281.

2   "OHL at a glance: Who's where in this year's OHL," *The Ottawa Citizen*, 26 September 1985; "13 players from Valley on NHL list," *The Ottawa Citizen*, 12 February 1986.

3   "Two Americans stunned in Italian tennis," *The Montreal Gazette*, 15 May 1985; "Roundup Hockey," *The Globe and Mail*, 30 July 1985; "Hockey," *The Globe and Mail*, 7 August 1985; "OHL at a glance," *The Ottawa Citizen*, 26 September 1985.

4   "Wolves win opener with spirited effort," *The Sudbury Star*, 28 September 1985; "Wolves blast Greyhounds in first rivalry showdown," *The Sudbury Star*, 19 October 1985.

5   "Wolves' Middendorf eyes elusive 100-point plateau," *The Sudbury Star*, 19 November 1985.

6   "Sudbury Wolves send Duncanson, goalie Evoy to Cornwall for Patrick, Smith and Rouleau," *The Ottawa Citizen*, 3 December 1985.

7   Craig Duncanson, interview by Scott Miller, 23 September 2020.

8   "Titus shines as Royals upset Wolves," *The Sudbury Star*, 7 December 1985.

9   Gord Ewin, interview by Scott Miller, 2 November 2020.

10   "Second spot in Emms Division until new year," *The Sudbury Star*, 21 December 1985; "Wolves nip league leading Petes," *The Sudbury Star*, 6 January 1986; "Is LaForge's days numbered in Hamilton?" *The Sudbury Star*, 22 February 1986; "At long last – Wolves in the playoffs," *The Sudbury Star*, 8 March 1986; "Nine straight losses on the road," *The Sudbury Star*, 17 March 1986.

11   "Solid showing by Wolves, but Platers win game one," *The Sudbury Star*, 24 March 1986; "Platers now lead series 4-0," *The Sudbury Star*, 26 March 1986; "It's all over! Wolves eliminated in four games," *The Sudbury Star*, 29 March 1986.

12   "OHL's Wolves have something to prove this season," *The Sudbury Star*, 25 September 1986.

13   "New to pro ranks girl, 14, upsets tourney's 9th seed," *The Toronto Star*, 16 April 1986.

14   "OHL's Wolves have something to prove this season," *The Sudbury Star*, 25 September 1986; "Spitfires have right elements to win first OHL title," *The Ottawa Citizen*, 9 October 1986.

15   "Wolves lose road opener for only the second time," *The Sudbury Star*, 26 September 1986; "Wolves triumph at long last under full moon," *The Sudbury Star*, 18 October 1986.

16   "Wound Wolves going nowhere fast," *The Sudbury Star*, 12 November 1986.

17   "Wolves shuffle pack again," *The Sudbury Star*, 19 November 1986.

18   Ken Campbell, interview by Scott Miller, 15 June 2020.

19   Joe Drago, interview by Scott Miller, 16 January 2021.

20   "Wolves president Joe Drago quits," *The Sudbury Star*, 22 November 1986.

21   Joe Drago, interview by Scott Miller, 16 January 2021.

22   "Burgess buys out all Wolves shares," *The Sudbury Star*, 25 November 1986; "Death Notices: Burgess, Kenneth 'Ken' Murray," *The Sudbury Star*, 25 February 1998.

23   "Tale of a Tiger who shone in Wolves' clothing," *The Sudbury Star*, 15 December 2020.

24   Ken Campbell, interview by Scott Miller, 15 June 2020.

25   "Wolfpak booster club gains new popularity," *The Sudbury Star*, 18 February 1987.

26   "It's all over: Wolves lose to Centennials to ending frustrating campaign," *The Sudbury Star*, 21 March 1987.

27   Ken Campbell, interview by Scott Miller, 15 June 2020.

28   "Canadians trade Laforges to Wolves for Turner, draft," *The Kingston Whig-Standard*, 21 May 1987.

29   "…And Marc Laforge is not," *The Kingston Whig-Standard*, 27 May 1987; "Top pick happy to be with Marlies," *The Toronto Star*, 31 May 1987.

30   "Happiness key for Wolves' coach," *The Globe and Mail*, 31 October 1987.

31   "One down, 65 to go: Wolves open new season with win," *The Sudbury Star*, 26 September 1987.

32   "Wallin's disciplinary moves will benefit team in long run," *The Sudbury Star*, 17 October 1987.

33   "Full slate of Gardens events rock Marlboros' schedule," *The Toronto Star*, 22 October 1987; "Happiness key for Wolves' coach," *The Globe and Mail*, 31 October 1987.

34   "A little bit of everything for the fans," *The Sudbury Star*, 7 November 1987; "OHL Roundup: One OHL award a waste of time," *The Windsor Star*, 14 November 1987; "Hockey goons are learning that crime doesn't pay," *The Gazette*, 19 November 1987.

35   "OHL player handed severest penalty in history of league," *The Ottawa Citizen*, 18 November 1987; "Ban ends player's OHL career," *The Windsor Star*, 18 November 1987; "Lengthy suspension to Laforge likely to be appealed, says agent," *The Toronto Star*, 19 November 1987.

36   "Banned player keeps on punching," *The Toronto Star*, 8 November 1998.

37   "OHL Roundup: Wolves see light at end of tunnel," *The Windsor Star*, 23 January 1988; "Wounded Wolves near death after ridiculed in Kitchener," *The Sudbury Star*, 20 February 1988.

38   "Wolves coach exaggerates Vietnam exploits," *The Sudbury Star*, 22 February 1988; "Coach resigns post after his war record found exaggerated," *The Toronto Star*, 25 February 1988.

39   "Hyped war record, Wallin quits Wolves," *The Sudbury Star*, 24 February 1988.

40   "Tall tales cost coach," *The Ottawa Citizen*, 25 February 1988; "False war stories cost coach job," *The Globe and Mail*, 25 February 1988; "Coach resigns post after his war record found exaggerated," *The Toronto Star*, 25 February 1988; "War stories cost coach hockey job," *The Vancouver Sun*, 25 February 1998; "Sudbury coach no 'war hero'," *The Windsor Star*, 25 February 1988.

41   "OHL Roundup: Wallin's exploits still in the news," *The Windsor Star*, 5 March 1988.

42   "Where are they now?: John Wallin Hockey," *The Globe and Mail*, 26 July 1988.

43   "Crawford gets wish: Wolves beat Rangers," *The Sudbury Star*, 5 March 1988.

44 "Wolves end OHL season with loss," *The Sudbury Star*, 19 March 1988; "OHL poised to put cap on trades," *The Toronto Star*, 6 December 1988.

45 Sarlo, 18-36; "HOCKEY Geoff Courtnall may join Canucks," *The Globe and Mail*, 16 July 1988; "Wolves seeking respect," *The Windsor Star*, 29 September 1988; "Wolves no longer laughing stock," *The Sudbury Star*, 30 May 1988; "Wolves opt for defence with top pick," *The Sudbury Star*, 28 May 1988.

46 "OHL Roundup: Neilson cannot forget old team," *The Windsor Star*, 28 April 1988; "Wolves known playoff promise must be kept," *The Sudbury Star*, 23 September 1988.

47 "1989-90 Sudbury Wolves interviews," https://www.youtube.com/watch?v=mcOgZsxua9w (accessed 6 November 2020).

48 "Wolves owner truly loved the game," *The Sudbury Star*, 24 February 1998.

49 Ken Campbell, interview by Scott Miller, 15 June 2020.

50 "Pennell the hero in his first overtime game," *The Sudbury Star*, 24 September 1988; "Winless streak finally over as Wolves triumph over Bulls," *The Sudbury Star*, 22 October 1988.

51 "McMaster says trade improves Wolves," *The Sudbury Star*, 4 November 1988; "Copps Coliseum and Marlboros have struck tentative agreement," *The Toronto Star*, 10 November 1988; "Wolves goalie seeing stars," *The Sudbury Star*, 7 January 1989; "Wolves Dirty Dozen line reunited against in loss to Rangers," *The Sudbury Star*, 4 March 1989.

52 "Wolves miss playoffs – again," *The Sudbury Star*, 17 March 1989.

53 "Wolves, city police benefit game raises $5,000 for cancer centre," *The Sudbury Star*, 11 March 1989.

CHAPTER 6: SUDBURY'S RENAISSANCE, 1989-1994

1 Nicola Ross, *Healing the Landscape: Celebrating Sudbury's Reclamation Story* (City of Greater Sudbury, 2008), 32-121.

2 Peter C. Newman, "Sudbury's sunny renaissance," *Maclean's*, 1 April 1991, https://archive.macleans.ca/article/1991/4/1/sudburys-sunny-renaissance#!&pid=40 (accessed 1 February 2021).

3 "1990 London Knights at Sudbury Wolves – Part 1," https://www.

youtube.com/watch?v=Vc4R1PuGN4c (accessed 10 October 2020).

4   David Cruise and Alison Griffiths, *Net Worth: Exploding the Myths of Pro Hockey* (Toronto: Penguin Books Canada, 1991), 339-353; Sarlo, 50-60; "Scouts label Lindros as can't miss prospect," *The Ottawa Citizen*, 26 May 1989.

5   "Wolves open new season with tie," *The Sudbury Star*, 23 September 1989; "Wolves end '89 with win," *The Sudbury Star*, 2 January 1990.

6   "Wolves attract record London crowd of 5,531," *The Sudbury Star*, 20 January 1990.

7   "1989-90 Sudbury Wolves Interviews," https://www.youtube.com/watch?v=mcOgZsxua9w (accessed 25 November 2020).

8   "OHL leading scorer's trade wish comes true," *The Ottawa Citizen*, 12 January 1990; "Wolves captain on a howling mission," *The Sudbury Star*, 2 February 1990; "At last – DiPietro nets No. 50," *The Sudbury Star*, 9 February 1990; "Fairy-tale comeback for the bad Wolves," *The Ottawa Citizen*, 4 February 1990; "Curling, hockey pioneers to be inducted June 13," *The Sudbury Star*, 15 May 2001.

9   "1989-90 Sudbury Wolves Interviews," https://www.youtube.com/watch?v=mcOgZsxua9w (accessed 25 November 2020).

10   "Fairy-tale comeback for the bad Wolves," *The Ottawa Citizen*, 4 February 1990.

11   "Tanner stands up Wolves as Knights take big game," *The Sudbury Star*, 28 February 1990; "Junior hockey enjoying fan renaissance," *The Ottawa Citizen*, 6 February 1990.

12   "OHL Roundup," *The Windsor Star*, 30 December 1989; "Owen Sound to face Wolves: Playoff wait is finally over," *The Sudbury Star*, 12 March 1990.

13   "Wolves beaten in wild, crazy game," *The Sudbury Star*, 19 March 1990; "Wolves face a must-win situation," *The Sudbury Star*, 20 March 1990.

14   "Back in it: Wolves hang in for first playoff win in 10 years," *The Sudbury Star*, 21 March 1990; "Wolves grind out battle over Platers," *The Sudbury Star*, 23 March 1990.

15   "Wolves blow chance to dump Platers," *The Sudbury Star*, 27 March 1990; "It's right down to the wire for the Wolves," *The Sudbury Star*, 28 March 1990.

16   "Wolves can wrap it up tonight," *The Sudbury Star*, 26 March 1990; "Wolves blow chance to dump Platers," *The Sudbury Star*, 27 March 1990; "It's right down to the wire for the Wolves," *The Sudbury Star*, 28 March 1990; "It just wasn't meant to be for the Wolves," *The Sudbury Star*, 29 March 1990; "Wolves feel robbed of playoff series win," *The Sudbury Star*, 29 March 1990; "Wolves howling mad," *The Gazette*, 30 March 1990; "Carson ready to become franchise games leader on Thursday," *The Sudbury Star*, 5 March 2020.

17   "DiPietro scores with the big boys," *The Windsor Star*, 29 September 1989; "1993 Stanley Cup archive: Canadiens win final game and their 24th Cup," *The Montreal Gazette*, 9 June 2018.

18   "1989-90 Sudbury Wolves Interviews," https://www.youtube.com/watch?v=mcOgZsxua9w (accessed 30 November 2020).

19   "OHL welcomes Detroit franchise back in fold," *The Ottawa Citizen*, 12 December 1989; "Peca surprise pick on OHL draft day," *The Toronto Star*, 27 May 1990; "Wolves Corner," *The Sudbury Star*, 7 January 1991.

20   "Wolves fall flat in home-opener," *The Sudbury Star*, 22 September 1990; "OHL Roundup: No junior venue for Memorial Cup," *The Windsor Star*, 6 October 1990; "Wolves Corner," *The Sudbury Star*, 27 November 1990; "OHL Roundup: Season suspension in boarding incident," *The Windsor Star*, 22 December 1990.

21   "Toronto gymnast Umeh third at French meet," *The Gazette*, 17 December 1990; "Trouble follows quipster goalie," *Edmonton Journal*, 7 February 1991.

22   "Wolves' Young suspended for rest of season," *The Ottawa Citizen*, 21 December 1990; "Stiff penalty jars Sudbury juniors," *The Globe and Mail*, 22 December 1990; "Will Jason Young be back?" *The Sudbury Star*, 1 March 1991; "Young rejoins Wolves," *The Toronto Star*, 12 March 1991; "Playoffs: Sudbury has shot," *The Sudbury Star*, 15 March 1991.

23   "Wolves season analyzed," *The Sudbury Star*, 15 March 1991.

24   "Wolves prove they can match best," *The Sudbury Star*, 9 March 1991.

25   Ibid.

26   "Oshawa takes series opener," *The Sudbury Star*, 18 March 1991; "Wolves bomb Generals," *The Sudbury Star*, 23 March 1991; "Wolves one loss

away from season's end," *The Sudbury Star*, 25 March 1991; "Wolves bite bullet," *The Sudbury Star*, 27 March 1991.

27   "Wolves bite bullet," *The Sudbury Star*, 27 March 1991.

28   Sarlo, 65-66.

29   "Leyden division preview: Young star steals hype in Leyden," *The Windsor Star*, 26 September 1991.

30   Mike Commito, "Jamie Rivers Reflects on 40-Win Season in 1994-95," https://sudburywolves.com/article/jamie-rivers-reflects-on-40-win-season-in-1994-95 (accessed 14 December 2020).

31   "Wolves whip Knights," *The Sudbury Star*, 21 September 1991.

32   "Wolves bent on revenge," *The Sudbury Star*, 15 March 1992.

33   Mike Commito, "Jamie Rivers Reflects on 40-Win Season in 1994-95," https://sudburywolves.com/article/jamie-rivers-reflects-on-40-win-season-in-1994-95 (accessed 14 December 2020).

34   "Junior rivalries attract American fans," *The Calgary Herald*, 11 February 1992.

35   "No peals pending as deadline looms," *The Ottawa Citizen*, 10 January 1992; "Wolves hammer Ambassadors," *The Sudbury Star*, 11 January 1992.

36   "Chorus of boos greet Lindros," *The Sudbury Star*, 14 March 1992.

37   "Wolves bent on revenge," *The Sudbury Star*, 15 March 1992; "Good effort, but Wolves lose in playoff opener," *The Sudbury Star*, 17 March 1992; "Wolves win at last," *The Sudbury Star*, 21 March 1992; "Wolves win at last," *The Sudbury Star*, 21 March 1992; "Wolves in trouble after OT loss," *The Sudbury Star*, 23 March 1992.

38   "Still alive: Wolves force a sixth game in Oshawa tonight," *The Sudbury Star*, 24 March 1992; "Wolves survive for at least one more game," *The Sudbury Star*, 25 March 1992.

39   "Wolves-Generals finale tonight a complete sellout," *The Sudbury Star*, 26 March 1992.

40   "Finally! Wolves give fans reason to celebrate," *The Sudbury Star*, 27 March 1992; "Wolves win OT thriller," *The Sudbury Star*, 27 March 1992.

41   "Wolves-mania hits Sudbury," *The Sudbury Star*, 29 March 1992; "Playoff rivalry begins for Wolves, Cents," *The Sudbury Star*, 29 March 1992.

42   "Rough night for Wolves in opener," *The Sudbury Star*, 30 March 1992; "Give me a break! Sudbury Wolves certainly can't find any in home loss to North Bay," *The Sudbury Star*, 1 April 1992; "Ouch! Wolves on the ropes after loss to North Bay," *The Sudbury Star*, 3 April 1992; "Wolves dumped in four," *The Sudbury Star*, 5 April 1992.

43   Sarlo, 69-71.

44   "Bye Bye Wolves," *The Sudbury Star*, 7 April 1992.

45   "MacKenzie steps down as Wolves GM, coach," *The Sudbury Star*, 6 May 1992.

46   "The wait is over! Wolves hire new coach," *The Sudbury Star*, 25 May 1992; "Local Roundup: Way closes in on Olympics," *The Windsor Star*, 27 May 1992; "Potvin helps Baby Leafs extend series," *The Toronto Star*, 28 May 1992.

47   "Wolves win season opener," *The Sudbury Star*, 25 September 1992.

48   "Wolves, Cents rivalry heats up," *The Sudbury Star*, 26 September 1992; "Good deal, Sam: Many approve of Convery going to Thunder," *The Sudbury Star*, 30 October 1992.

49   "Playoff opener at home," *The Sudbury Star*, 20 March 1993.

50   "100-point club," *The Sudbury Star*, 12 March 1993.

51   "Junior hockey," *The Ottawa Citizen*, 16 January 1993.

52   "Stuffed wolf, community work add to Sudbury's team success," *The Toronto Star*, 7 March 1993.

53   "Wolves win opener: Armstrong's five goals spark Sudbury in Game 1," *The Sudbury Star*, 22 March 1993; "Wolves one win away," *The Sudbury Star*, 29 March 1993; "Shell-shocked: Wolves take a Royal pounding in Newmarket," *The Sudbury Star*, 1 April 1993.

54   "Sudbury tastes playoff victory," *The Sudbury Star*, 2 April 1993.

55   "Wolves get last laugh," *The Sudbury Star*, 2 April 1993.

56   "Wolves take early lead," *The Sudbury Star*, 5 April 1993; "Wolves coach looks on bright side of Thursday's loss," *The Sudbury Star*, 10 April 1993; "Wolves bow out: Sudbury loses to Peterborough in dramatic Game 7," *The Sudbury Star*, 16 April 1993.

57   Sarlo, 77-84.

58   "Wolves slump as season about to start," *The Sudbury Star*, 20 September

1993; "Wolves rated high," *The Sudbury Star*, 24 September 1993; "Wolves player at crossroads," *The Sudbury Star*, 1 February 1994.

59 "Wolves down Generals," *The Sudbury Star*, 31 October 1993.

60 "Wolves give fans Halloween treat," *The Sudbury Star*, 1 November 1993.

61 "Fresh start for new Wolves," *The Sudbury Star*, 10 December 1993; "Wolves wonder what might have been," *The Sudbury Star*, 13 April 1993.

62 Mike Commito, "Macauley Carson Set to Make Wolves History," https://sudburywolves.com/article/macauley-carson-set-to-make-wolves-history (accessed 14 December 2020).

63 "Milley ready to make history," *The Sudbury Star*, 17 March 2000.

64 "Major Junior: Rivers CHL player of the month," *The Ottawa Citizen*, 9 March 1994.

65 "Wolves down 67's: Rivers hits milestone with six-point game," *The Sudbury Star*, 19 February 1994.

66 Mike Commito, "Jamie Rivers Reflects on 40-Win Season in 1994-95," https://sudburywolves.com/article/jamie-rivers-reflects-on-40-win-season-in-1994-95 (accessed 14 December 2020).

67 "Wolves set new record," *The Sudbury Star*, 5 March 1994; "Sudbury Wolves clinch third," *The Sudbury Star*, 19 March 1994.

68 "Commanding lead: Mullin, Venedam lead Wolves to playoff win," *The Sudbury Star*, 28 March 1994; "Wolves advance: Sudbury eliminates Oshawa with overtime win," *The Sudbury Star*, 30 March 1994.

69 "Round 2: Wolves hope to reach third round for the first time in 13 seasons," *The Sudbury Star*, 2 April 1994.

70 "Today," *The Ottawa Citizen*, 3 April 1994; "Hockey: Simpson hero again as 67's advance," *The Ottawa Citizen*, 11 April 1994.

71 "Goodbye Wolves," *The Sudbury Star*, 11 April 1994; "Wolves wonder what might have been," *The Sudbury Star*, 13 April 1994.

CHAPTER 7: HOWLING ALONG, 1995-1999

1 "Hockey: OHL agrees to realign into three divisions," *The Ottawa Citizen*, 4 June 1994.

2 "McMaster resigns: But, he will stay on to handle next OHL draft," *The Sudbury Star*, 16 April 1994.

3   "Kings crown new GM," *Edmonton Journal*, 25 May 1994; "Gretzky finally traded to Blues," *The Globe and Mail*, 28 February 1996; "McMaster loses his crown in L.A.: Kings fire GM after missing play-offs," *The Montreal Gazette*, 23 April 1997.

4   "Howling to a championship?" *The Sudbury Star*, 23 September 1994.

5   "Siberian via Israel cracks Ranger lineup," *The Toronto Star*, 12 October 1994.

6   "Windsor deals Adams for draft pick," *The Windsor Star*, 10 January 1995; "Wolves, Thunder trade," *The Globe and Mail*, 11 January 1995.

7   "Wolves' Coupal suspended for season," *The Toronto Star*, 22 November 1994; "Commissioner not picking on Wolves," *The Sudbury Star*, 25 November 1994.

8   "Ouch! Wolves blow 4-1 lead in loss to Centennials," *The Sudbury Star*, 13 March 1995.

9   "Season ends on winning note," *The Sudbury Star*, 18 March 1995.

10   Mike Commito, "Jamie Rivers Reflects on 40-Win Season in 1994-95," https://sudburywolves.com/article/jamie-rivers-reflects-on-40-win-season-in-1994-95 (accessed 17 December 2020).

11   "Wolves, Rangers set to clash in OHL playoff opener Sunday," *The Sudbury Star*, 17 March 1995; "A blowout: Wolves go 7-for-9 on the powerplay in lopsided playoff win over Rangers," *The Sudbury Star*, 20 March 1995; "Blowout II: Wolves hit double figures again to take commanding 2-0 lead," *The Sudbury Star*, 22 March 1995; "No sweep: Goalie Belitski hot as Wolves lose to Rangers," *The Sudbury Star*, 23 March 1995; "Finally: Wolves need 71 minutes to win 4-3," *The Sudbury Star*, 25 March 1995; "One down, three to go," *The Sudbury Star*, 27 March 1995.

12   "Solid effort: Moore's penalty shot marker sparks Wolves," *The Sudbury Star*, 1 April 1995; "Brutal effort: Wolves not much of a threat in loss to Spits," *The Sudbury Star*, 3 April 1995; "Spitfires even score," *The Windsor Star*, 3 April 1995.

13   "Wolves bark worse than their bite," *The Windsor Star*, 6 April 1995.

14   "Spitfires take 2-1 lead in series: Wolves rally falls short," *The Sudbury Star*, 7 April 1995.

15   "Sudbury wins in Windsor: Wolves deadlock series with Spits," *The Sudbury Star*, 8 April 1995; "Unbelievable! Wolves take 3-2 lead in series over Spitfires after scoring six goals in the first nine minutes," *The Sudbury Star*, 10 April 1995.

16   "Spitfires crash," *The Windsor Star*, 12 April 1995; "Bye Bye Spitfires: Wolves now advance to the OHL's semifinals," *The Sudbury Star*, 12 April 1995.

17   "Last-minute collapse," *The Sudbury Star*, 16 April 1995; "Close again, but Wolves suffer another one-goal loss," *The Sudbury Star*, 18 April 1995.

18   "Close again, but Wolves suffer another one-goal loss," *The Sudbury Star*, 18 April 1995.

19   "Back in the hunt," *The Sudbury Star*, 19 April 1995; "All tied up: Wolves nip Jr. Red Wings 4-3 again at home," *The Sudbury Star*, 21 April 1995; "On the road: Weekend trip to Detroit for Wolves fans was an exciting one," *The Sudbury Star*, 24 April 1995.

20   "One to go: Wolves one win away from berth in OHL final," *The Sudbury Star*, 23 April 1995.

21   Mike Commito, "Jamie Rivers Reflects on 40-Win Season in 1994-95," https://sudburywolves.com/article/jamie-rivers-reflects-on-40-win-season-in-1994-95 (accessed 21 December 2020); "Down to the wire: Wolves, Red Wings going to a seventh game," *The Sudbury Star*, 25 April 1995.

22   "Massacre in Motown," *The Sudbury Star*, 27 April 1995.

23   Mike Commito, "Jamie Rivers Reflects on 40-Win Season in 1994-95," https://sudburywolves.com/article/jamie-rivers-reflects-on-40-win-season-in-1994-95 (accessed 21 December 2020).

24   "Wolves opening the season on the road for only the sixth time," *The Sudbury Star*, 22 September 1995; "Wolves run out of gas in Soo season opener," *The Sudbury Star*, 23 September 1995.

25   "OHL Standings," *The Sudbury Star*, 29 December 1995; "Bleeding's getting worse for Wolves," *The Sudbury Star*, 15 January 1996.

26   "Call him head coach: Lalonde becomes bench boss No. 20 for the OHL's Wolves," *The Sudbury Star*, 16 January 1996.

27   "So far, so good: Lalonde wins his first game as Wolves coach," *The Sudbury Star*, 20 January 1996; "Wolves are knocking at death's door," *The Sudbury Star*, 11 March 1996; "It's all over! No playoffs for the Wolves this season," *The Sudbury Star*, 13 March 1996; "Wolves win meaningless game," *The Sudbury Star*, 16 March 1996.

28   "What went wrong? Plenty of problems plagued the Wolves," *The Sudbury Star*, 13 March 1996.

29   "Foligno's night to remember," *The Sudbury Star*, 21 September 1996.

30   Ibid.

31   "Now it's for real: Wolves open 25th season tonight," *The Sudbury Star*, 20 September 1996.

32   "Blue line special – Defenceman Paul Mara is top rated American in NHL draft," *Pittsburgh Post-Gazette*, 17 June 1997, https://news.google.com/newspapers?nid=1129&dat=19970617&id=CogNAAAAIBAJ&sjid=mm8DAAAAIBAJ&pg=3421,261676 (accessed 4 January 2021).

33   "It's all over: Wolves win 5-3 to finish season with 50 points," *The Sudbury Star*, 15 March 1997.

34   "22 games to go: Wolves hope for win to start final third of season," *The Sudbury Star*, 31 January 1997; "Lalonde fires himself," *The Sudbury Star*, 4 February 1997; "Win greets start of Nystrom Era," *The Sudbury Star*, 5 February 1997.

35   Mike Commito, "Perseverance and determination: Sean Venedam's incredible comeback," https://sudburywolves.com/article/perseverance-and-determination-sean-venedams-incredible-story-back-onto-the-ice (accessed 25 October 2019).

36   Ibid.

37   Ibid.; "Behind the covers of human books," *The Toronto Star*, 26 January 2013.

38   "Sudbury starts season with eight rookies," *The Sudbury Star*, 19 September 1997; "Otters spoil Wolves 1997 debut," *The Sudbury Star*, 20 September 1997; "Wolves' 1997 draft class possibly best ever," *The Sudbury Star*, 20 October 2000.

39   "Axed: Wolves head coach fired," *The Sudbury Star*, 8 October 1997; "Wolves hire Watt to spark players," *The Sudbury Star*, 9 October 1997;

"Fired Wolves coach caught off guard by dismissal," *The Sudbury Star*, 9 October 1997; "Watt takes over: New coach puts Wolves through their paces," *The Sudbury Star*, 10 October 1997; "Watt(a) start! Wolves play for two periods, but still win," *The Sudbury Star*, 11 October 1997.

40   "Lalonde gets full support from Burgess," *The Sudbury Star*, 25 October 1997; "Finally … it's official!" *The Sudbury Star*, 19 December 1997; "Wolves' power play stalls again," *The Sudbury Star*, 20 December 1997.

41   "Death Notices: Burgess, Kenneth 'Ken' Murray," *The Sudbury Star*, 25 February 1998; "Wolves owner truly loved the game," *The Sudbury Star*, 24 February 1998; "Wolves clinch playoff spot," *The Sudbury Star*, 28 February 1998.

42   "Sloppy effort, but Wolves end regular season with win," *The Sudbury Star*, 14 March 1998; "Sudbury's tying goal waved off," *The Sudbury Star*, 16 March 1998; "Two-goal lead slips away from Sudbury," *The Sudbury Star*, 18 March 1998; "Wolves refuse to roll over," *The Sudbury Star*, 20 March 1998.

43   "Whole new series: Wolves deadlock series 2-2 after winning in OT," *The Sudbury Star*, 21 March 1998.

44   "Campbell does it again for the Wolves," *The Sudbury Star*, 23 March 1998; "Stormy weather ahead," *The Sudbury Star*, 25 March 1998.

45   "Storm take opener," *The Sudbury Star*, 28 March 1998; "Storm sweep past Wolves," *The Sudbury Star*, 4 April 1998.

46   "Higgs banking on Wolves' youth," *The Sudbury Star*, 25 September 1998; "The OHL's oldest rookie," *The Sudbury Star*, 25 September 1998.

47   "Episode 293: Featuring Andrew Raycroft," *Spittin' Chiclets*, 10 September 2020. https://www.barstoolsports.com/shows/18/spittin-chiclets (accessed 17 June 2021).

48   "Barnes goes to Guelph, then to St. Mike's," *The Sudbury Star*, 15 October 1998; "Wolves make history in loss to Battalion," *The Sudbury Star*, 19 October 1998.

49   "Wolves fall back to earth," *The Sudbury Star*, 23 November 1998; "Wolves by the numbers," *The Sudbury Star*, 27 November 1998; "Record night: Wolves' No. 1 line reunited for 17-point effort over Colts," *The Sudbury Star*, 19 December 1998.

50   "Second locked up," *The Sudbury Star*, 6 March 1999; "50 for Milley,"
     The Sudbury Star, 13 March 1999; "Wolves get big effort from Mikes,"
     The Sudbury Star, 18 March 1999; "OHL Award Winners," *The Windsor
     Star*, 5 June 1999.

51   "Several Wolves finish in top 10," *The Sudbury Star*, 21 March 1999.

52   "Wolves open playoffs against Bulls tonight," *The Sudbury Star*, 20
     March 1999; "Playoff opener goes to Bulls," *The Sudbury Star*, 21
     March 1999; "Wolves bullied again," *The Sudbury Star*, 22 March 1999;
     "Wolves' top line needs to produce," *The Sudbury Star*, 23 March 1999;
     "It's almost over for Wolves," *The Sudbury Star*, 24 March 1999; "A quick
     death: Bulls eliminate Wolves in four straight games," *The Sudbury Star*,
     26 March 1999.

CHAPTER 8: GREAT EXPECTATIONS, 1999-2003

1   "Wolves' training camp starts Sept. 1: Sudbury's regular season
     home-opener will be against Erie Otters Sept. 24 at Sudbury Arena," *The
     Sudbury Star* 29 July 1999, page B5.

2   "Wolves trade veteran goalie: Andrew Raycroft dealt to the Kingston
     Frontenacs for a fourth-round draft pick in 2000," *The Sudbury Star*, 10
     July 1999. Raycroft went on to win the Red Tilson Trophy that season,
     awarded to the most outstanding player (MVP) in the OHL. He was the
     first goaltender to do so in almost fifty years.

3   "Wolves ranked fifth in CHL," *The Sudbury Star*, 16 September 1999.

4   "Wolves sign Templeton," *National Post*, 28 May 1995.

5   "'Hockey was his life'," *The Sudbury Star*, 10 December 2003.

6   Bobby Chaumont, interview by Scott Miller, 15 November 2021.

7   "Wolves humbled by Hounds," *The Sudbury Star*, 19 September 1999.

8   "Wolves remain confident: Despite 0-5-0 record, team feels the wins will
     come soon," *The Sudbury Star*, 7 October 1999; "Templeton sounds off
     (again)," *The Sudbury Star*, 11 December 1999; "Wolves expect more fans
     for second half," *The Sudbury Star*, 28 January 2000; "Finally!: Wolves
     playing over .500 mark for the first time in five seasons," *The Sudbury
     Star*, 29 January 2000.

9 "Wolves' win streak ends at 13 games," *The Sudbury Star*, 19 March 2000.

10 "Sudbury Wolves blank visiting Huskies 4-0 in interlocking tilt," *The Sudbury Star*, 14 February 2000; "Wolves put pounding on 67s," *The Sudbury Star*, 23 February 2000; "Wolves rewrite record book," *The Sudbury Star*, 15 March 2000; "Milley ties Foligno's mark," *The Sudbury Star*, 18 March 2000.

11 "Wolves' win streak ends at 13 games," *The Sudbury Star*, 19 March 2000.

12 "Magnificent Milley: Norm Milley breaks Mike Foligno's career record of 166 goals," *The Sudbury Wolves*, 20 March 2000.

13 "Wolves in total control," *The Sudbury Star*, 28 March 2000.

14 "Fronts can't afford to lose," *The Kingston Whig*, 3 April 2000; "Injury-riddled Frontenacs bow out: Wolves win series in five games," *The Kingston Whig*, 4 April 2000.

15 "What a comeback!" *The Sudbury Star*, 15 April 2000.

16 "Season's over for Wolves," *The Sudbury Star*, 21 April 2000; "One week later, Wolves still furious at Game 7 loss," *The Sudbury Star*, 28 April 2000.

17 "Sudbury Wolves still tinkering with roster: Goaltender Mike Smith added Wednesday," *The Sudbury Star*, 26 October 2000.

18 "Wolves reel in Sturgeon as first pick," *The Sudbury Star*, 4 June 2000; "Wolves add three new faces to lineup," *The Sudbury Star*, 19 September 2000; "MacKenzie – new captain of the Wolves," *The Sudbury Star*, 22 October 2000.

19 "Semenov says Sudbury 'sucks': Big defenceman doesn't want to return to Wolves; ask for trade," *The Sudbury Star*, 7 September 2000; "Semenov denies statements," *The Sudbury Star*, 8 September 2000; "Wolves owner comes to the defence of Semenov," *The Sudbury Star*, 10 September 2000.

20 "Wolves' first round pick still at home: Adam Sturgeon left team Sunday night," *The Sudbury Star*, 28 September 2000; "Wolves acquire two defenceman from Bulls," *The Sudbury Star*, 3 September 2001.

21 "Wolves defender has no intention of returning: Dennis Wideman is expecting to be traded," *The Sudbury Star*, 25 November 2000.

22 "Wideman speaks with Waterloo police," *The Sudbury Star*, 9 December 2000; "Wideman affair winding down: It's unclear if OHL will investigate after police drop investigation," *The Sudbury Star*, 12 January 2001.

23 "Templeton takes on accusers: Sudbury Wolves head coach/GM reveals Wideman accusing him of physical assault," *The Sudbury Star*, 7 December 2000.

24 "Templeton cleared in Wideman affair," *The Sudbury Star*, 11 January 2001; "Wolves load up at OHL's trade deadline," *The Sudbury Star*, 11 January 2001.

25 "Wolves unbeaten streak ends," *The Sudbury Star*, 11 March 2001.

26 "Long wait to celebrate: It's been 25 years since the Sudbury Wolves captured a division championship banner," *The Sudbury Star*, 25 March 2001.

27 "Mackenzie named Best Faceoff Man: Sudbury native among those honoured by the Ontario Hockey League," *The Sudbury Star*, 2 May 2001.

28 "Wolves No.9 this week in CHL rankings," *The Sudbury Star*, 13 March 2001.

29 "Semenov may get serious consideration for MVP," *The Sudbury Star*, 29 March 2001; "Semenov named OHL defender of the year," *The Sudbury Star*, 4 May 2001.

30 "Wolves in total control: Sudbury wins 6-0 and could wrap up series in Barrie tonight," *The Sudbury Star*, 30 March 2001; "Wolves eliminate Colts in 5: Sudbury blanks Barrie 2-0 to take the Eastern Conference quarter-final series 4-1," *The Sudbury Star*, 2 April 2001.

31 "Wolves meet Majors tonight," *The Sudbury Star*, 6 April 2001; "Wolves net Major first win," *The Sudbury Star*, 07 April 2001.

32 "OHL game postponed," *The Kingston Whig*, 9 April 2001.

33 "Majors win in OT one day later," *The Toronto Star*, 10 April 2001.

34 "Wolves back in control," *The Sudbury Star*, 12 April 2001; "Close to another series win," *The Sudbury Star*, 13 April 2001; "Majors keep hopes alive," *The Sudbury Star*, 15 April 2001; "Majors push Wolves to Game 7 with gritty effort," *The Toronto Star*, 18 April 2001; "Seventh game needed," *The Sudbury Star*, 18 April 2001.

35 "Make or break," *The Sudbury Star*, 19 April 2001; "Stunned: Two shots,

two goals, Wolves' season over; Fast start by St. Mike's key to 3-1 win over Sudbury," *The Sudbury Star*, 20 April 2001.

36   "Banner frustrating reminder of greatness," *The Sudbury Star*, 3 May 2001.

37   "Stortini thrilled to be drafted by the Wolves," *The Sudbury Star*, 12 May 2001.

38   Bobby Chaumont, interview by Scott Miller, 15 November 2021.

39   Zack Stortini, interview by Scott Miller, 24 September 2020.

40   "Tie closes out Wolves' preseason," *The Sudbury Star*, 13 September 2001; "Wolves' opener postponed," *The Sudbury Star*, 14 September 2001.

41   "Rookies spark Wolves to win," *The Sudbury Star*, 16 September 2001.

42   "Templeton not surprised Winstanley left Wolves: Wolves head coach/GM comments on losing second leading scorer," *The Sudbury Star*, 8 January 2002; "Loss of Centennials blow to North: Wolves' official," *The Sudbury Star*, 29 December 2001; "Wolves management paints wrong picture," *The Sudbury Star*, 5 January 2002; "Attendance figures show how much Sudbury loves the Wolves," *The Sudbury Star*, 16 March 2002.

43   "Cents end rivalry with 4-1 win," *The Sudbury Star*, 10 March 2002.

44   Randy Carlyle, interview by Scott Miller, 26 September 2020.

45   "Attack spoil Carlyle's night: Owen Sound downs Sudbury 4-1 on the night Randy Carlyle's number was retired," *The Sudbury Star*, 29 December 2001.

46   "Wolves claw out 4-3 OT win," *The Sudbury Star*, 27 March 2002.

47   "Colts put Wolves on ropes," *The Sudbury Star*, 29 March 2002; "Wolves call it a season," *The Sudbury Star*, 31 March 2002.

48   "Templeton celebrates 25 years: Sudbury Wolves head coach/GM is enjoying his silver anniversary in the OHL," *The Sudbury Star*, 12 March 2002.

49   "April Fool's joke lights up radio phone lines," *The Sudbury Star*, 2 April 2002.

50   Zack Stortini, interview by Scott Miller, 24 September 2020.

51   "There's no limit to potential," *The Sudbury Star*, 18 September 2002;

"Stortini named OHL's youngest captain," *The Sudbury Star*, 22 September 2002.

52   "Templeton," *The Sudbury Star*, 18 September 2002.

53   "Wolves trounced in opener: 67's third-period butt-kicking decided factor in 7-1 loss," *The Sudbury Star*, 21 September 2002.

54   "Whitmarsh makes 29 saves as Wolves shut out Majors," *The Sudbury Star*, 23 November 2002.

55   Bobby Chaumont, interview by Scott Miller, 15 November 2021.

56   "Wolves desperate for win to keep playoff hopes alive as they take on the Bulls tonight," *The Sudbury Star*, 17 January 2003; "Fewer fans, fewer dollars for Wolves," *The Sudbury Star*, 19 January 2003; "Wolves owner impatient with losing," *The Sudbury Star*, 31 January 2003; "Difficult season so far for Wolves' top pick," *The Sudbury Star*, 5 February 2003.

57   "Wolves need new coach, GM," *The Sudbury Star*, 21 March 2003.

58   "Templeton, Wolves in nasty court battle," *The Sudbury Star*, 13 September 2003; "Wolves eager to settle Templeton suit," *The Sudbury Star*, 17 September 2003; "Templeton, Wolves settle: Team pays former coach last year of contract, retracts allegations," *The Sudbury Star*, 30 September 2003; "Obituary: Templeton dead at 63: Tributes pour in from across hockey world for one of the OHL's best coaches," *The Sudbury Star*, 6 December 2003; "'Hockey was his life': Friends, family pay tribute to the memory of Bert Templeton," *The Sudbury Star*, 10 December 2003.

59   Zack Stortini, interview by Scott Miller, 24 September 2020.

CHAPTER 9: CINDERELLA STORY, 2003–2007

1   "Wolves ready to draft without a head coach," *The Sudbury Star*, 23 April 2003.

2   "Wolves to pick defenceman Staal," *The Sudbury Star*, 3 May 2003; "Wolves shore up blueline at OHL Draft: Defender Marc Staal, chosen first by the Wolves, second overall," *The Sudbury Star*, 5 May 2003.

3   Bobby Chaumont, interview by Scott Miller, 15 November 2021.

4   "Mike Foligno brings hope: New coach/GM of the Sudbury Wolves is

a good-news story the entire city can share in," *The Sudbury Star*, 17 June 2003; "Foligno ready to lead Wolves: Former Wolves star makes his return to junior team official," *The Sudbury Star*, 16 June 2003; "Three coaches, five players call Sudbury home: Not since 1995 has the Sudbury Wolves had so much local talent," *The Sudbury Star*, 20 February 2004.

5   "Building a solid relationship: - The Sudbury Wolves' plan to build corporate boxes shows a commitment to Sudbury," *The Sudbury Star*, 30 September 2002; "Sudbury Wolves drawing up plans for $2.4-M Sudbury Arena facelift," *The Sudbury Star*, 12 January 2003.

6   "Foligno not concerned about OHL prognosticators: Wolves picked to finish last by OHL watchers," *The Sudbury Star*, 19 September 2003; "Foligno perfect so far: Mike Foligno, Sudbury's favourite son, coaches Wolves to 4-0 win over Erie in OHL regular season opener," *The Sudbury Star*, 20 September 2003.

7   "OHL Notebook: Homecoming for Spits' Smith," *The Windsor Star*, 1 November 2003; "Column: Chaumont named to OHL all-star team: Local boy first Wolves player in three seasons to be named an all-star," *The Sudbury Star*, 15 January 2004.

8   "Wolves to meet Majors: Opening game in the best-of-seven Eastern Conference quarter-final goes Friday in Toronto," *The Sudbury Star*, 15 March 2004; "Editorial: Go Wolves Go," *The Sudbury Star*, 15 March 2004.

9   "Majors blank Wolves in opener," *The Sudbury Star*, 20 March 2004; "Wolves, Majors all tied up," *The Sudbury Star*, 22 March 2004; "St. Mike's roll over Wolves," *The Sudbury Star*, 24 March 2004.

10   "Wolves score 'major' blowout," *The Sudbury Star*, 30 March 2004.

11   "Fans cram buses after Wolves upset St. Mike's," *The Sudbury Star*, 30 March 2004; "Ecstasy and agony: Wolves season ends on Toronto ice – Toronto scores 5-2 win over Sudbury," *The Sudbury Star*, 31 March 2004; "Majors have last howl on Wolves in Game 7 win," *The Toronto Star*, 31 March 2004.

12   "They Said It," *The Sudbury Star*, 25 March 2005.

13   "Wolves import and export: Sudbury trades disgruntled rookie for No. 7 pick in CHL import draft," *The Sudbury Star*, 30 June 2005.

14 "Wolves whump Otters," *The Sudbury Star*, 27 September 2004; "Wolves' Pouliot doesn't have to listen to the hype about his play," *The Sudbury Star*, 4 March 2005.

15 "Pouliot named OHL's top rookie: Wolves forward becomes the second player in franchise history to be named OHL rookie of the year," *The Sudbury Star*, 21 April 2005.

16 "Wolves' Pouliot named CHL Rookie of the Year: Sidney Crosby first player to win back-to-back MVP awards," *The Sudbury Star*, 25 May 2005.

17 Mike Commito, "Sudbury's Iron Man: Bobby Chaumont," https://sudburywolves.com/article/sudburys-iron-man-bobby-chaumont (accessed 25 August 2019).

18 Bobby Chaumont, interview by Scott Miller, 15 November 2021.

19 "Wolves put halt to Knights' streak," *The Sudbury Star*, 18 December 2004.

20 "Wolves set to dance with elimination tonight," *The Sudbury Star*, 15 April 2005.

21 "Wolves prepare for battle," *The Sudbury Star*, 22 March 2005; "Wolves give fans what they want: The Sudbury Wolves bring entertainment and a sense of pride when they perform, and the fans have taken notice," *The Sudbury Star*, 31 March 2005.

22 "Wolves 3, Battalion 2," *The Globe and Mail*, 25 March 2005; "Wolves top Brampton in OT," *The Sudbury Star*, 25 March 2005; "Brampton bounces back," *The Sudbury Star*, 2 April 2005.

23 "Big Ben strikes in overtime," *The Sudbury Star*, 5 April 2005.

24 "Former Wolves player dies in Toronto auto accident," *The Sudbury Star*, 5 April 2005; "Home-ice advantage," *The Sudbury Star*, 6 April 2005; "Playing for hometown fans helpful: 67's 3 Wolves 2," *The National Post*, 8 April 2005; "This year's Wolves are nothing like 2001 edition," *The Sudbury Star*, 9 April 2005; "Wolves bounce back," *The Ottawa Citizen*, 10 April 2005; "Wolves even series with overtime win," *The Ottawa Citizen*, 10 April 2005.

25 "Attack overshadows 67's win," *The Ottawa Citizen*, 12 April 2005; "Wolves reel from 'The Punch': 'We have to get our focus back,' Foligno

says after Musselman suspended for decking Mancari," *The Sudbury Star*, 13 April 2005; "Musselman banned, team fined $10K for hit: Wolves forward 'shocked' by severity of punishment for his hit on Mark Mancari," *The Sudbury Star*, 16 April 2005; "Sudbury stays alive in series despite suffering off-ice blow," *The Globe and Mail*, 16 April 2005.

26   "Wolves lost a backbreaker," *The Sudbury Star*, 14 April 2005; "Sudbury stays alive in series despite suffering off-ice blow," *The Globe and Mail*, 16 April 2005.

27   "Wolves sent packing: Ottawa ends Sudbury's playoff run in Game 6," *The Sudbury Star*, 18 April 2005; "Column: Goaltending is huge in the OHL playoffs," *The Sudbury Star*, 23 April 2005; Bobby Chaumont, interview by Scott Miller, 15 November 2021.

28   Zack Stortini, email message to Scott Miller, 17 September 2020.

29   "Wolves set roster, for now," *The Sudbury Star*, 6 September 2005; "Staal returns to find letter on sweater," *The Sudbury Star*, 26 September 2005; "Wolves win second straight: Pouliot nets hat trick in 7-4 thumping of Petes," *The Sudbury Star*, 3 October 2005.

30   "Wolves swing two big deals," *The Sudbury Star*, 9 January 2006; Akim Aliu, "Hockey Is Not for Everyone," https://www.theplayerstribune.com/articles/hockey-is-not-for-everyone-akim-aliu-nhl (accessed 11 January 2022).

31   "Hockey phenom holds city dear: John Tavares grew up dreaming of playing in Sudbury Arena," *The Sudbury Star*, 30 September 2005; "Wolves find win column: Sudbury takes command against Generals in 6-2 win," *The Sudbury Star*, 1 October 2005.

32   "Staal stands out as Canada wins junior crown: Sudbury cheers as Wolves player named top defenceman," *The Sudbury Star*, 6 January 2006; "Playoff push on for the Wolves and their opponents tonight," *The Sudbury Star*, 3 March 2006.

33   "Frontenacs gain early edge," *The Sudbury Star*, 25 March 2006; "Wolves return with home ice," *The Sudbury Star*, 27 March 2006; "Wolves shut out Kingston," *The Sudbury Star*, 29 March 2006; "Fronts eliminated," *The Kingston Whig*, 3 April 2006; "Bring on the Petes!," *The Sudbury Star*, 3 April 2006.

34 "Wolves face tough test in deep Peters," *The Sudbury Star*, 5 April 2006; "Staal vs. Staal," *The Sudbury Star*, 6 April 2006; "Power play pushes Petes to win," *The Sudbury Star*, 7 April 2006; "Wolves fall again, for Pete's sake," *The Sudbury Star*, 8 April 2006.

35 "Wolves season comes to an end," *The Sudbury Star*, 12 April 2006; "Wolf pack packs up another OHL season: Players say team under-achieved this season," *The Sudbury Star*, 14 April 2006.

36 "Bleak outlook," *The Sudbury Star*, 25 September 2006; "Second Staal coming: Wolves draft fourth brother in first round," *The Sudbury Star*, 8 May 2006; "14 Sudbury players taken in OHL Draft," *The Sudbury Star*, 8 May 2006.

37 "Duguay honoured," *The Sudbury Star*, 29 September 2006.

38 "Wolves open 35th season with style," https://www.sudbury.com/sports/wolves-open-35th-season-with-style-213804 (accessed 20 January 2021).

39 "Wolves get left winger," *The Sudbury Star*, 23 November 2006.

40 "Justin Donati joins Wolves," *The Ottawa Citizen*, 10 January 2007; "Wolves retooled and ready," *The Sudbury Star*, 12 January 2007.

41 "The jobs came back," *The Sudbury Star*, 30 December 2006.

42 "Voters don't like Wolves' chances," *The Sudbury Star*, 28 March 2007.

43 Mike Commito, "Ten Years Later: Remembering the Wolves' Historic Run," https://sudburywolves.com/article/10year_anniversary_magic_run (accessed 30 September 2019). Unless noted otherwise, direct quotes from members of the 2006-2007 Wolves as it pertains to this playoff run have been drawn from this article.

44 "True Self emerges," *The Sudbury Star*, 3 April 2007; "Dahm named player of the week," *The Sudbury Star*, 5 April 2007; "Wolves bite IceDogs," *The Sudbury Star*, 28 March 2007; "Wolves take command," *The Sudbury Star*, 30 March 2007; "Big-minute guys eye Colts," *The Sudbury Star*, 5 April 2007.

45 "Wolves corral Colts," *The Sudbury Star*, 9 April 2007; "Wolves trip up Colts on the road," *The Sudbury Star*, 10 April 2007; "Dahm-inated," *The Sudbury Star*, 12 April 2007.

46 Commito, "Ten Years Later."

47 "Wolves reveal 'Secret' to success," *The Sudbury Star*, 16 May 2007.

48   Commito, "Ten Years Later."

49   "Wolves fever spreading," *The Sudbury Star*, 25 April 2007; "Sudbury ready to celebrate if Wolves victorious," *The Sudbury Star*, 27 April 2007.

50   "Donati twins know mother would relish on-ice duel," *The National Post*, 19 April 2007.

51   "Wolves stumble in opener," *The Sudbury Star*, 19 April 2007; "Belleville 'Staals' out in OT," *The Sudbury Star*, 20 April 2007; "Wolves hit hard by Snow," *The Sudbury Star*, 23 April 2007; "Donati breaks through," *The Sudbury Star*, 24 April 2007; "Wolves have Bulls by the horns," *The Sudbury Star*, 26 April 2007.

52   "Wolves urge fans to be loud," *The Sudbury Star*, 27 April 2007; "Wolves win!" *The Sudbury Star*, 28 April 2007; "Thrilled Wolves fans confident team can take Whalers," *The Sudbury Star*, 28 April 2007.

53   Commito, "Ten Years Later."

54   "The Plymouth Whalers are good. So what?" *The Sudbury Star*, 30 April 2007.

55   Commito, "Ten Years Later."

56   "MPPs support Sudbury Wolves," *The Sudbury Star*, 2 May 2007; "Fans rally for the Wolves," *The Sudbury Star*, 3 May 2007.

57   "Foligno key to Wolves," *The Toronto Star*, 4 May 2007.

58   "Whalers win opener," *The Sudbury Star*, 5 May 2007.

59   "Wolves whump Whalers," *The Sudbury Star*, 7 May 2007.

60   "Wolves' impress playoff run 'icing on the cake' in Sudbury," *The National Post*, 8 May 2007.

61   Ibid.

62   "Hockey Notes," *The Ottawa Citizen*, 12 May 2007.

63   "Donati does it again," *The Sudbury Star*, 9 May 2007.

64   "Tough loss, but Wolves fans still optimistic," *The Sudbury Star*, 10 May 2007; "Hockey: Wolves goalie shines in loss," *The Ottawa Citizen*, 12 May 2007.

65   "Midnight chimes for Wolves," *The Sudbury Star*, 14 May 2007.

66   Ibid; "Staal top defenceman," *The Ottawa Citizen*, 8 May 2007.

67   Commito, "Ten Years Later."

CHAPTER 10: AFTERMATH, 2007-2012

1   "Wolves add another Foligno to the fold," *The Sudbury Star*, 7 May 2007; "Maggio finds right fit with Wolves," *The Sudbury Star*, 8 May 2007; "Sudbury Wolves announce a trio of trades," *The Sudbury Star*, 2 June 2007; "Carlyle keeps his word," *The Sudbury Star*, 18 August 2007; "Wolves name Baker captain," *The Sudbury Star*, 20 September 2007; "Fine day for Foligno family," *The Sudbury Star*, 9 October 2007.

2   "Sudbury's old barn gets a brand new look: New revenues will put the Wolves in big leagues," *The Sudbury Star*, 17 May 2006; "For the right price, arena's on block," *The Sudbury Star*, 1 May 2007.

3   "Sudbury Community Arena renovations don't impress," *The Sudbury Star*, 14 November 2007.

4   "Wolves hit win column," *The Sudbury Star*, 6 October 2007; "Wolves raise banner," *The Sudbury Star*, 19 October 2007; "Battalion blank Wolves," *The Sudbury Star*, 20 October 2007.

5   "Young Foligno gives Wolves win," *The Sudbury Star*, 17 November 2007; "Wolves lose 10th straight," *The Sudbury Star*, 10 December 2007; "Still focused on playoffs, despite streak: Foligno," *The Sudbury Star*, 14 December 2007; "Wolves snap losing streak," *The Sudbury Star*, 15 December 2007; "Wolves' Gill blazes OHL trail," *The Sudbury Star*, 25 January 2008.

6   "Bye-bye Baker," *The Sudbury Star*, 9 January 2008; "The other skate drops for Wolves," *The Sudbury Star*, 10 January 2008; "Wolves newcomers want to make impact," *The Sudbury Star*, 11 January 2008; "Trade puts Giudice at head of pack," *The Sudbury Star*, 18 January 2008.

7   "Optimistic Wolves fans already eager for next year," *The Sudbury Star*, 8 March 2008; "Wolves losing the right way," *The Sudbury Star*, 14 March 2008; "Wolves wrap up season with loss," *The Sudbury Star*, 17 March 2008; "Wolves hoping history repeats," *The Sudbury Star*, 16 April 2008.

8   "Nickel Caps hang with Thrashers," *The Sudbury Star*, 26 April 2008; "Nickel Caps capture national crown," *The Sudbury Star*, 28 April 2008; "Nickel Capitals Canada's team," *The Sudbury Star*, 29 April 2008.

9   "A new Sudbury Wolves era to dawn on Friday," *The Sudbury Star*, 30 April 2008; "Bad boy edge could work for McFarland," *The Sudbury Star*, 3 May 2008.

10   "The buzz is back," *The Sudbury Star*, 3 May 2008; "Arena becomes Russia House: Foligno takes Filatov with first import draft pick," *The Sudbury Star*, 27 June 2008.

11   "Wolves' road to redemption starts tonight," *The Sudbury Star*, 19 September 2008.

12   "Wolves win season opener; Sudbury whups Oshawa," *The Sudbury Star*, 20 September 2008; "Wolves run record 3-0," *The Sudbury Star*, 4 October 2008; "Full steam ahead for McFarland," *The Sudbury Star*, 3 November 2008.

13   "The mysterious case of the Sudbury Wolves," *The Sudbury Star*, 13 January 2009; "Few thought they'd do it," *The Sudbury Star*, 16 March 2009.

14   "Aliu makes surprise return to Wolf pack," *The Sudbury Star*, 5 January 2009; "Command performance: Aliu bucks the odds with return to wolf pack," *The Sudbury Star*, 6 January 2009.

15   "Major mastery over Wolves," *The Sudbury Star*, 21 February 2009; "Captain Kurtz channels Renaud; Wolves new captain credits former Windsor teammate for his success," *The Sudbury Star*, 23 February 2009.

16   "Another Foligno eyes NHL: Scouts drool over Marcus's size, work ethic," *The Sudbury Star*, 21 January 2009; "Post-season dream comes true," *The Sudbury Star*, 16 March 2009.

17   "Wolves stumble," *The Sudbury Star*, 19 March 2009; "Bouyant Wolves coming home," *The Sudbury Star*, 20 March 2009; "Wolves eager to hear home crowd roar," *The Sudbury Star*, 21 March 2009.

18   "It's back to Belleville," *The Sudbury Star*, 26 March 2009; "Wolves' season over," *The Sudbury Star*, 31 March 2009.

19   "Wolves fans in get on big draft," *The Sudbury Star*, 9 May 2009; "Lots of talent at Wolves spring camp," *The Sudbury Star*, 8 June 2009.

20   "McFarland returns to help out," *The Sudbury Star*, 8 June 2009.

21   "Wolves fans feel optimistic," *The Sudbury Star*, 7 September 2009.

22   "Foligno leaves the bench; DEPARTURE: Wolves head coach steps

back," *The Sudbury Star*, 28 August 2009; "Verreault deserving of Wolves head coaching job," *The Sudbury Star*, 3 September 2009.

23   "Wolves having Groundhog season," *The Sudbury Wolves*, 4 February 2010.

24   "Wolves drop season opener," *The Sudbury Star*, 19 September 2009.

25   "Wolves snap losing skid," *The Sudbury Star*, 19 October 2009.

26   "Verreault leaves Wolves," *The Sudbury Star*, 21 October 2009.

27   "Foligno triumphant in return to bench," *The Sudbury Star*, 24 October 2009.

28   "Wolves look for boost from overager," *The Sudbury Star*, 3 November 2009; "Wolves add depth to blue-line," *The Sudbury Star*, 5 November 2009; "Chiarot trade a gutsy move by Wolves management," *The Sudbury Wolves*, 14 January 2010.

29   "Sudbury recovers from first-game pounding against the Barrie Colts," *The Kingston Whig*, 20 March 2010.

30   "Wolves face Colts in Round 1; OHL PLAYOFFS: Barrie ranked No.1 in Canada," *The Sudbury Star*, 17 March 2010; "Colts hammer Wolves," *The Sudbury Star*, 19 March 2010; "First-round series gets nasty," *The Kingston Whig*, 24 March 2010; "Colts sweep Wolves; OHL PLAYOFFS: Wolves reason comes to an end as Colts complete sweep," *The Sudbury Star*, 25 March 2010.

31   "Foligno steps aside," *The Sudbury Star*, 7 April 2010.

32   "Foligno joins Carlyle, Ducks," *The Sudbury Star*, 25 June 2010.

33   "Eager to put his stamp on the Wolves; OHL: Sudbury names Trent Cull new head coach," *The Sudbury Star*, 12 May 2010; "Blaine Smith the Wolves' new GM; OHL: Been with the club for 23 years," *The Sudbury Star*, 12 May 2010.

34   "Wolves pick slick forward; OHL PRIORITY SELECTION: Take Campagna fifth overall," *The Sudbury Star*, 3 May 2010; "Wolves move in speedy, skilled direction," *The Sudbury Star*, 4 May 2010; "Wolves hope pick brings offence," *The Sudbury Star*, 11 August 2010; "New-look Wolves ready for camp," *The Sudbury Star*, 31 August 2010; "Wolves swing another deal," *The Sudbury Star*, 1 September 2010; "'Fresh start' to year," *The Sudbury Star*, 2 September 2010; "Wolves new look,

changes offer hope; OHL: Column," *The Sudbury Star*, 8 September 2010.

35 "Wolves drop season opener," *The Sudbury Star*, 25 September 2010; "Wolves make deal for defenceman," *The Sudbury Wolves*, 29 September 2010; "Wolves whumped by Majors," *The Sudbury Star*, 18 October 2010.

36 "Wolves earn feisty win," *The Sudbury Star*, 6 November 2010.

37 "Wolves deal McFarland, Chiarot to Saginaw," *The Sudbury Star*, 10 December 2010; "Deal shakes up Wolves," *The Sudbury Star*, 11 December 2010; "McFarland never reached his promise," *The Sudbury Star*, 14 December 2010

38 "Round 1: Expect three favourites to win, one upset," *The Sudbury Star*, 24 March 2011.

39 "Foligno stays in Sudbury," *The Sudbury Star*, 11 January 2011.

40 "Sudbury's last goal wins," *The Ottawa Citizen*, 27 March 2011; "Wolves stun 67's in opener," *The Sudbury Star*, 28 March 2011; "Fans applaud GM, coach for team's success," *The Sudbury Star*, 29 March 2011; "Wolves take control," *The Sudbury Star*, 30 March 2011.

41 "Wolves complete sweep," *The Sudbury Star*, 1 April 2011.

42 "67's fail to step up," *The Ottawa Citizen*, 1 April 2011.

43 "Like team, Wolves fans hitting their stride," *The Sudbury Star*, 5 April 2011.

44 "Wolves riding wave of spectacular second-half surge; COLUMN: Wolves won only five of first 20 games this season," *The Sudbury Star*, 2 April 2011; "Major collapse," *The Sudbury Star*, 14 April 2011; "Fans proud of Wolves' playoff run."

45 "Wolves unveil 40th anniversary jerseys; ONTARIO HOCKEY LEAGUE: Classic green," *The Sudbury Star*, 21 September 2011.

46 "Wolves win one for Burgesses," *The Sudbury Star*, 26 November 2011.

47 "Berk Keaney Sr.; You have your diehard sports fans and then you have…," *The Sudbury Star*, 3 December 2011; "Wolves give Keaney great send-off; ONTARIO HOCKEY LEAGUE: Vienneau posts shutout as Sudbury tops Brampton 4-0," *The Sudbury Star*, 3 December 2011; "End of an Era," https://sudburywolves.com/end-of-an-era (accessed 29 August 2020).

48 "Wolves add scoring punch in Sunday deal," *The Sudbury Star*, 23 November 2010; "MacDonald gets the 'C'," *The Sudbury Star*, 10 November 2011.

49 "Vienneau leaves USHL for Wolves," *The Sudbury Star*, 3 September 2011.

50 "Friday brings one of the most anticipated openers for Wolves in years," *The Sudbury Star*, 22 September 2011.

51 "Wolves lanced by Knights," *The Sudbury Star*, 1 October 2011; "Pominville sparks Wolves," *The Sudbury Star*, 6 October 2011.

52 "Win revs up the Wolves," *The Sudbury Star*, 8 October 2011.

53 "Wolves spend wise at trade deadline," *The Sudbury Wolves*, 12 January 2012.

54 "Sgarbossa makes history in Wolves win," *The Sudbury Star*, 19 March 2012.

55 Ibid.; "NHL rights traded to Avs; Sgarbossa," *The Sudbury Star*, 28 February 2012.

56 "Wolves go down in four," *The Sudbury Star*, 29 March 2011; "Hard to blame coach Cull," *The Sudbury Star*, 29 March 2012.

CHAPTER 11: PEAKS AND VALLEYS, 2012-2016

1 "Wolves bolster blueline with early picks," *The Sudbury Star*, 9 April 2012; "Young Burgess deserves a chance to shine; COLUMN: Owner's son drafted in third round by Sudbury Wolves," *The Sudbury Star*, 12 April 2012.

2 "Wolves opt for offence," *The Sudbury Star*, 28 June 2012.

3 "Wolves ready for Russia," *The Sudbury Star*, 11 August 2012; "Wolves extend Cull; OHL: Head coach signed till 2013-14 season," *The Sudbury Star*, 14 August 2012; "Howl to the champions; HOCKEY: Wolves win Junior Club World Cup," *The Sudbury Star*, 27 August 2012; "Wolves still basking in golden glow; OHL: World Cup champs eager for training camp," *The Sudbury Star*, 29 August 2012.

4 "New rink needed: Wolves GM: POWER OUTAGE: Glitch on game night highlights arena shortcomings," *The Sudbury Star*, 15 September 2012; "Reviving the rink; RECREATION: Sudbury could follow

example of the Sault by replacing its aging barn with a modern facility," *The Sudbury Star*, 25 September 2012; "Barbeau wants new arena," *The Sudbury Star*, 26 September 2012.

5   "Wolves looking for slump-busting win tonight," *The Sudbury Star*, 14 November 2012.

6   "Wolves' streak comes to an end," *The Sudbury Star*, 14 January 2013.

7   "OHL: Sudbury sells as deadline looms; Wolves make waves," *The Sudbury Star*, 9 January 2013; "In wake of blockbuster, Wolves deal another," *The Sudbury Wolves*, 10 January 2013; "Blockbuster deal offers hope better days may be in the cards," *The Sudbury Star*, 10 January 2013; "Palazzese posts shutout in debut; ONTARIO HOCKEY LEAGUE: Wolves 2, Steelheads 0," *The Sudbury Star*, 12 January 2013.

8   "Campagna still leading the way; OHL: Skilled centre leads Sudbury point-getters," *The Sudbury Star*, 25 January 2013; "Captain Kantor relishes his role," *The Sudbury Star*, 2 February 2013.

9   "Cull deserves high marks for work with Wolves," *The Sudbury Star*, 16 March 2013.

10   "Wolves bound for 2nd round; OHL PLAYOFFS: Sudbury 1, Brampton 0 (OT)," *The Sudbury Star*, 30 March 2013.

11   "Pack sacked by Bulls; OHL PLAYOFFS: Belleville 5, Sudbury 0," *The Sudbury Star*, 12 April 2013.

12   "Fixter gets warm welcome; SUDBURY WOVLES: New associated coach happy to join the Pack," *The Sudbury Star*, 18 June 2013; "Wolves coach headed to the AHL," *The Sudbury Star*, 4 July 2013; "Moving on all about opportunity, Cull says; ONTARIO HOCKEY LEAGUE: Took assistant coach job with Syracuse Crunch," *The Sudbury Star*, 5 July 2013.

13   "Wolves get first win at Jr. World Cup; HOCKEY: Not enough to make tournament semifinals, however," *The Sudbury Star*, 29 August 2013.

14   "No need to panic Wolves fans," *The Sudbury Star*, 31 August 2013; "Wolves trade Genovese, acquire Crisp, McDowell," *The Sudbury Star*, 4 September 2013; "Raine gets the 'C' for Sudbury," *The Sudbury Star*, 20 September 2013.

15   "Wolves add offence in trade with Otters," *The Sudbury Star*, 5 September 2013; "Wolves hit ice with high hopes," *The Sudbury Star*, 20 September 2013.

16   "Wolves open with lopsided loss," *The Sudbury Star*, 23 September 2013.

17   "Hounds snap Wolves' win streak," *The Sudbury Star*, 30 December 2013.

18   "Wolves make big splash," *The Sudbury Star*, 10 January 2014.

19   "Hunter's No. 15 raised to rafters," *The Sudbury Star*, 1 February 2014; Nathaniel Oliver, "Dale Hunter's Unbreakable Record," https://the-hockeywriters.com/dale-hunter-unbreakable-record/ (accessed 11 January 2022).

20   "Despite lapses, Wolves are still contenders," *The Sudbury Star*, 5 December 2013; "Central Division lead at stake," *The Sudbury Star*, 6 February 2014; "'We have to get wins'," *The Sudbury Star*, 5 March 2014; "Will the real Wolves please stand up?" *The Sudbury Star*, 11 March 2014; "Wolves lose grip on title," *The Sudbury Star*, 15 March; "Wolves wrap up with win," *The Sudbury Star*, 17 March 2014.

21   "Lots of history with Wolves-Colts; COLUMN: Seventh playoff meeting between two squads," *The Sudbury Star*, 20 March 2014.

22   "Colts hold off Wolves in Game 1," *The Sudbury Star*, 21 March 2014; "Close not good enough," *The Sudbury Star*, 24 March 2014.

23   "Wolves pushed to the brink," *The Sudbury Star*, 26 March 2014; "Wolves send it back to Barrie," *The Sudbury Star*, 28 March 2014; "Lots of blame to go around in Wolves collapse," *The Sudbury Star*, 31 March 2014.

24   "'I had to move along'; OHL: Wolves trade Campagna to Plymouth for picks," *The Sudbury Star*, 16 August 2014; "Wolves eager to prove predictions wrong," *The Sudbury Star*, 26 September 2014.

25   Michael Pezzetta, interview by Branden Scott, https://www.youtube.com/watch?v=S2cIXujgQh4 (accessed 11 August 2020).

26   "Wolves import size," *The Sudbury Star*, 3 July 2014; "Long journey for Tanguay," *The Sudbury Star*, 11 September 2014.

27   "Wolves name captains," *The Sudbury Star*, 25 September 2014.

28   "Timpano steady as Wolves win opener," *The Sudbury Star*, 27

September 2014.

29   Micheal Pezzetta, interview by Branden Scott, https://www.youtube.com/watch?v=S2cIXujgQh4 (accessed 11 August 2020).

30   "Wolves try to stay positive; OHL: Erie 8, Sudbury 1," *The Sudbury Star*, 27 October 2014.

31   "Sudbury Wolves coach Paul Fixter: 'I lost my cool'", https://www.cbc.ca/news/canada/sudbury/sudbury-wolves-coach-paul-fixter-i-lost-my-cool-1.2814204 (accessed 11 January 2022).

32   "Timpano brilliant as Wolves win," *The Sudbury Star*, 7 February 2015.

33   "OHL: Ottawa 6, Sudbury 0; Worst season in Wolves history comes to end," *The Sudbury Star*, 23 March 2015.

34   "Wolves and 67s swap blueliners," *The Sudbury Star*, 5 November 2014; "Wolves deal Baptiste to Erie," *The Sudbury Star*, 25 November 2014; "Wolves fire head coach Paul Fixter," *The Sudbury Star*, 5 January 2015; "Wolves beat deadline," *The Sudbury Star*, 9 January 2015.

35   "Burgess says boo-birds don't bug him," *The Sudbury Star*, 5 October 2013; Ken Campbell, "OHL owner's son retires after scoring zero goals in 95 games," *The Hockey News*, 16 October 2014, https://the-hockeynews.com/news/ohl-owners-son-retires-after-scoring-zero-goals-in-95-games (accessed 11 January 2022); Ben Leeson, "Lesson: Burgess issue drove wedge between Sudbury Wolves and their fans," https://www.thesudburystar.com/2014/10/15/leeson-burgess-issue-drove-wedge-be-tween-sudbury-wolves-and-their-fans (accessed 11 January 2022); "ONE-ON-ONE with Sudbury Wolves Owner Mark Burgess," https://www.youtube.com/watch?v=XbbV96eQj2k (accessed 11 January 2022).

36   "David Levin's amazing story; OHL DRAFT: Sudbury Wolves slated to pick Israeli hockey star first," *The Sudbury Star*, 8 April 2015; "'Best feeling ever': OHL DRAFT: Wolves select Levin No. 1," *The Sudbury Star*, 11 April 2015.

37   "Wolves take highly regarded Russian; HOCKEY: Dmitri Sokolov a possible top-10 pick in next year's NHL draft," *The Sudbury Star*, 2 July 2015.

38   "Patrick Murphy expected to bring experience, versatility," *The Sudbury Star*, 11 August 2015.

39   "Wolves hire new GM; HOCKEY: Barclay Branch excited about team's young talent," *The Sudbury Star*, 12 August 2015.

40   "Coach, family enjoying Sudbury," *The Sudbury Star*, 3 September 2015.

41   "Desrochers gets the 'C'," *The Sudbury Star*, 25 September 2015.

42   "Wolves snap skid; Sudbury 4, Guelph 3," *The Sudbury Star*, 14 December 2015; "Birthday boy shines; Sudbury 6, Sault 4, as Wolves enjoy balanced attack," *The Sudbury Star*, 7 January 2016.

43   "Wolves add netminder," *The Sudbury Star*, 21 October 2015.

44   "Wolves deal Jenys to 'Dogs," *The Sudbury Star*, 24 November 2015; "Murphy moves up front," *The Sudbury Star*, 27 November 2015.

45   "Levin seeks extra gear," *The Sudbury Star*, 28 March 2016; "I can do better: Sokolov; Rookie import the fifth Wolf to score 30 as a rookie," *The Sudbury Star*, 29 March 2016; "Pezzetta, Sokolov drafted," *The Sudbury Star*, 27 June 2016.

46   "Captain finds new home: Desrochers signs with his hometown Lakers," *The Sudbury Star*, 29 April 2016.

47   "Playoffs a must: Wolves GM; Barclay Branch reflects on past season, and plans for next year," *The Sudbury Star*, 16 April 2016.

CHAPTER 12: NEW ERA, 2016-2022

1   "Windsor product signs with Wolves; Lalonde joins OHL club after big season in Alliance league," *The Sudbury Star*, 6 July 2016.

2   "Wolves take defenceman Lalonde at No.2; Sudbury brass see Windsor product logging big minutes," *The Sudbury Star*, 11 April 2016; "Banner draft day for locals; OHL teams select nine Sudbury players," *The Sudbury Star*, 11 April 2016; "Playoffs a must: Wolves GM; Barclay Branch reflects on past season, and plans for next year," *The Sudbury Star*, 16 April 2016.

3   "Wolves change hands," *The Sudbury Star*, 30 July 2016.

4   Dario Zulich, interview by Scott Miller, 25 September 2020.

5   "Wolves sale approved," *The Sudbury Star*, 19 August 2016.

6   Dario Zulich, interview by Scott Miller, 25 September 2020.

7   "New Wolves owner welcomed," *The Sudbury Star*, 10 August 2016.

8   "City to proceed with arena plans," *The Sudbury Star*, 4 August

2016; "Arena belongs downtown," *The Sudbury Star*, 11 August 2016; "Kingsway crowned," *The Sudbury Star*, 28 June 2017.

9   "Gateway committed to Sudbury, company says," *The Sudbury Star*, 28 July 2020.

10   "Wolves 'raise the roof'," *The Sudbury Star*, 16 September 2016.

11   Dario Zulich, interview by Scott Miller, 25 September 2020.

12   "Wolves trade Timpano," *The Sudbury Star*, 25 August 2016; "Wolves name captain," *The Sudbury Star*, 30 September 2016.

13   "Wolves start on right foot," *The Sudbury Star*, 24 September 2016.

14   "Wolves head to post-season," *The Sudbury Star*, 18 March 2017.

15   "Wolves ready for Generals," *The Sudbury Star*, 24 March 2017; "Statement win for Wolves," *The Sudbury Star*, 25 March 2017.

16   "Wolves retake series lead," *The Sudbury Star*, 29 March 2017; "Wolves season over," *The Sudbury Star*, 3 April 2017; "Wolves season a success," *The Sudbury Star*, 11 April 2017.

17   Micheal Pezzetta, interview by Branden Scott, https://www.youtube.com/watch?v=S2cIXujgQh4 (accessed 11 August 2020).

18   "Papineau 'excited' to be GM," *The Sudbury Star*, 18 April 2017.

19   "Wolves, head coach part ways," *The Sudbury Star*, 24 May 2017; "'Humble': Stillman takes over," *The Sudbury Star*, 26 May 2017; "Sudbury Wolves finalizes scouting staff," *The Sudbury Star*, 12 August 2017.

20   "Wolves unveil new outfit," *The Sudbury Star*, 15 August 2017.

21   "Wolves ship out Lalonde," *The Sudbury Star*, 24 August 2017; "Wolves deal some more," *The Sudbury Star*, 25 August 2017; "Blueline bolstered," *The Sudbury Star*, 21 September 2017.

22   "Wolves name captain," *The Sudbury Star*, 26 October 2017.

23   "Wolves collapse in 3rd," *The Sudbury Star*, 25 September 2017; "Murray snipes three, but Wolves fall in OT," *The Sudbury Star*, 28 September 2017.

24   "Six deals in under 48 hours," *The Sudbury Star*, 11 January 2018; "Wolves move on after deals," *The Sudbury Star*, 11 January 2018.

25   "Israeli player sets sight on NHL," *The Sudbury Star*, 28 June 2018.

26   "Bowen backstops win," *The Sudbury Star*, 9 March 2018.

27 "Sniper haunts old team," *The Sudbury Star*, 17 March 2018.

28 "Wolves battle to the losing end," *The Sudbury Star*, 19 March 2018.

29 "Zulich remains optimistic," *The Sudbury Star*, 28 February 2018.

30 "Byfield a big-time talent," *The Sudbury Star*, 31 March 2018; "Wolves bag Byfield," *The Sudbury Star*, 7 April 2018.

31 "Wolves too woo goalie," *The Sudbury Star*, 29 June 2018; "Luukkonen commits to Wolves," *The Sudbury Star*, 3 August 2018.

32 "Wolves start on right foot," *The Sudbury Star*, 22 September 2018; "Wolves bounce back," *The Sudbury Star*, 29 September 2018.

33 "Luukkonen wins world junior goal with Team Finland," *The Sudbury Star*, 5 January 2019; "Much better effort, same result for Wolves," *The Sudbury Star*, 6 January 2019.

34 "Wolves to retire Schutt's No. 8," *The Sudbury Star*, 12 October 2018; "Wolves strike early," *The Sudbury Star*, 3 November 2018.

35 Dario Zulich, interview by Scott Miller, 25 September 2020.

36 "Wolves' streak ends in Mississauga," *The Sudbury Star*, 16 December 2018; "Hounds outgun Wolves," *The Sudbury Star*, 16 February 2019.

37 "'We believe in them' – Wolves GM pleased with roster after trade deadline," *The Sudbury Star*, 10 January 2019.

38 "Papineau pleased with season," *The Sudbury Star*, 20 March 2019.

39 "Wolves draw first blood," *The Sudbury Star*, 23 March 2019; "Levin, Luukkonen, help life Wolves to OT win," *The Sudbury Star*, 23 March 2019; "Power play heats up as Wolves beat Steelheads 5-3," *The Sudbury Star*, 24 March 2019; "Wolves complete sweep," *The Sudbury Star*, 28 March 2019.

40 "Hat tricks a big treat for 67's Veterans," *The Ottawa Citizen*, 6 April 2019; "Wolves' season ends in triple-OT heartbreaker," *The Sudbury Star*, 12 April 2019.

41 "Luukkonen named OHL goalie of the year," *The Sudbury Star*, 26 April 2019; "Luukkonen wins Red Tilson as OHL's most outstanding player," *The Sudbury Star*, 9 May 2019.

42 "Byfield named rookie of the year," *The Sudbury Star*, 28 May 2019.

43 "Big draft day for Sudbury and the North," *The Sudbury Star*, 6 April 2019; "Sudbury Wolves 2019 draft picks – full list," *The Sudbury Star*, 7

April 2019; "Wolves' Luukkonen, Byfield accept OHL awards at Hockey Hall of Fame," *The Sudbury Star*, 7 June 2019.

44   Zack Stortini, interview by Scott Miller, 24 September 2020.

45   "Big Zack is back," *The Sudbury Wolves*, 2 August 2019.

46   "A 31-year ride, filled with just about everything junior hockey can offer," *The Sudbury Star*, 18 September 2019.

47   "'Really excited' – Wolves' new netminder eager to get started," *The Sudbury Star*, 4 September 2019; "Wolf Tracks: Captains who bleed blue," *The Sudbury Star*, 18 September 2019; "Wolves run wild on Troops," *The Sudbury Star*, 27 September 2019.

48   "Murray called to the Canes," *The Sudbury Star*, 22 June 2019.

49   "One deal down as the clock ticks on OHL trade deadline," *The Sudbury Star*, 9 January 2020.

50   Mike Commito, "Macauley Carson Set to Make Wolves History," https://sudburywolves.com/article/macauley-carson-set-to-make-wolves-history (accessed 25 January 2021); "Carson ready to become franchise games leader on Thursday," *The Sudbury Star*, 5 March 2020.

51   "OHL cancels rest of regular season," *The Sudbury Star*, 19 March 2020; "Sudbury Wolves' season over as CHL cancels play offs, Memorial Cup," *The Sudbury Star*, 24 March 2020.

52   "'We have liked him for a long time' – Sudbury Wolves pick up Pekar," *The Sudbury Star*, 8 January 2020; "Battalion trade Sudbury native Chenier to Sudbury Wolves," *The Sudbury Star*, 9 January 2020; "Wolves make some noise at the right time of year," *The Sudbury Star*, 10 March 2020.

53   "Season a learning experience for Byfield," *The Sudbury Star*, 11 April 2020.

54   "Sudbury Wolves, OHL target Dec. 1 start date," *The Sudbury Star*, 6 August 2020.

55   "OHL delays season again," *The Sudbury Star*, 24 December 2020; "Zulich addresses OHL season cancellation," *The Sudbury Star*, 22 April 2021.

56   "High-end forwards highlight Wolves' 2020 draft," *The Sudbury Star*, 7 April 2020.

57 "'I really enjoyed coaching in Sudbury': Stillman leaving Wolves for NHL gig," *The Sudbury Star*, 16 December 2020.

58 "'So thankful for this day': Kings crown Byfield in NHL draft," *The Sudbury Star*, 7 October 2020.

59 "U.S. shuts out Canada for gold," *The Toronto Star*, 6 January 2021.

60 "Wolves' top scout thrilled for chance to pick No.1," *The Sudbury Star*, 7 May 2021; "Sudbury Wolves to select first overall in 2021 OHL Priority Selection," https://ontariohockeyleague.com/article/sudbury-wolves-to-select-first-overall-in-2021-ohl-priority-selection-presented-by-real-canadian-superstore (accessed 18 June 2021).

61 "Meet Quentin Musty, the Top Pick in the OHL Draft," https://www.si.com/hockey/news/meet-quentin-musty-the-top-pick-in-the-ohl-draft (accessed 18 June 2021); "No.1 pick 'a tremendous young man': Sudbury Wolves GM says Musty wants to win, 'does everything' well," *The Sudbury Star*, 5 June 2021; "Musty joins the pack; No. 1 pick in OHL draft officially commits to Wolves," *The Sudbury Star*, 8 June 2021.

62 "Laurentian owes banks $91 million, has liabilities of $321 million – report," *The Sudbury Star*, 3 February 2021; "Laurentian coach still baffled by decision to cut sports programs," *The Sudbury Star*, 30 April 2021; "Wolves Name Craig Duncanson Head Coach," https://sudburywolves.com/article/wolves-name-craig-duncanson-head-coach (accessed 9 December 2021).

63 "Thompson gets the C," *The Sudbury Star*, 7 October, 2021; "Wolves open season with win," *The Sudbury Star*, 9 October 2021; "Home-away contrast continues for Wolves," *The Sudbury Star*, 23 November 2021.

64 "Wolves suspend team activities after 12 players test positive," *The Sudbury Star*, 1 December 2021; "Thompson unable to attend Hockey Canada Selection camp," *The Sudbury Star*, 10 December 2021; "Wolves shake off rust, earn point on road," *The Sudbury Star*, 30 December 2021.

65 "Wolves deal Stillman to Petes, Biondi to Bulldogs," *The Sudbury Star*, 11 January 2022; "Wolves name Liam Ross captain," *The Sudbury Star*, 14 January 2022.

66 "Wolves clip Kingston 8-4," *The Sudbury Star*, 15 January 2022; "Wolves

fall to Hounds, will finish outside playoff picture," *The Sudbury Star*, 10 April 2022.

CONCLUSION: MORE THAN A HOCKEY TEAM

1   Zack Stortini, interview by Scott Miller, 24 September 2020.
2   Dario Zulich, interview by Scott Miller, 25 September 2020.
3   Joe Bowen, interview by Scott Miller, 21 September 2020.
4   Randy Carlyle, interview by Scott Miller, 26 September 2020.